Studying the Jew

Studying the Jew

Scholarly Antisemitism in Nazi Germany

Alan E. Steinweis

First Harvard University Press paperback edition, 2008

Library of Congress Cataloging-in-Publication Data

Steinweis, Alan E.
   Studying the Jew : scholarly antisemitism in Nazi Germany / Alan Steinweis.
      p.   cm.
   Includes bibliographical references and index.
   ISBN 978-0-674-02205-8 (cloth : alk paper)
   ISBN 978-0-674-02761-9 (pbk.)
      1. Antisemitism—Germany—History—20th century.   2. National socialism
and scholarship.   3. National socialism and intellectuals.   4. Holocaust,
Jewish (1939–1945)—Causes.   5. Germany—Intellectual life—20th century.
6. Germany—Ethnic relations.   I. Title.

DS146.G4S73 2006
940.53'180943—dc22

                                                                              2005052831

For Susanna

Contents

Studying the Jew

Introduction

This book is about the perversion of scholarship by politics and ideology. It follows the careers and publications of a few dozen German scholars who developed expertise about the Jews, their religion, and their
history, and placed that expertise at the disposal of the Third Reich.
These scholars were, in many instances, talented people who acknowledged no contradiction between intellectual respectability and hatred for
Jews. In retrospect we can easily recognize the mendacious, disingenuous, or ideologically reductionist nature of their work. But in the Third
Reich they were taken seriously as experts on an urgent matter of public
policy.

During the Nazi era, several terms were used to describe antisemitic
scholarship about Jews. The most common were "Jewish research" (*Judenforschung*) and "research on the Jewish question" (*Forschung zur Judenfrage*), the latter connoting an emphasis not so much on Jews themselves
as on Jewish-Christian relations. Although the term "Jewish studies"
(*jüdische Studien*) was not employed in Nazi Germany, it suggests what
the Nazi regime actually undertook to put in place during its short
12-year existence: an interdisciplinary academic field drawing upon
scholarship in anthropology, biology, religion, history, and the social sciences, with its own institutes, libraries, conferences, and journals.

For many years the standard work on this subject has been *Hitler's
Professors: The Part of Scholarship in Germany's Crimes against the Jewish
People,* published in 1946 by the eminent Yiddishist Max Weinreich.[1] As
the research director of the Jewish Scientific Institute in New York

1

(YIVO), Weinreich traveled immediately after the end of the war to Germany, where he collected antisemitic publications that had appeared in Germany during the Nazi period. The book amounted to an indictment of German scholars whose role in the Nazi persecution of the Jews had gone insufficiently recognized. *Hitler's Professors* was an angry book, and understandably so, as it reflected the German-educated Weinreich's deep personal revulsion over the conduct of his German counterparts. But Weinreich's anger did not stand in the way of a detailed and carefully documented reporting of facts, and when one considers how quickly the book was researched and written—Weinreich finished it in March 1946—then his achievement becomes all the more impressive. Reviewing the book in the periodical *Commentary,* Hannah Arendt praised Weinreich for calling attention to the collaboration by serious German scholars with the Nazi regime. Weinreich's book, wrote Arendt, "provides a good trunk to which supplements and additions can be grafted."[2]

Some supplementing and grafting has indeed been accomplished in the six decades since Weinreich. Much of the earliest research on the subject was contained in studies of Nazi organizations. Helmut Heiber's gigantic book on the historian Walter Frank and his Institute for History of the New Germany generated a wealth of information on one of the most important Nazi research institutions.[3] Works by Herbert Rothfeder and Reinhard Bollmus did the same for Alfred Rosenberg's organization,[4] while Michael Kater produced a formidable study of scholarship within the SS.[5] Two especially important studies appeared in the 1980s. Robert Ericksen's book on theologians in Nazi Germany presented the first thorough assessment of the antisemitic writings of Gerhard Kittel, one of the most prominent of the Nazi scholars active in this field.[6] Meanwhile, Michael Burleigh's study of Nazi research on eastern Europe documented how scholars helped to legitimize and plan a program of German territorial expansion that would necessitate the displacement of the Jews.[7] In the early 1990s, work by Götz Aly and Susanne Heim added further important details of the involvement of German scholars in the brutal German occupation of Poland and other places.[8]

Nonetheless, with the exception of Ericksen's study of theologians, none of these works offered intensive analysis of the intellectual qualities of antisemitic scholarship, and none were informed by a thorough knowledge of Jewish history, society, and religion. Beginning only in the late 1990s, a new wave of scholarship devoted to an in-depth appraisal of both the institutional and the intellectual features of Nazi Jewish studies began to emerge. The most notable of the recent studies have been Susannah Heschel's work on antisemitic Protestant theology,[9] Patricia von Papen's examination of Nazi historical writing on the Jewish question,[10] and Maria-Kühn Ludewig's biography of Johannes Pohl,[11] the Nazi Hebraist and plunderer of Jewish libraries. Most recently, Dirk Rupnow has contributed two very useful interpretive articles surveying the subject and historiography.[12]

In view of the immense and still growing body of scholarship about Nazi Jewish policy and the Holocaust, it seems curious that more has not been written on Nazi anti-Jewish research. This raises interesting questions about the basic assumptions of post-1945 historiography. One of these assumptions may have been that the writings of Nazi antisemites were pure propaganda, and thus did not merit serious intellectual consideration. In 1946, Max Weinreich warned against dismissing Nazi scholarship as simple "scurrilous literature," but his admonition went largely unheeded.[13] In general, moral revulsion toward National Socialism may well have discouraged scholars from taking seriously (not the same, it should be emphasized, as validating) the intellectual, cultural, and scientific production of that regime. Although we have now moved well beyond this point, we must still grapple with the disturbing question of whether Nazi Jewish research, or at least some of it, could be considered legitimate scholarship, despite its repugnant ideological bias.

The chief historical importance of Nazi Jewish studies is not, in any case, to be found in its contributions to the intellectual understanding of Jews and Judaism. Rather, it lay in its contribution to the Nazi regime's efforts to win intellectual and social respectability for anti-Jewish policies by supplying an empirical basis for longstanding antisemitic prejudices. Even though broad segments of German society subscribed to antisemitic beliefs before the Nazis came to power, such sentiments were by no means universal or uniform. Many Germans were not antisemitic, and others were only moderately so.[14] The Nazi regime endeavored to intensify and spread antisemitism, working through the media, the education system, and mass organizations.[15] The promotion of antisemitic scholarship must be seen as part of this broader effort to justify the persecution, and ultimately the removal, of the Jews.

The core of this book is formed by the published writings and statements of the antisemitic scholars—the actual scholarship and the people who produced it. While some necessary details about institutional contexts are provided, the emphasis here is on people and their ideas. This book offers a close, critical reading of the actual antisemitic texts, with attention given to their sources, methodologies, and conclusions, as well as their relationship to the bigger picture of Nazi ideology and anti-Jewish policy. This study limits itself to scholarship that was particularly focused on elucidating the racial characteristics, religion, history, and society of the Jews. It is organized into chapters devoted to academic disciplines, or clusters of disciplines. Although many of the Nazi scholars who are examined here regarded themselves as participants in an interdisciplinary enterprise, their scholarship usually tended to be anchored in the discipline of their training. Understanding the academic genealogy of the scholarship is no less important than understanding the political, ideological, and personal motivations of the people who produced it.

The organization of this book reflects the process by which Nazi scholars ascribed to Jews characteristics and behaviors that defined them as racially alien, religiously and morally corrupted, inassimilable, and dangerous. Chapter 1 describes the ideological, political, and institutional background of the emergence of Nazi Jewish studies. It addresses how Nazi ideas about Jews fit into the longer historical context of anti-Judaism and antisemitism. Early in his career, Hitler advocated what he called an "Antisemitism of Reason," a racial doctrine that would be a departure from the religiously, culturally, and economically based anti-Judaism of previous centuries. After Hitler's movement attained power, scholars who were sympathetic to its agenda moved to create and institutionalize an antisemitic Jewish studies founded precisely on the supposedly "scientific" principle of Jewish racial distinctiveness.

Chapters 2 through 5 examine antisemitic scholarship in a number of disciplines. They follow Nazi scholarship as its focus shifted from race to religion to history to sociology. The sequence of these chapters reflects the broad chronological sweep of Nazi Jewish studies, starting with the supposed ancient racial origins of the Jews and moving on to the creation of the Jewish religion, then to Jewish-Christian relations in modern times, and finally to social scientific studies of contemporary Jewry.

Chapter 2 traces the persistent effort to racialize the Jews, which involved the attempted reconstruction of their racial history since ancient times, as well as the description of the physical and behavioral characteristics that set them apart from other peoples. The attempt to define the Jews biologically was accompanied by scholarly efforts to define the essence of their religion. This is the focus of Chapter 3. Nazi ideology stipulated that biological race constituted the basis of all peoples, while cultural characteristics such as religion were merely the superstructure. Chapter 4 turns to Nazi historical scholarship on the evolution of the so-called Jewish question in early modern and modern times. The focus of such work was on Jewish-Christian relations in Europe, and in particular on the emancipation of the Jews and their assimilation into European societies. Chapter 5 examines how Nazi scholars in the social sciences analyzed Jewish communities of their own day, and provided quantitative evidence for the alleged pathological behavior of the Jews as aliens, criminals, capitalists, social parasites, agents of cultural decay, and defilers of the German race. The post-1945 legacy of Nazi Jewish studies is assessed in the Epilogue, but it is a theme that arises in many other parts of the book as well. What happened to the antisemitic scholars after the end of the Third Reich? Were they successful in finding academic positions? Did their ideas continue to resonate in German scholarship and society?

In his conclusion to *Hitler's Professors,* Max Weinreich claimed that German scholars "prepared, instituted, and blessed the program of vilification, disfranchisement, dispossession, expatriation, imprisonment, deportation, enslavement, torture, and murder."[16] Taking advantage of sixty years of historical perspective, a wealth of additional sources, and a far more detailed understanding of Nazi society, we must once again undertake a close interrogation of the antisemitic texts and the careers of their authors. We must continue to ask how and why scholarship, the very existence of which is (or should be) predicated on the search for enlightenment and truth, was produced in the service of an ideology of exclusion and domination.

1

An "Antisemitism of Reason"

On September 16, 1919, Adolf Hitler committed to paper one of his earliest ideological statements regarding the "Jewish question." The 30-year-old war veteran was still in the infancy of his political career, having just gravitated into the orbit of the small ultranationalistic, anti-Marxist, and antisemitic German Workers Party. His statement on the Jewish question came in the form of a letter to Adolf Gemlich, another recently decommissioned soldier.[1] The Gemlich letter began with an attack on what Hitler regarded as an outmoded, emotional form of antisemitism. For most Germans who were negatively disposed toward Jews, Hitler explained, antisemitism had more the character of a personal sentiment than a political doctrine. Most anti-Jewish antipathy arose from the bad impressions that ordinary Germans took away from their direct personal interactions with Jews. Unfortunately, Hitler maintained, when hostility toward Jews remained a "simple manifestation of emotion" it could not translate into a "clear understanding of the consciously or unconsciously systematic degenerative effect of the Jews on the totality of our nation." Emotional antisemitism, Hitler argued, could not provide the basis for a political program. "Antisemitism as a political movement," he insisted, "may not and can not be determined by flashes of emotion, but rather through the understanding facts."

Chief among these facts, Hitler continued, was that "Jewry is without question a race and not a religious community." Much more so than the peoples around them, the Jews had maintained their racial character "through a thousand years of inbreeding." For him, the essence of that character consisted of materialism and greed. Combining religious and racial motifs, which would remain a hallmark of his anti-Jewish rhetoric, Hitler asserted that "the dance around the golden calf" had been preserved in the racial essence of Jewry. Among Jews, he claimed, only money mattered, for Jews lacked the higher moral or spiritual aspirations of other peoples. Their craving for money was matched only by their desire for political power, the purpose of which was to protect and expand Jewish wealth. Whether it be through the purchase of influence from princes or through the manipulation of public opinion through their control of the press, Hitler asserted that Jews exploited whatever means might be at their disposal to acquire power. Invoking the kind of medical metaphor that came to be characteristic of Nazi antisemitic rhetoric, Hitler described the Jews as a "racial tuberculosis" among other peoples.

Old-fashioned emotional antisemitism, Hitler argued, was insufficient, and would lead only to pogroms, which contribute little to a permanent solution. This is why, Hitler maintained, it was important to promote "an antisemitism of reason," one that acknowledged the racial basis of Jewry. The solution, Hitler argued to Gemlich, should begin with the "systematic legal combating and removal of Jewish privileges" and lead ultimately to "the removal of the Jews altogether."

Hitler reiterated his belief in the importance of a racially conscious, scientifically sound "antisemitism of reason" in a number of speeches. The most important of these was delivered at a Nazi party meeting in the Munich Hofbräuhaus on 13 August 1920. Known as Hitler's "foundational speech" on the Jewish question, the detailed, several-hour-long oration carried the official title "Why Are We Antisemites?"[2] Hitler again underscored the need for a "scientific understanding" of the Jewish question but, in a new twist, admitted that this would remain worthless unless it were to become the "basis of a mass organization" that was determined to put antisemitic principles into practice. Hitler's new recognition of the indispensability of old-fashioned emotional Jew-hatred probably arose from his growing experience with political rabble-rousing. He raised the subject yet again a year later, on 8 September 1921, in another speech in Munich, for which his handwritten outline contained the following point: "Scientific antisemitism can here be combined with the emotional kind."[3] From the very beginning of his political career, therefore, Hitler believed in the importance of placing antisemitism on a racial, scientific footing, yet he came to understand that it would not suffice alone. It would have to be combined with the more emotional antisemitism he had derided earlier.

It has long been recognized that it was Nazism's preoccupation with race that distinguished it from antisemitic movements and ideologies of previous centuries, and that endowed it with an iron logic of exclusion and separation that led ultimately (if not inevitably) to the Holocaust.[4] Religious anti-Judaism had always promoted Jewish conversion to Christianity (or Islam), and an antisemitism that emphasized the cultural patterns or economic conduct of Jews had always allowed for the possibility of Jewish assimilation. In rejecting this tradition, Hitler placed himself in a fairly direct line of thought dating back to the second half of the nineteenth century. In 1879 Wilhelm Marr had promoted the concept of "antisemitism" as a way of underlining the racial, rather than religious, characteristics of the Jews. Theodor Fritsch had reinforced this racist antisemitism in his *Handbook of the Jewish Question,* which had first appeared in 1887, went through 36 editions before World War I, and continued to be published into the 1940s.[5] Hitler's "antisemitism of reason" followed in this tradition and posited the racial origin of Jewishness. Hence he assumed that the fundamental error committed by generations of Jew-haters had been to try to coerce, cajole, or seduce Jews into conforming to the Gentile majority. Jewishness, in the Nazi worldview, was fundamentally innate and hereditary, and a key aim of Nazi policy was to separate out and dissimilate the Jews, in effect undoing the damage supposedly done by well-intentioned but misguided antisemites of previous eras.

After the failed Putsch of 1923, the Nazi party moved away from its early revolutionary strategy for seizing power and toward one that was designed to attract voters. Consequently, Hitler's early emphasis on antisemitism gave way to a more multifaceted propaganda campaign intended to attract a diverse constituency. But antisemitism nonetheless remained an important plank in the Nazi platform. Hitler's rhetoric and that of his party continued to resonate with emotional anti-Jewish metaphors. Persistent recourse to a cruder and more emotional antisemitism as a mobilizing tactic did not preclude pursuing an "antisemitism of reason" simultaneously. The Nazi movement employed precisely the kind of approach outlined early on by Hitler, cultivating a "scientific antisemitism" that would provide a rational basis for an anti-Jewish policy, while at the same time exploiting traditional Christian accusations and stereotypical images to manipulate the baser instincts of the population. During the Weimar Republic, antisemitic writers associated with the Nazi movement produced a host of works attempting to demonstrate the innate, intractable, racial basis of Jewish behavior. Among these were Hans-Severus Ziegler, Paul Schultze-Naumburg, and Hans F. K. Günther, all three of whom were appointed to teaching positions after the Nazis had entered a coalition government in the German state of Thuringia in 1930. Günther's book *The Racial Characteristics of the Jewish People* (*Rassenkunde des jüdischen Volkes*), published the same year, offered a summary of the then current state of antisemitic racial anthropology, and would become a touchstone work in the soon-to-emerge field of Nazi Jewish studies.

Nazi Jewish Studies: The Institutional Framework

Despite the ideological mandate for a "scientific antisemitism," the Nazi movement never systematically developed a plan to realize it. After Hitler's assumption of power in 1933, the field began to emerge through encouragement and financial support from the upper echelons of the Nazi hierarchy as well as through initiatives from below, from academic and Nazi activists who recognized political and career opportunities when they saw them. The enterprise was shaped by improvisation at almost every step along the way. Nazi officials and agencies competed against each other to control the scholars and their scholarship. Traditional centers of power, such as the universities, sometimes resisted the pressure of Nazification and at other times acquiesced all too readily. Thus, the institutional beginnings and subsequent development of Nazi Jewish studies followed a pattern that was quite typical for the Third Reich. They conformed to the "polycratic" structure of the Nazi dictatorship, which was characterized by multiple centers of power, persistent interagency rivalry, and perpetual feuding among Hitler's lieutenants.[6]

Partly as a result of this Nazi polycratic syndrome, and partly because of the traditional organization of German academic life, Jewish studies in the Third Reich took the form of a loosely organized interdisciplinary enterprise. It drew upon the combined expertise of scholars based at universities, at free-standing research institutes, and at government agencies. Even though it never constituted more than but a small segment of German academic life, the field underwent significant growth in the relatively short span of its existence. In academic and intellectual life, then as now, twelve years do not amount to a significant period of time. We must keep this very limited time-frame in mind when assessing the successes and failures of this Nazi project.

The post-1933 Nazification of faculty, curricula, and course content at German universities was, from the Nazi perspective, a radical and often frustrating task.[7] The usual pattern was one of party and government pressure from above combined with accommodation of faculty from below. The speed and thoroughness with which the metamorphosis was accomplished, however, could differ drastically from one department and one university to the next. There were several obstacles the Nazis had to overcome. One was the inherent slowness of change in an academic establishment that was controlled by a small number of senior professors. Another was the intellectual and institutional conservatism of a large segment of the German academic world, which resented too overt a politicization of academic life, and feared, with some degree of justification, an influx of party hacks into the faculty. An obstacle peculiar to the introduction of antisemitic Jewish studies was the absence of qualified non-Jewish scholars who possessed expertise about Jews. The main exceptions to this rule tended to be found in the fields of ancient Oriental studies and Protestant theology. It was not by coincidence that one of the first universities to institutionalize Jewish studies was Tübingen, where Gerhard Kittel and Karl Georg Kuhn taught courses on ancient Judaism and the Talmud. As time passed, Jewish studies made increasing inroads in academic life. Professorships came open, funding was rechanneled, established scholars were retooled, and a new generation of graduate students proved willing to devote their energies to a subject area they perceived as politically advantageous and professionally opportune. By the early 1940s, courses on Jews or on the Jewish question were being offered at the universities of Berlin, Halle, Jena, Munich, Münster, Marburg, Vienna, Graz, and Heidelberg. The courses were based in a variety of disciplines, mainly history and theology but also psychology, economics, anthropology, and Slavic languages.[8] At least 32 doctoral dissertations were completed in Germany between 1939 and 1942 that dealt in some way with the Jews.[9]

Early in the regime, when the universities' embrace of antisemitic Jewish studies still seemed tentative, Nazi supporters decided to fill the gap by creating their own free-standing Jewish studies institute. The main force behind this initiative was the historian Walter Frank. In 1935, with support from high-ranking Nazis such as Alfred Rosenberg and Rudolf Hess, Frank founded the Institute for History of the New Germany (Institut für Geschichte des neuen Deutschlands), the purpose of which was to infuse a National Socialist perspective into German historical scholarship.[10] A short time later, this so-called Reich Institute established its special Research Department for the Jewish Question, based in Munich, and placed it under the direction of the historian Wilhelm Grau. Walter Frank publicly admitted that Grau's unit had been made necessary by the reluctance of university faculties to embrace and promote scholarship on the Jewish question.[11] Operating under the administrative protection of the Reich Education Ministry, during the second half of the 1930s the Research Department occupied a central position in the emerging field of Nazi Jewish studies. It sponsored research projects at universities, convened conferences that drew participants from a variety of academic disciplines, and published the conference proceedings in a scholarly yearbook, *Forschungen zur Judenfrage* (*Research on the Jewish Question*). This yearbook was published by the Hamburg-based Hanseatische Verlagsanstalt, a press that specialized in Nazi-oriented scholarship.[12]

Alfred Rosenberg, the longtime Nazi ideologue, had originally been among Walter Frank's patrons in the promotion of antisemitic scholarship. But the alliance deteriorated rapidly, and the two men, both stubborn and self-righteous by nature, became bitter rivals. Frank regarded Rosenberg as ideologically rigid and unscholarly, whereas Rosenberg saw Frank as an obstacle to his primacy as the Nazi movement's chief spokesman on ideological matters. This rivalry was a driving force behind Rosenberg's attempts in the late 1930s to establish a Jewish studies institute of his own.[13] After lengthy negotiations and some intrigue at the highest levels of the Nazi regime, Rosenberg finally got his way. The Institute for Research on the Jewish Question was created in 1941 as a branch of Rosenberg's planned Nazi University. Based in Frankfurt, where it had taken control of the large Hebraica and Judaica collections of the city library, Rosenberg's institute duplicated Frank's in some respects. It convened scholarly conferences, published a journal, and underwrote antisemitic research. It did, however, depart from Frank's in both substance and tone, making fewer pretenses to academic objectivity, and enjoying less cooperation from scholars with academic appointments. Its antisemitic rhetoric was more strident, and its usage of scholarship to justify anti-Jewish measures, such as the deportation of Jews from Europe, was more direct.[14] Its journal, *Weltkampf (World Struggle)* published articles that were much shorter and more thinly documented with evidence than those appearing in the *Forschungen zur Judenfrage*.[15] In one especially notorious respect, the ambitions of Rosenberg's institute extended beyond those of Frank's. Armed with a special commission from Hitler, Rosenberg organized a massive program for the plundering of libraries throughout Nazi-occupied Europe. The booty facilitated the extraordinary build-up of the research collections of the various branches of the new Nazi party university. As a result, hundreds of thousands of books stolen from Jewish libraries around Europe flowed into the Institute's Frankfurt library. Had Germany won the war, this would have remained the largest and most impressive Jewish library in Europe.

Research on Jews and the Jewish question was promoted by several further extrauniversity institutes in pursuit of the Nazi ideological agenda. The Institute for the Study and Eradication of Jewish Influence on German Religious Life, founded in 1939 by the Protestant theologian Walter Grundmann, supported research intended to justify the use of dejudaized Bibles and hymnals by church congregations.[16] The Publikationsstelle Dahlem specialized in statistical studies of the societies of eastern Europe, where the largest concentration of Jews in Europe was found.[17] In the field of race science, studies of Jews took place under the auspices of the Kaiser Wilhelm Institute for Anthropology, Human Heredity, and Eugenics in Berlin, which had been founded in 1927 and was presided over by the prominent racial anthropologist Eugen Fischer.[18] The same held true for the scientific research department of the SS, the so-called Ahnenerbe, under whose auspices some Jews were killed so that their skeletons could be preserved for racial and anatomical study.[19] Several government agencies established their own research institutes in which, among other subjects, the study of Jews was pursued. These included the Nazi occupation authority in Poland, the General Government, which employed antisemitic scholars in its Cracow-based Institute for German Work in the East (Institut für deutsche Ostarbeit).[20] Finally, the Reich Security Main Office (RSHA) initiated an ambitious program of research on Jews during the war. It hoped ultimately to achieve a primacy in this field consistent with its central role in the implementation of the Final Solution, seizing a huge number of books from Jewish libraries in the hope of building a major research collection. But the historians hired by the RSHA possessed little expertise about Jews, and they produced little actual scholarship before the Nazi regime came to an end.[21]

While the proliferation of institutes might convey the impression that Nazi Jewish studies was beset by disorganization or even chaos, such was not the case. The many centers of Jewish research all drew on a finite network of scholars, many of whom were employed by one institute or university while engaged in a commissioned project by another. A division of labor among university faculties, free-standing institutes, and government agencies is quite typical in the world of scholarship. Notwithstanding the abhorrent purpose of the scholarship itself, the decentralized institutional structure of Jewish studies in Nazi Germany would not be unfamiliar to American or European scholars working in a variety of fields in our own day.

The Social and Political Function of Antisemitic Scholarship

The intellectual characteristics and broad social function of Nazi Jewish studies must be understood within the larger context of how the "Jewish question" was publicly represented in the Third Reich. Although Hitler himself distinguished between two types of antisemitism, the antisemitic discourse of the Nazi era can best be viewed as a three-tiered phenomenon. The bottom tier consisted of the crasser forms of anti-Jewish propaganda, designed to appeal to the less intellectually discerning among the masses of the German population.[22] The propaganda was delivered in various forms, including newspapers that were read by millions, films such as *Jud Süss (The Jew Süss)* and *Der ewige Jude (The Eternal Jew)*, and innumerable speeches by Nazi leaders. A notch above this lowbrow propaganda was a middlebrow discourse designed to secure social and intellectual respectability for antisemitism among educated Germans, or at least among those with higher intellectual standards. This genre usually took the form of nonfiction books aimed at a general readership, and political-cultural periodicals such as the *NS-Monatshefte (National Socialist Monthly)* with a circulation of 52,500, and the SS newspaper *Das Schwarze Korps (Black Corps)*, with a circulation of 189,000.[23] Textbooks designed for classroom use in primary and secondary schools might also be included in this category.[24] Finally, the products of Nazi Jewish studies constituted a top tier of Nazi antisemitism, one based ostensibly on scientific and factual knowledge. This tier was by no means isolated from the tiers below it but rather funneled ideas down to them.

The scholars who were active in Nazi Jewish studies wrote and published first and foremost for each other, and then for the rest of the academic community, Nazi officials, and educated laypersons more broadly. Such intellectual elitism was consistent with their strong self-identification as serious scholars. It was also a practical consequence of their desire to secure academic appointments. But they did not pursue their scholarship sealed away in an ivory tower. Although most of their books and articles attracted a limited readership, their arguments often surfaced in the middlebrow antisemitic publications, and were reported fairly widely in the German press, trickling down to a mass readership and providing "scientific" legitimation for Nazi antisemitism and anti-Jewish policies. For example, the organ of Wilhelm Grau's Research Department for the Jewish Question, the *Forschungen zur Judenfrage,* contained abstruse language and a dense academic apparatus that made it inaccessible to the vast majority of the German reading public. But the content of these volumes (and the lectures on which they had been based) received frequent coverage in mass-circulation newspapers. The *Völkischer Beobachter,* the Nazi party's newspaper, which had a circulation of almost two hundred thousand in Berlin alone, and hundreds of thousands more in other regional editions, reported regularly on lectures and conferences sponsored by the antisemitic research institutes. Similar reports appeared in daily newspapers such as the *Deutsche Allgemeine Zeitung* (circulation 60,000), the *Berliner Tageblatt* (60,000), the *Frankfurter Zeitung* (72,000), the *Westdeutscher Beobachter* (200,000) and a host of other newspapers that, taken together, reached a large percentage of the German population.[25] In 1941, the opening of Alfred Rosenberg's Institute for Research on the Jewish Question was the subject of a splashy report in the *Illustrierter Beobachter,* a national publication with a circulation of almost seven hundred thousand.[26]

Public lectures, and the attendant coverage in the mainstream press, were an important conduit through which scholars channeled their "scientific antisemitism" to broader audiences. In the late 1930s, Walter Frank's Reich Institute organized two series of public presentations by several of the scholars who had contributed to the *Forschungen*. The first series of lectures was offered in Munich in late 1937, in conjunction with the exhibition "The Eternal Jew." This exhibition, sponsored by the Munich district of the Nazi party, attracted over four hundred thousand visitors. The lecture series included presentations about the Dreyfus Affair, the Jewish influence on German philosophy, Baruch Spinoza, the racial development of ancient Jewry, the Talmud, the Jews and capitalism, and Goethe and the Jewish question. German newspapers devoted extensive coverage to the lectures, reporting that they attracted overflow crowds to the main auditorium of the University of Munich.[27] Frank's Reich Institute organized a similar lecture series in January 1939, held in the main auditorium of the University of Berlin on Unter den Linden just a few weeks after the "Kristallnacht" pogrom of 9–10 November. According to German press reports, the audiences were so large that many listeners had to sit in the aisles. In the opinion of the *Völkischer Beobachter,* this turnout demonstrated the determination of the people of Berlin to address the Jewish problem with the "weapons of scholarship."[28] German Radio broadcast a three-minute summary of the proceedings on the evening of each lecture.[29] Media coverage of the same scale was granted to the opening conference of Alfred Rosenberg's antisemitic research institute in March 1941. The *Völkischer Beobachter* celebrated "Research in the Struggle against World Jewry" with a front-page banner headline and over the next two days described the contents of some of the scholarly lectures.[30] Through this mechanism, ordinary Germans were persuaded that the policies of their government accorded with the research findings of learned university professors and other scholars.

An example of how the trickle-down effect could work is found in the now-famous diary of Victor Klemperer, a Romance languages scholar of Jewish heritage who survived the Nazi years by virtue of his marriage to a so-called Aryan woman. On 12 July 1938, Klemperer recorded in his diary: "Antisemitism again greatly increased. I wrote to the Blumenfelds about the declaration of Jewish assets. In addition to the ban on practicing certain trades, yellow visitor's cards for baths. The ideology also rages with a more scientific touch. The Academic Society for Research into Jewry is meeting in Munich; a professor (German university professor) identifies the eternal traits of Jews: cruelty, hatred, violent emotion, adaptability—another sees 'ancient Asiatic hate flickering in Harden's and Rathenau's eyes.'"[31]

Klemperer read German newspapers in order to keep abreast of the news, and also to collect material for his study of the Nazi use of language.[32] His information on the meeting of the "Academic Society for Re-search into Jewry" might well have come from the *Völkischer Beobachter,* which reported on the conference in three consecutive editions a few days earlier.[33] Klemperer committed one minor error: the actual name of the sponsoring organization was the Research Department for the Jewish Question of the Institute for History of the New Germany. Its annual conference, held 5–7 July in Munich, had featured presentations by the historian Walter Frank, the racial anthropologist Eugen Fischer, the bi-ologist Otmar von Verschuer, and the theologian Gerhard Kittel. The text of Klemperer's diary entry is telling: first he related new concrete Nazi anti-Jewish measures, and then he immediately noted the attempt to anchor antisemitism in science. Klemperer recognized how the two fit together. He understood that a science of antisemitism was designed to legitimize a policy of antisemitism. And in all likelihood he had learned about the conference of antisemitic scholars from one of the very same newspapers that ordinary Germans could and did read.

The education system provided a further channel through which "sci-entific antisemitism" entered the mainstream of German society. Text-books and curricula targeted at students in primary and secondary schools resonated with messages about the racial otherness of the Jews. In many cases they drew heavily from the standard works of scholarship in race science, yet they also transmitted simplistic and mean-spirited anti-Jewish stereotypes that were designed to instill in students a visceral revulsion toward the Jews.[34] These educational materials, with their hy-brid content of "science" and propaganda, may well have best embodied what Hitler had in mind when he spoke of the need to combine scientific and emotional antisemitism.

In addition to its legitimizing function, antisemitic scholarship pro-vided a form of "intelligence," that is, practical information about Jews and Judaism that could be applied directly to the formulation and im-plementation of the regime's anti-Jewish policies. Max Weinreich's 1946 book, which underscored instances of such direct participation, served as an indictment of what he regarded as a class of German criminals who had not been prosecuted at Nuremberg.[35] A similar emphasis on direct complicity in the genesis and implementation of the Final Solution is to be found in recent German work about the careers of scholars and other "experts" in the Nazi period. One prominent German specialist on the Nazi era has gone so far as to describe such experts and scholars as the "guiding forces of extermination."[36] Yet this characterization is questionable. In Nazi Germany, the key policy decisions were made by a state and party elite that was prepared to exploit, or to ignore, the advice of scholars as convenience dictated. Scholars and other experts did not so much determine the main contours of Nazi anti-Jewish policy as they contributed to decision-making by helping to define and articulate the alleged "problem," generating concrete information about Jewish communities, recommending a range of possible solutions, and providing arguments that could be invoked by Nazi leaders seeking to justify one policy or another. This did indeed amount to a substantial involvement in the formulation of policy, but one that was probably less significant than their contribution to the legitimization of Jew-hatred within German society.

"Scientific Antisemitism": An Intellectual Sketch

The careers and works of the Nazi experts on Jews reveal certain repeated themes and common patterns. Perhaps the most salient is the explicitly stated intention to modernize antisemitism by placing it on a racial footing. Relying on the developing field of race science, Nazi scholars identified racial difference as a fundamental, if not always obvious, factor of historical causation. Because, as they maintained, all humans possess an instinctive sense of racial identity and racial difference, antisemitism in Germany could be explained as the manifestation of a natural revulsion of Germans toward Jews. Similarly, they regarded the Jewish religion as an external manifestation of the Jewish racial essence rather than as a faith system that could and should be understood on its own terms. In the social sciences, a preoccupation with maintaining racial purity underlay attempts to quantify the extent and social consequences of miscegenation and intermarriage between Germans and Jews. Empirical data about the partners who breached the racial divide and their progeny, derived from statistical studies of fertility, fecundity, economic standing, and criminality, were marshaled to demonstrate the degenerative consequences of racial mixing.

The scholars who pursued the new antisemitic sciences took their roles as professional academics seriously, seeking to anchor their antisemitic research and writing in the established or emerging methodologies of their disciplines. In the field of race science they endeavored to identify genetic, and not merely anthropological, markers for Jewishness. In the field of religious studies they tried to augment traditional Christian theological critiques of Judaism with insights into the psychological and sociological consequences of Jewish religious and legal practices. In the field of history they worked in the archives to reconstruct in detail the nature of Jewish-Christian relations in specific communities over time, and to situate the role of antisemitism in the popular consciousness of ordinary people in past centuries. In the social sciences they revisited and reevaluated the theories of earlier scholars who had hypothesized about the nature of Jewish society, such as Werner Sombart and Arthur Ruppin, in the light of new data.

The insistence on academic standards for research, documentation, and publication was intended to clearly set the antisemitic scholars apart from the cruder forms of antisemitism that were common in Nazi Germany. Even though the arguments of "scientific antisemitism" filtered through to a wide public through mass-circulation newspapers, the scholars endeavored to keep a safe distance from the coarse antisemitic propaganda appearing in the popular media. The *Völkischer Beobachter* and other propaganda organs resonated with age-old antisemitic accusations, such as that Jews had engaged in the ritual murder of Christian children and used their blood to make Passover matzo. They mongered the common allegations about Jewish conspiracies, the most defamatory of which was represented by the myth of the Protocols of the Elders of Zion. Julius Streicher's newspaper *Der Stürmer* (circulation 486,000) was particularly notorious for its semipornographic caricatures of Jews as seducers and molesters. Relatively little of this perverse fare was present in Nazi Jewish studies. This is not to say, however, that the scholarship was not virulently antisemitic in its own way. Its viciousness was of a more subtle kind, deriving from the tendentious and often cynical manipulation of scientific knowledge, historical events, religious texts, and statistical data. As a "respectable" means for justifying the disenfranchisement, expropriation, and removal of Jews from German society, the Nazi scholarship served a purpose essentially like that of the cruder propaganda.

Ironically, a hallmark of Nazi Jewish studies was its exploitation of voluminous scholarship produced by Jewish scholars past and present. Long before 1933, the use of Jewish texts as a basis for attacking Jews and Judaism had become a well-established antisemitic strategy. In medieval and early modern times, Christian scholars pored over Jewish religious and legal texts in search of evidence of the theological error of

Judaism, Jewish hostility to people of other faiths, the unethical nature of Jewish business practices, and a wide array of further transgressions. While many of these earlier attacks took the form of vituperative polemics against Judaism, not all did. During the Reformation, the movement known as Christian Hebraism produced dozens, if not hundreds, of Protestant scholars who specialized in Jewish texts. While their ultimate purpose, namely the refutation of Judaism and the conversion of the Jews, may have been identical to that of anti-Jewish polemicists, their idiom differed dramatically. They valued a careful and rigorous assessment of Jewish texts, as read in their original languages, carried on cordial relationships with Jewish scholars, and in some cases defended the rights of Jewish printers to publish the Talmud at a time when authorities desired to ban it. These scholars were convinced that the more information available about Judaism the better, and that the fatal flaws at the core of Judaism could most effectively be exposed by using the Jews' own words. Later antisemites, such as Johann Eisenmenger, who worked in the seventeenth century, and Theodor Fritsch, who worked two centuries later, were a good deal less polite, but they carried on the tradition of mining Jewish texts for antisemitic material.

In the Nazi period, Jewish religious texts, especially the Talmud, remained important sources for anti-Jewish research, but antisemitic scholars now had a far greater bounty with which to work than did their predecessors from earlier centuries. In the intervening period, Jews had produced an immense body of nonreligious scholarship about themselves and their history. This began with the nineteenth-century movement known as the "science of Judaism" (*Wissenschaft des Judentums*), continued late in that century with the emergence of an *anti*-antisemitic race science, and advanced further in the early decades of the twentieth century with the advent of Jewish social science, specifically sociology and statistics, epitomized by the work of Arthur Ruppin. Much of this Jewish scholarship, written from reformist or Zionist perspectives, focused on what were deemed to be the problematic, even pathological characteristics of Jewish society, which were believed to be the consequences of persecution and life in the Diaspora. The purpose of this scholarship had been to improve Jewish society.[37] Jewish scholars had produced a constructive, self-critical, and empirically based body of knowledge as part of a grand emancipatory project. What they could not anticipate was that their work would become source material for antisemitic scholarship that itself aspired to scientific respectability. During the Nazi era, antisemitic scholars pored over the works of their Jewish counterparts, acknowledged the factual veracity of the data contained in the Jewish works, selected what they needed, and cited them extensively in support of their own racist ideology.

The heavy use of Jewish materials was only to be expected of scholars who wished to be taken seriously as experts on Jewish life and history. As a rhetorical strategy for legitimizing antisemitism, however, it was potentially a double-edged sword. Exploiting the Talmud and other traditional Jewish texts for antisemitic arguments was one thing, but citing modern-day secular Jewish scholarship was quite another. Could Jewish scholars be cited without according their point of view some validity? Antisemitic scholars skirted this problem by insisting on the distinction between data and interpretation. They thus credited Jewish scholars with the technical competence to collect information and report it accurately. But when it came to interpretation, they asserted the need to consider, and correct for, the cultural and even racial bias of Jewish authors.

Even as they presumed that neutrality was impossible for Jewish scholars, the Nazi scholars often laid claim to objectivity and scientific rigor in their own work. For some, this assertion may well have been the result of a sincere conviction that Nazism did indeed embody the essential truth about Germans, Jews, and race. For others who were less deluded, it was a convenient means for obfuscating the obvious contradiction between scholarly integrity on the one hand and intellectual work on behalf of an official state ideology on the other.

Like most scholars, the Jew experts of the Third Reich acted out of a combination of personal self-interest, ideological conviction, and career-oriented opportunism. Genuine antisemitic conviction clearly was at work in many cases, even though explaining the psychological or biographical origins of such hatred can be difficult. For its part, careerist opportunism can be easily discerned among scholars who had exhibited no antisemitic tendencies before 1933, and then emerged as Jew-haters once the Nazis were in power. But it is hard to know what sentiments they may have kept to themselves until they felt confident to express them. There is also the common human tendency to reduce intellectual and moral dissonance by adjusting one's ideological beliefs to one's social and professional circumstances. For many, the adoption of an antisemitic worldview may well have been an entirely inevitable adjustment to life in Nazi Germany. Finally, we need to keep in mind that anti-semitism of one form or another had been quite a common feature of life in Germany before 1933. Such sentiments had been held by many Germans of all social and economic classes, and had been by no means uncommon in academic circles. With regard to their attitudes toward Jews, the changed political situation in Germany after January 1933 required no adjustment at all.

Whatever their individual motivations may have been, German scholars set about to create a Nazi version of Jewish studies that would fulfill Hitler's call for an "antisemitism of reason." Many of them were people of high intelligence and formidable discipline, people who would have likely succeeded in political circumstances much different from those of the Third Reich. Yet however much they may have perceived themselves as contributing to knowledge and to the pursuit of truth, their most significant contribution would be to the legitimation of the barbaric policies of a brutal regime.

2

Racializing the Jew

is more, Felix Mendelssohn had been Jewish only by virtue of Nazi racial definitions. In actuality, Mendelssohn had been a Christian whose notable compositions had included the Reformation Symphony. On all of these levels, Weil exposes the crude racist stereotype that was at the heart of Nazi antisemitism.

During the Third Reich, the Nazi preoccupation with race and heredity manifested itself in almost every area of policy, both inside Germany and in German-occupied Europe. With good reason, the Nazi regime has been referred to as a "racial state."[2] Race, rather than religion or political orientation, lay at the core of the most fundamental policy decisions regarding membership in the so-called German "community of the people" (*Volksgemeinschaft*). Exclusion from this community initially took the form of social marginalization and economic disfranchisement, and later escalated to physical segregation, deportation, forced labor, and murder. Jews were not the only people to suffer this fate. It befell others as well, most notably the Roma and Sinti ("Gypsies"). In the name of protecting a racially defined "community of the German people," the Nazi regime also persecuted homosexuals, stigmatized social nonconformism as a hereditary abnormality, and forcibly sterilized disabled Germans, eventually murdering hundreds of thousands of them. The entire structure of exclusion and persecution rested on a foundation of racist and eugenic thought that specified the boundaries between German and alien, healthy and unhealthy. One of the chief functions of the regime's racial experts was to define those boundaries and to endow them with intellectual legitimacy.

The racialization of the Jews—the definition of their peoplehood primarily in biological rather than religious, social, or cultural terms—had begun in the nineteenth century. It developed as part of a more general tendency to divide humanity into racial groups, to define behaviors typical to each group, and to attribute those behaviors to heredity.[3] The Nazi regime inherited a large and often contradictory body of racial theory that had been produced in Europe and the United States by scholars with a variety of backgrounds and motivations; some had themselves been Jewish.

The Nazis came to power determined to rid Germany of its Jewish "problem." The state of racial "knowledge" as of 1933 provided an inadequate basis for the anti-Jewish legislation that would follow. Nazi scholars pressed forward with research on the racial origins and characteristics of the Jews. They pursued this mandate for diverse personal reasons: their belief in its correctness; their yearning for status and significance in the new order; and their concern to secure steady employment. Beyond these personal motives, they hoped to enhance the intellectual legitimacy of antisemitism, to influence state and party policy, and to contribute to what they believed to be the advancement of science.

The Foundation: Hans F. K. Günther

A reader immersed in the output of Nazi Jewish studies will inevitably notice that one book was cited more often than any other: Hans F. K. Günther's *Racial Characteristics of the Jewish People (Rassenkunde des jüdischen Volkes)*, which was published in 1930.[4] Although many of Günther's own Nazi contemporaries harbored serious doubts about the scientific qualities of his work, his writings succeeded in framing academic discussions about race in Nazi Germany. His works performed three important functions: they embodied an apotheosis of the racist tradition in German anthropology of the late nineteenth and early twentieth centuries; they provided a bridge between that tradition and the ostensibly more scientifically based race science of the Nazi era; and they encapsulated a racial interpretation of human existence that seemed to be based on rigorous research, even as it was relatively easy to understand for nonspecialist readers.

Born in 1891 in Freiburg, Günther had trained as a linguist specializing in Germanic and Romantic languages, as well as in Finnish and Hungarian.[5] After receiving his doctorate in 1920, he served as a secondary school teacher in Dresden. He frequented the Anthropological Institute in that city, where he consulted the literature that would establish his reputation as "Race-Günther." In 1922 he published *The Racial Characteristics of the German People (Rassenkunde des deutschen Volkes)*, a study that would become a touchstone work for German racists in the Weimar and Nazi periods. The book, which was published by J. F. Lehmanns, one of Germany's most prominent right-wing presses and a chief exponent of race ideology, went through 16 editions by the end of 1934.[6] The first 11 editions contained special appendices on the racial origins of the Jews, but in the late 1920s Günther resolved to devote an entire book to that subject. When the Nazis assumed power in the German state of Thuringia in 1930, Günther was appointed to a professorship for social anthropology at the University of Jena. The appointment provoked a good deal of controversy within the faculty, some of whose members regarded Günther as more of a party hack and a dilettante than a serious scholar.[7] The appointment, which came at about the same time that *Racial Characteristics of the Jewish People* was appearing,[8] was the first high-profile, ideologically motivated academic decision made by a Nazi government, and a harbinger of things to come. Günther officially joined the Nazi party in 1932, and continued to enjoy professional success and notoriety after the Nazi seizure of power. In 1935 he moved from Jena to the University of Berlin, where he took over an institute for "Race Studies, the Biology of Peoples, and Rural Sociology." In 1939 he accepted a professorship at the University of Freiburg. After the war, Günther continued to publish in a racist vein, but he was not able to secure another academic appointment. He died in 1968, but remains to this day an iconic figure among "Nordic" supremacists.

Although Günther was the Third Reich's most prominent and widely cited expert on race, his work was not considered cutting edge in its time. His publications remained for the most part uninformed by insights from modern genetics, a field that received a great deal of official support from the Nazi regime. Günther depended instead on softer methodologies inherited from the racialist discourses of the nineteenth and early twentieth centuries. First and foremost among these was a physical anthropology that concentrated mainly on the classification of human beings into racial groups or typologies based on external physiological characteristics, such as the size and proportions of the body, the shape of the face and head, and the color of the skin, eyes, and hair. Günther synthesized this sort of anthropological data with observations drawn from philology, art, religion, and Jewish history. He performed little or no original research of his own. His technique was to consume and sort through the large and growing literature on race, synthesize his own conclusions based on the research of others, and explain it all in a clear, straightforward manner to a broad readership. Enhancing the accessibility of his books was the profusion of photographs and other illustrations that Günther harvested from anthropological collections.

Günther presented his *Racial Characteristics of the Jewish People* as the synthesis and culmination of the research carried out over the past century by non-Jewish as well as Jewish scholars. There was nothing especially novel to his claim that the Jews were a mixture of races rather than a singular or pure race per se. This argument had attained common currency in race theory by the turn of the twentieth century. The most prominent exponent of this view had been the University of Berlin anthropologist Felix von Luschan.[9] Writing in the 1890s, Luschan had insisted on a clear distinction between linguistic and racial categories, dismissing the notion that Jews could be thought of simply as "semites," as the recently coined term "antisemitism" had implied. Instead Luschan had maintained that the Jews represented an amalgamation of three races: the Arabic-Semitic, the Nordic-Amoritic, and the ancient Hittite. Inasmuch as Günther also depicted the Jews of modern times as the product of several "hereditary racial dispositions" that had been sharpened through a process of "selection" over the centuries, he belonged to the same school as Luschan.[10] For its part, Günther's account of the racial development of the Jewish people over thousands of years was based on a more elaborate racial typology than Luschan's had been, and also incorporated the extensive historical and anthropological literature on Jews that had appeared between 1900 and 1930.

Even though race was the central idea in Günther's writing, he insisted on respecting a crucial distinction between the concept of "race" and that of *Volk*. Referring to the popular discourse about race within the Nazi and other right-wing movements, Günther conceded that in "nonscientific contexts" it perhaps "doesn't hurt" to refer to the Jews simply as a race. But scholarly treatments of the subject, he emphasized, required semantic distinctions. The Jews should be properly understood not as a race but rather as a mixture of races constituting a *Volk*. Moreover, he argued, both "semitic" as well as "Aryan" were linguistic and not racial concepts, and the frequent use of these terms generated, in his opinion, more confusion than enlightenment about the racial origins of Germans and Jews.[11]

Günther reflected mainstream race theory in arguing that all of the peoples of the modern era had been produced by the mixing of prehistoric races that long ago had ceased to exist in their pure forms. The identities and locations of these original races, as well as their physical and cultural characteristics, had been matters of debate for decades. In various works published during the 1920s, Günther posited a racial typology in which 10 ur-races accounted for the composition of the peoples of modern Europe. The Nordic race, based originally in Scandinavia and the northern part of present-day Germany, constituted the dominant element

(*Einschlag*) of the modern German *Volk,* albeit in combination with elements from other European ur-races, such as the Eastern (*Ostische*) race, the Western (*Westische*) race, and the Dinaric (Balkan) race. Central to Günther's argument about the racial composition of the Jews was his assertion that they had descended by and large from non-European races, most notably the Near Eastern (*Vorderasiatische*) race, an origin that rendered them fundamentally different and incompatible with Germans and most other Europeans.

Günther devoted a significant chapter of *Racial Characteristics of the Jewish People* to describing the traits of this Near Eastern race. Previous race theorists had referred to this group by a variety of labels, including Assyroid, Proto-Armenian, and Hittite. It had supposedly originated in the Caucasus and in the fifth and fourth millennia B.C.E. had expanded into Asia Minor and Mesopotamia, and eventually to the eastern coast of the Mediterranean Sea.[12] The original race, Günther maintained, was preserved in its most hereditarily unadulterated form in the modern-day Armenians. Günther adduced from this fact that the characteristics of the ur-race could be determined from close observation of contemporary Armenians. This circular logic was as absurd as it was common in such racist discourse. First it designated the (supposed) characteristics of modern peoples as echoes of the attributes of ancient forebears, and then it cited the similarities between ancients and moderns as proof of hereditary continuity. People of the Near Eastern race, according to Günther, had been of medium physical stature, and had possessed short heads, moderately broad faces, and large, protruding, downwardly curving noses. The stereotypical Ashkenazic Jewish nose, Günther claimed, needed to be understood as a physiognomic legacy of the Near Eastern racial influence. It was not so much the size of this nose that Günther considered racially distinctive but its geometry and, more specifically, its "nostrility," a term Günther borrowed from the article about "Nose" in the *Jewish Encyclopedia.*[13] This feature, as Günther described it, derived from fleshy outer nostrils set conspicuously high on the face. Aside from the nose, other facial features of the Near Eastern race included fleshy lips, a wide mouth, and a weak, receding chin, which, in combination with the distinctive nose, were seen to give the Near Eastern face its unmistakable profile. Günther's list of typical features also included large, fleshy ears, brown or black hair, brown eyes, brownish skin, heavy body hair, thick converging eyebrows among men, and, among women, a tendency toward corpulence often resulting in double chins.[14] It was a racial por-

pushing dislike

trait that Günther knew would strike most of his readers as aesthetically unpleasing.

In Günther's racist thinking, it was axiomatic that races and peoples possessed psychological and cultural qualities that were linked by heredity to their external physiological characteristics. Circular reasoning was at work here as well. Günther based his description of the personality of the Near Eastern ur-race on characteristics he attributed to modern Greeks, Turks, Jews, Syrians, Armenians, and Iranians ("Persians"), whose similarities to the ancient race were presumed to serve as proof of the explanatory power of race and heredity. Many Nazi-era scholars who cited Günther reproduced this fallacious reasoning.

The salient cultural trait of the Near Eastern race was, in Günther's view, its "commercial spirit" (*Handelsgeist*). Günther noted that on this point he was in full agreement with the Jewish race theorist Samuel Weissenberg, who had described Armenians, Greeks, and Jews as "artful traders."[15] The "commercial spirit" was seen to be the product of a "supple mind," a "gift of the gab," a good feel for the psychology of other peoples, an ability to assess opportunities and circumstances, and an ability to understand foreign cultures. While some of these qualities might be considered admirable, Günther left no doubt that they were menacing. He maintained that the Near Eastern race had been "bred not so much for the conquest and exploitation of nature as it was for the conquest and exploitation of people." Moreover, the race possessed a tendency for "calculated cruelty," which manifested itself in the kind of money-lending caricatured by Shakespeare in the figure of Shylock.[16]

merchant spirit
Economics

Günther regarded peoples of Near Eastern origin as deficient in the area of state-building and statecraft. The Armenians, Günther asserted (citing Luschan), were the most ungovernable people of all. Only when a strong Nordic racial element had been added had peoples of predominantly Near Eastern racial origin been able to establish effective polities.[17] Near Eastern peoples, Günther believed, possessed an aptitude for building religious communities, although they also tended to get carried away with their emotions. Günther viewed their emotional volatility as destructive, producing an ambivalence between an "unbridaled lust for flesh" on the one hand and a predilection for "mortification of the flesh" on the other.[18]

For Günther, Europeans had an instinctive, racially inbred aversion to peoples of Near Eastern racial origin and the traits they exhibited. As evidence for this assertion, he pointed to the frequency with which satanic figures were represented with Near Eastern physiognomies in European art. He provided an illustration from a medieval English manuscript showing a devil with a hooked nose, as well as a sculpture on the Cathedral of Notre Dame in Paris depicting an evil spirit.[19] Along similar lines, he devoted a chapter to ancient expressions of the Jewish ideal of physical beauty, with special attention given to the Song of Songs.[20] In so doing, Günther invoked aesthetic preferences as evidence of racially determined tendencies, a common line of argument in Nazi racist scholarship.[21]

Racial Alientin About half of Günther's book attempted to explain how European Jews came to be a racial hybrid of predominantly Near Eastern origin, and were thus racially alien to Europe. Fundamental to his argument was the assertion that the prebiblical Canaanites had belonged mainly to this race. The ancient Hebrews, on the other hand, who later entered Canaan and merged with its inhabitants, had been of Oriental racial stock, originating in northern Syria, or perhaps Arabia. In the modern world, Günther claimed, the Oriental race was most pronounced in the Arab world, and in parts of Central Asia.[22] The chief physical traits of this group included medium stature, slender build, and long, narrow heads. The Oriental nose did not protrude especially, and tended to curve down lower than Near Eastern noses. The face was also marked by slightly bulging lips, almond-shaped eyes, and small ears. Peoples of predominantly Oriental origin tended to have light brown skin and dark hair.[23]

The cultural and psychological qualities of the Oriental race, Günther claimed, were best observed among modern-day Bedouin. One noticed an "aloof dignity," a "gloomy seriousness," and a "pronounced obduracy," the last of which may help explain the severity of religious belief among peoples of Oriental origin.[24] These qualities corresponded to the impressionistic observations of Orientalists who were contemporary to Günther. The British Orientalist Archibald Henry Sayce, for example, was quoted by Günther as ascribing to the Arabs "intensity of faith, ferocity, exclusiveness, [and] imagination." Sayce saw these as "Semitic" traits, but Günther claimed that Sayce, and others, had confused the Semites, a linguistic-cultural classification, with Oriental racial elements.[25] Why it was that Europeans had also exhibited a penchant for religious fanaticism was a question that Günther did not think to address.

Citing works by Immanuel Benzinger and other prominent scholars of ancient Israel, Günther identified two migrations into Canaan, the first by Hebrews, and the second by Israelites, Hebrews who had spent several generations in Egypt. Günther maintained that these migrations had resulted in a racial amalgamation between the Near Eastern Canaanites and the oriental Hebrew/Israelites. Günther called the result an "Oriental-Near Eastern-Nordic-Hamite-Negro mix of races."[26] This mix contained Negro and Hamite (Ethiopian) racial elements that the Israelites had acquired in Egypt. Both of these ur-races had been native to sub-Saharan Africa. Günther was eager to demonstrate that modern Jews often exhibited African features, a desire best exemplified by his juxtaposition of a picture of Benjamin Disraeli with that of a Hottentot.[27] As for the Nordic element, Günther held that it had already been present in the Canaanite population as the result of prehistoric migrations from Europe, and was later reinforced by the arrival of Philistines and other peoples who contained some Nordic blood.[28]

According to Günther, the Babylonian exile of the Israelites increased the Near Eastern element in their racial composition.[29] Upon return from this exile in the sixth century B.C.E., Nehemiah and Ezra undertook to stabilize and standardize the religion of Judaism. Günther interpreted their reforms as major steps toward the racial "sealing off" (*Abschliessung*) of the Jews. The measures included the discouragement of exogamy and the branding of non-Jews as impure.[30] Many such strictures and prejudices were later carried over into the Talmud, which Günther and other racist antisemites understood as the protector of Jewish racial purity after the forced dispersion from the ancestral homeland.[31]

To Günther, racial instincts were essential for understanding the situation of Jews in the Diaspora. In Hellenistic-Roman times, the commercial possibilities offered by the Mediterranean world proved irresistible to "people of primarily Near Eastern race" whose "commercial spirit" made them restless.[32] Günther's explanation for the origins of the Jewish Diaspora focused far more on this voluntary dispersion than on the later forced dispersion under the Romans, thus underscoring the point that Jews of subsequent centuries owed their predicament as a homeless people to their own racial instincts rather than to oppression by others.

The same racial instincts (reinforced by Talmudic prohibitions) limited Jews' racial mixing with the peoples around them, even if a good deal of cultural assimilation took place. But the prohibition of exogamy did not preclude conversions to Judaism, and through such means additional external racial elements were infused into the Jews.[33] The most notable infusion, in Günther's view, was the mass conversion of the

Khazars in the eighth century. Günther saw the Khazars as having been predominantly of the Near Eastern race. Their conversion to Judaism further strengthened the Near Eastern racial element among the Ashkenazic Jews (whom Günther called "Eastern Jews"), rendering it, rather than the Oriental, predominant.[34] Among the Sephardic Jews (in Günther's terminology, "Southern Jews"), who lived primarily in the Middle East and North Africa, mixing took place with peoples of primarily Oriental racial background. As a consequence, a racial divergence emerged between Ashkenazic Jews, whom Günther characterized as a mix of Near Eastern, Oriental, East Baltic, Eastern, Inner-Asian, Nordic, Hamite, and Negro, and Sephardic Jews, whom he described as a mix of Oriental, Near Eastern, Western, Hamite, Nordic, and Negro.[35]

Günther's emphasis on the impact of the conversion of the Khazars on the racial composition of the Jews becomes all the more notable when considered in the context of racial theory as it had developed in Germany since the late nineteenth century. Most race theorists had insisted that the Jews of modern times represented a pure race descended from their ancient ancestors. The racial mixing that had produced the Jews was assumed to have taken place at least two thousand years earlier. This essentially had been von Luschan's argument. The most significant challenge to this position had come from Samuel Weissenberg, a distinguished Jewish physician and anthropologist working in Russia around the turn of the century.[36] Weissenberg, who had received his medical training in Germany, was aghast at the antisemitic intentions (or at least implications) of race theory, inasmuch as one of its basic points was the essential, hereditary otherness of the Jews. His own ambitious anthropological fieldwork among Jews in Russia and the Middle East led him to conclude not only that the Jews were much more racially diverse than the dominant race theory had presumed but also that this diversity was the result of mixing that was far more historically recent. Equally important, Weissenberg emphasized the significance of environment, rather than heredity, for explaining both the physiological and cultural characteristics that made the Jews distinctive. The hereditarian Günther rejected Weissenberg's environmentalism but, ironically enough, argued that the Jewish Weissenberg had been correct (and the non-Jewish von Luschan incorrect) about the extent of Jewish racial mixing since ancient times. But Günther's agreement with Weissenberg would take him only so far. The Jews of modern times, in Günther's view, were still a highly inbred people, so much so that they might be considered a "race of the second order."[37]

Having established the racial origin of the Jews, Günther proceeded to describe at great length the defining attributes of modern-day European Jews. His catalog of Jewish stereotypes intended to explain what made the Jews recognizable as a specific *Volk* to other Europeans. The characteristics noted were morphological and behavioral, having to do with the way Jews looked, the way they walked, gestured, spoke, and smelled. Günther emphasized that Jews themselves had observed and written frequently about peculiarly Jewish features. He cited studies published by Jewish scholars, and emphasized that much of his presentation rested on the observations of Samuel Weissenberg.[38] Günther's use of Weissenberg's scholarship to promote conclusions that would have been anathema to Weissenberg himself (Weissenberg died in 1928) typified the antisemitic exploitation and distortion of Jewish scholarship that would become routine in the Third Reich.

Günther pointed out that the physical characteristics of Jews that were conspicuous to other Europeans were not specifically Jewish but rather were typical for peoples of Near Eastern and Oriental racial origin.[39] Jews, Günther noted, were set apart by their size, tending to be small relative to the peoples around them.[40] Jews were marked not only by their size but also by their unusual shape and proportions, which included short limbs, small breasts, and rounded backs. Günther speculated that the rounded back was not a hereditary feature in and of itself but rather the result of a physically degenerate lifestyle that was itself the product of a racially determined psychology.[41] Along similar lines, Günther argued that the Jewish propensity for fatty faces, necks, and shoulders was the consequence of an "opulent" lifestyle of overconsumption and little exercise or physical labor.[42] Even as he presented his racial portrait as the findings of scientific inquiry, Günther's disdain for the Jews was never far from the surface.

Physical anthropologists had long employed measurement of the size and shape of human heads as a methodology for racial classification. Borrowing from the anthropological literature, Günther observed that modern-day Jews usually had moderately, but not overly, short heads. (In the jargon of the physical anthrolopologists, they were mesocephalic rather than brachycephalic.) The shape and size of Jewish heads did, however, show variation from one region to the next. Günther discussed

Franz Boas's study of the "Changes in Bodily Forms of Descendants of Immigrants," published in 1910, according to which North American Jews had heads that were longer than those of European Jews. Boas had ascribed this difference to environmental influences in the United States, a conclusion that racist anthropologists found threatening. Günther speculated whether the real explanation for Boas's findings might well have been that the Jews of North America contained a disproportionately heavy Oriental racial element. This itself, Günther argued, might have been the result of the process by which European Jews of particular geographic origins were "selected" by political circumstances for migration to America.[43]

Günther's depiction of Jewish facial features could not have been calculated to be more unflattering. He described "bulging" lips, heavy eyelids, large, fleshy ears, loose skin, hairiness, and a prominent nose. To the heavy eyelids he attributed the stereotypical "furtive gaze," which many had interpreted as "sensual and brooding" or "sly." Günther supported this observation with quotations from the *Jewish Encyclopedia* as well as from the influential German Jewish magazine *Ost und West*.[44] Jewish ears, he wrote, were not merely large but also relatively fleshy, and tended to protrude more perpendicularly from the head than the ears of non-Jewish Europeans. This feature, particularly noticeable among children, Günther pointed out, had given rise to the Austrian expression "Moritz ears," a form of derision that associated large ears with a common Jewish name.[45] Jewish skin, Günther maintained, was often dark, loose, and matted, and betrayed Jewish heritage when no other distinctive Jewish features were present.[46] As for the most familiar stereotypical feature, the nose, Günther emphasized the association of Jews with the "nostrility" typical of the Near Eastern race. He acknowledged, however, that this Near Eastern racial feature was actually a good deal less common than was widely believed. In fact, he argued, it was found among only a minority of Jews. Weissenberg, for example, had contended that only 10 percent of Russian Jews possessed this form of nose, an estimate that Günther did not contest. Yet this nose had somehow become the foremost physical marker of Jewishness. Günther hypothesized that the Near Eastern nose had come to be associated with the "authentic Jew" by virtue of its virtual absence among European non-Jews. Rare as it might have been, it stood out as a marker of difference between Jews and other Europeans.[47]

Jews with blond hair and blue eyes were not uncommon in Europe, and presented a special challenge to Günther, as they seemed to fly in the face of the normal racial taxonomies. Günther took pains to fit this phenomenon into his theory. For Günther, an exponent of the virtues of the Nordic race, the key question was the degree to which blond-haired, blue-eyed Jews contained Nordic blood. He admitted that this was indeed part of the explanation, as there had been a Nordic racial element in the Jews since ancient times. But Günther ascribed greater importance to the infusion of an "East Baltic" racial element into the Jews. His source for this assertion was the work of Maurice Fishberg, a Jewish scholar who had been a contemporary of Weissenberg.[48] Light hair and green or blue eyes, Günther maintained, were common characteristics of the East Baltic race, which had originated in the northwestern regions of modern-day Russia. Decisive for Günther was the observation that among peoples of East Baltic background, these features were hereditarily linked to short heads, just as they were among the minority of Jews who exhibited them. Blond-haired, blue-eyed Nordic peoples, in contrast, had longer heads. Citing both Fishberg and another Jewish scholar, Sigmund Feist, Günther pointed out the tendency of contemporary German Jews to seek blue-eyed, blond-haired spouses. Fishberg and Feist had based this assertion on surveys of classified advertisements published in Jewish newspapers for persons seeking partners. To Günther, the significance of this pattern was twofold. First, it reflected the strong influence of a Nordic ideal of beauty that had taken hold among Jews, and second, it reflected an attempt by Jews to camouflage their heritage.[49] Had it been Günther's intention to elucidate the psychological dimensions of the drive among many German Jews to assimilate, these would not have been unreasonable conclusions.[50] But in the context of Günther's work, the implication was a good deal more sinister, suggesting that the alteration of the physical appearance of Jews promoted their infiltration into a society in which they were racially alien.

Günther's racial stereotyping of the Jews was not limited to physical appearance. He made much of supposedly distinctive Jewish body movements and gestures, which, he claimed, struck non-Jews as "essentially different" (*andersartig*).[51] These qualities of the body were in part the result of hereditary physiology and in part habitual, although, Günther insisted, physical habits were themselves often rooted in psychological qualities that were passed down through heredity. Whether through heredity or culture, Jewish movements and gestures were innate to the group—something that Jewish observers had long recognized, Günther pointed out. He provided the example of Walther Rathenau, the prominent Jewish businessman and politician who had been assassinated in 1922. Rathenau has often been presented as the epitome of the nationalistic, ultraassimilated German Jew, whose eagerness to fit in to German society manifested itself as Jewish self-denial or even self-hatred.[52] By virtue of their "dilapidated and crooked" way of walking, Günther cites Rathenau as having written in 1902, Jews had made a "laughingstock" of themselves in the midst of the Germans, a people that had been "educated and bred according to strict military standards." Günther further endorsed Rathenau's description of Jewish movements and gestures as signaling either "tail-wagging obsequiousness" or "contemptuous arrogance." Rathenau, however, had believed that the Jewish body and Jewish mannerisms had been environmentally determined; they were the product, in Rathenau's phrase, of "two thousand years of misery"—the implication being that the amelioration of the conditions under which Jews lived would normalize their bodies. Günther attacked this view as an example of misguided Lamarckianism, the belief in the "heritability of acquired traits" that enjoyed some popularity in the early twentieth century. According to Günther, these traits needed to be seen instead as those of the Near Eastern race "in their peculiarly Jewish manifestation."[53]

Jewish bodily movements, Günther observed, were set apart by their "softness" and "limpness." The "Jewish gait" was slow and "creeping." Jews tended to shuffle. The main cause for much of this, Günther contended, was the frequency of flat-footedness among Jews.[54] This longstanding stereotype had seemed to receive empirical validation in a study conducted during World War I by the Anglo-Jewish geneticist Redcliffe Salaman, who had measured the feet of Jewish and non-Jewish soldiers in the British army. Whereas only 1 out of 40 non-Jewish soldiers had flat feet, among Jews it had been 1 out of 6.[55] Salaman provided photographs to Günther for use in the latter's research.[56] Although Günther did not explicitly endorse the longstanding belief that flat feet made Jews unfit for military service, it served as the biological premise of his assertion of a "Jewish gait."

This distinct gait, as Günther described it, was determined in part by movements of the arms. During walking, Günther maintained, the upper arms of Jews tended to remain tucked in close to the body, while below the elbows their forearms moved energetically, as though to accompany talking. The configuration was similar during running, although in this case the lower arms were pointed downward and outward. The overall effect, Günther emphasized, impressed non-Jews as awkward and peculiarly Jewish.[57]

The Jewish face was distinguished by peculiar expressions, rooted physiologically in muscle structure and movement, and psychologically in Jewish attitudes toward life. To illustrate this point, Günther asked his reader to consider the familiar Jewish archetype of the "nebbish." Quoting an article from the Jewish magazine *Ost und West,* Günther described the "nebbish" as a Jewish type recognizable by certain expressions of tenderness and lamentation, by a certain manner of whimpering, crying, and showing fear.[58]

The Jewish persona, Günther argued, was further accentuated by a "particularly Jewish way of talking," the so-called *Mauscheln* (or *Gemauschel*). The designation for this stereotype has its origin in the word *Moshe,* the Hebrew name for Moses. For centuries this derisory characterization of Jewish speech patterns served as an important marker of Jewish otherness.[59] Quoting the early eighteenth-century work "The Peculiarities of the Jews," by the Christian scholar Johann Jakob Schudt, Günther pointed to the "peculiar accent and pronunciation and diction" that gave a Jew away "as soon as he opens his mouth." Günther also cited the antisemitic composer Richard Wagner as an authority on this subject. In his essay *Jews in Music,* Wagner had described the Jewish manner of speech as "hissing, shrilling, buzzing, and messy," attributes he also found in Jewish music. The Jews, Wagner maintained, might learn the language of their host nation but would always speak as foreigners.[60]

The *Mauscheln,* Günther explained, was not only noticeable among German Jews but manifested itself in different versions wherever Jews lived among other peoples. It was much more than a simple accent, he argued. Every *Volk* had its own peculiar "sound preference," which was determined hereditarily through the physiology of speech organs as well as by psychological characteristics. The *Mauscheln,* therefore, had to be seen as a manifestation of "racially specific" sound patterns among Jews who had taken on a new "racially alien" language. Jews who spoke without a noticeable *Mauscheln* had simply "repressed" their natural manner of producing sounds. The distinctively Jewish speech attributes included audible respiration ("stertorous breathing"), nasal intonation, and guttural pronunciation of the "ch" consonant. Günther allowed for the environmental explanation that the Jews had been using a Semitic language for millennia, but underscored the similarities between the Jewish *Mauscheln* and the "sound preference" of the modern peoples of the Caucasus, who, like the Jews, were of primarily Near Eastern racial origin.[61]

Among the most malicious of anti-Jewish stereotypes invoked by Günther was that of the "Jewish odor." The so-called *odor Judaeus* had been ascribed to Jews for many centuries, as Günther took pains to document in page after page of examples drawn from ancient and medieval sources. In an especially egregious exploitation of a Jewish text, Günther cited passages from the Talmud in which human body scents were mentioned, tendentiously interpreting them to prove that the Jews had possessed a strong collective olfactory consciousness already in ancient times.[62] Günther did not see the Jews as being unusual in this regard. Every *Volk* had a particular odor, he pointed out, substantiating this claim with a collection of impressionistic anecdotes drawn from diverse cultural contexts. Native South Americans, for example, were said to have attributed specific odors to Europeans, to Africans, and to themselves. Similarly, according to Günther, Chinese dogs were able to discern Europeans dressed in Chinese clothing on the basis of differences between European and Chinese body odors. Every culture records such observations about the distinctive smells emanating from those who are alien, and in Europe these observations applied primarily to Jews. The peculiar odor of every *Volk* often seemed unpleasant to persons from other peoples; it struck them as a "stench."[63] As Günther understood it, the distinctive odor of a people was determined by the interaction of "inherited odor" and "acquired odor." Whereas the first was the result of "racial hereditary disposition," the second was a product of environmental factors such as locality, dwelling, clothing, diet, occupation, and hygiene. Individual persons transmitted odor through perspiration, especially from the armpits, from their hair, and from their sexual organs. Chemically, odors were differentiated by the composition and combination of fatty acids in the perspiration. In the case of the Jews, Günther conceded that much of the odor may have been attributable to poor hygiene among eastern European Jews, as well as to an ancient and enduring Jewish partiality toward garlic. Günther expressed his hope that the developing field of "race physiology" would address the question of the degree of hereditary influence involved, mainly through analysis of blood and fatty acids.[64] In expressing this hope, Günther underscored the limitations of his own methodology, in effect acknowledging that modern science was in the process of overtaking the kind of old-fashioned analysis embodied by his own work.

Günther's *Racial Characteristics of the Jewish People* could (and did) serve as a handbook for racist antisemites, but Günther denied that he was an antisemite himself. At the heart of the "Jewish question," he wrote, was not the alleged racial inferiority of the Jews, but rather their racial "otherness" (*Andersartigkeit*), their "racial-psychological estrangement" from Germans and other Europeans.[65] This, he asserted, was an objective fact, subject increasingly to scientific proof, which both Jews and non-Jews would have to confront. The attempt to live together had, inevitably, produced negative consequences for all involved, so for the sake of the European *Völker* as well as that of the Jews, a separation would be necessary. In Germany this separation was all the more urgent because of the dramatic increase in "mixed marriages" in the first three decades of the twentieth century. Citing the conclusions of the Jewish scholar Max Marcuse, a German pioneer in research on sexuality, Günther pointed out that mixed marriages between Jews and non-Jewish Germans produced fewer children than did endogamous marriages. Whereas Marcuse had attributed this phenomenon to cultural, psychological, and economic preferences of Jews and their non-Jewish partners, Günther emphasized the role of "mutual racial dissimilarity," which inevitably lowered the fertility of both peoples.[66] Moreover, he believed, the children produced by such marriages included a disproportionately high number of "psychopaths and neurotics," "physical deviants," and criminals.[67] Of particular concern to Günther was the Jewish preference for German partners with blond hair and blue eyes, that is, precisely those Germans with a "strong Nordic element." The Germans, Günther argued, had good reason to be "horrified" at the increasing number of such marriages and their consequences: the "racial contamination [*Durchfremdung*] of the hereditary elements of their own *Volk*."[68]

Günther greeted Zionism as a positive development, praising it for recognizing the genuine racial consciousness (*Volkstum*) of the Jews. The "segment of Jewry that thinks in a Jewish-*Völkisch* way," he observed, properly recognized the "process of mixing" as a "process of decomposition" that threatened their own people.[69] The "racial-biological future of Jewry," he asserted, could take one of two paths, either that of Zionism or that of "destruction" (Untergang). The assimilation of the Jews into European society, Günther argued, was a chimera based on the erroneous universalistic worldviews of liberalism or Christianity. Mixing with non-Jews had led to Jewish degeneration, and as long as Jews remained among peoples who were racially alien to them, they would be subject to degradation and marginalization. "Only the clear separation of Jews from non-Jews, and of non-Jews from Jews," he concluded, would provide a "dignified solution to the Jewish question."[70]

Günther's rhetorical nod to evenhandedness and his pretension of showing concern for the welfare of the Jews did distinguish his brand of antisemitism from the cruder, more overtly vicious anti-Jewish propaganda that was common in Germany in his day. Even so, its antisemitic tenor was unmistakable. Günther's work embodied a combination of popular accessibility and a veneer of scientific legitimacy that made it ideal as an intellectual justification for later anti-Jewish legislation in Germany. Separation of Jews from Germans in the realm of marriage, sex, and reproduction was at the core of Nazi racial policy after 1933. Other Nazi measures were intended to create a separate cultural space for Jews living in Germany, or to encourage or badger Jews into emigrating from Germany altogether. The transfer of Jews from Germany to a prospective Jewish homeland in Palestine was consistent with Günther's call for separation and with his encouragement of Zionism. It was for this reason that some Jewish Zionists could even find some logic in Günther's ideas (even as they probably did not mistake him for a philosemite). A measure of Günther's legitimacy in this context was the visit he received in 1933 from Arthur Ruppin, the prominent Jewish scholar and Zionist. After dropping in on Günther at the latter's institute at the University of Jena, Ruppin noted that he had had a pleasant and satisfying meeting with the German professor. The two men agreed that the Germans and the Jews should be separated from one another.[71]

Günther represented an intellectual tradition that specialized in describing, and sometimes measuring, externally observable human physiological features and behaviors. Methods drawn from anthropology, however, could not explain the biological mechanisms underlying human heredity, and were, therefore, not capable of determining the precise influence of heredity on observed characteristics. Toward the end of his *Racial Characteristics of the Jewish People,* Günther suggested that race science in the future should head in the direction of the developing field of genetics. The study of Jewish blood types, he argued, and also that of Jewish pathology, that is, Jewish susceptibility to various kinds of illnesses, were only beginning to provide fruitful areas of research. Günther pointed to articles that had been published in the 1920s in mainstream medical journals, such as one on the optical physiology of the eyes of Jews that had appeared in the *Journal of Ophthalmology (Zeitschrift für Augenheilkunde).* Much of the emerging literature cited by Günther was also appearing in the *Archives of Racial and Social Biology (Archiv für Rassen- und Gesellschaftsbiologie),* a journal that was issued by J. F. Lehmann, Günther's own publisher, and whose board of editors included the prominent scientists Fritz Lenz and Eugen Fischer.

It would not be an overstatement to say that Günther's *Racial Characteristics of the Jewish People* became a touchstone work for Nazi Jewish studies, laying out a research agenda in a number of fields. Günther had presented the Jews as a people of diverse racial origin who, over time, had developed into a "race of the second order." He had promoted the notion that humans possessed a racial instinct that bred an innate aversion to racial difference. He had pointed to the racial consciousness that the Jews themselves had cultivated, had underlined the degenerative consequences of miscegenation, and had suggested the emigration of the Jews as a solution to the problems presented by their presence in Germany. For antisemitic scholars who followed Günther, these ideas provided both a foundation and a point of departure for further inquiry.

"Scientific Antisemitism" in Practice: The Nuremberg Laws

A fusion of Günther's "racial antisemitism" and practical anti-Jewish policy can be seen in the notorious legislation known as the Nuremberg Laws, which were promulgated by the Nazi regime in the autumn of 1935.[72] Two of these laws—the Reich Citizenship Law and the Law to Protect German Blood and Honor—were issued in September on the occasion of the annual Nazi party rally in Nuremberg, while the third—the Law to Protect the Hereditary Health of the German People—followed several weeks later. The three laws, as well as a plethora of related decrees regarding implementation, were intended to bring a modicum of order and consistency to the ongoing efforts to define and marginalize

Germany's Jews. There had been a great deal of racial legislation and administrative chicanery targeted at Jews since the Nazis had come to power in Germany in January 1933, but much of it had been improvised by ministerial bureaucracies, provincial governments, and quasi-official occupational guilds. It would be an exaggeration to say that "chaos" prevailed in the realm of anti-Jewish legislation in late 1935, but there were vagaries, ambiguities, and contradictions that would have to be resolved from the top down. The Nuremberg laws intended to do just that.

The laws established for the first time a fixed hierarchy of racial categories that would remain in place for the duration of the Nazi regime. The categories ranged from "full Jew" at the bottom of the scale to full "Aryan," or German, at the top. There were two intermediate categories of "mixed race" persons, so-called *Mischlinge,* in between.[73] Every German would be classified into one of these categories depending on the religious affiliations of his or her four grandparents in 1871, the year of the founding of the German Reich. Persons with three or four Jewish grandparents were classified as Jews, regardless of their religious faith. Persons with only one Jewish grandparent were classified as *Mischlinge* of the second degree, and in most respects were treated like Germans. The most complicated situation was that of persons with two Jewish grandparents, that is, "half-Jews," who were designated as *Mischlinge* of the first degree. If these were married to Jews or belonged officially to the Jewish community, they were classified as "Jews under the law" (*Geltungsjuden*). With regard to marriage, the Nuremberg Laws trapped the *Mischlinge* of the first degree in pincers, as they were prohibited from marrying or having sex with Germans or with *Mischlinge* of the second degree, and if they married Jews they would be classified as Jews and suffer the consequences. The laws, in effect, encouraged *Mischlinge* of the first degree either to marry other members of the same category or to remain single. This method of regulating sex and marriage intended to reinstitute a separation between Jewish and German bloodlines, which, from the Nazi perspective, had become dangerously intermingled as the result of extensive intermarriage in the late nineteenth and early twentieth centuries.[74]

The laws were intended to institutionalize a universal, smoothly functioning, and predictable system of racial definition, inclusion, exclusion, and separation. While the laws set down basic principles, the details of implementation were worked out in a series of further laws, decrees, en-

actments, and other administrative measures. The increasingly voluminous and complex body of Nazi racial legislation presented a challenge
to the bureaucrats and lawyers whose job was to make this new racial order function on a daily basis. Government experts tried to provide a
modicum of synthesis and clarity in a series of annotated legal compilations. The most influential, and notorious, of these commentaries was
published in 1936 by Wilhelm Stuckart and Hans Globke.[75] Both were
high-ranking functionaries in the Reich Ministry of the Interior. As the
state secretary, Stuckart was the senior professional civil servant in the
ministry, and, in effect, its second-in-command. The holder of a doctorate in jurisprudence, Stuckart was one of the Nazi regime's pivotal figures in the area of anti-Jewish legislation.

Stuckart's historical notoriety stems primarily from his participation
at the infamous Wannsee conference in January 1942, at which he represented his ministry and helped to work out the modalities of the "Final
Solution." As described in the well known Wannsee Protocol—the record
as written down by Adolf Eichmann—Stuckart's main contribution to
the deliberations was to oppose the inclusion of mixed-race Germans in
the deportation of German Jews "to the east." Such persons, Stuckart argued, contained valuable German racial characteristics that should not
be sacrificed. More pragmatically, he warned that the brutal treatment of
mixed-race Germans would damage morale among their many pure-
blooded German relatives, some of whom were in the Wehrmacht. Stuckart suggested the possibility of simply sterilizing the *Mischlinge* as a
compromise solution.

Stuckart's expertise in such matters derived from his years of elaborat-
ing the legal status of mixed-race Germans. Although fewer in number
than full Jews, there were tens of thousands of such persons in Germany,
and questions concerning their racial status, access to occupations, and
personal freedoms—including the freedom to choose whom they might
marry—were actually a good deal more complicated than those pertaining to the more cut-and-dried categories of Aryan and Jew. Many of the
administrative measures that were enacted with a view to implementing
the Nuremberg laws pointedly addressed the confounding status of
mixed-race Germans (as well as that of Aryans and Jews in "mixed marriages").[76] Stuckart's collaborator on the legal commentary, Hans Globke,
who also held a doctorate, was a high civil servant in the Interior Ministry. Globke would later go on to enjoy a successful career in govern-

ment in the post-1945 Federal Republic. His appointment as Chancellor Konrad Adenauer's chief of staff in 1953 led to one of West Germany's major early political embarrassments. Globke seemed to provide the classic example of the "bureaucratic perpetrator" (Schreibtischtäter), who had managed to escape justice by virtue of having engaged in persecution from behind a desk rather than from behind a rifle.[77]

In 1936, the positions of Stuckart and Globke in the Interior Ministry endowed their commentary on the Nuremberg laws with the status of a quasi-official publication. Most of their book addressed details of how specific provisions were to be interpreted for purposes of day-to-day practice. But it also contained an introduction that laid out the fundamental ideological principles upon which the Nuremberg laws were based. This introduction is instructive, not only because of the influential nature of the Stuckart-Globke commentary but also because it endeavored carefully and soberly to sort out a number of concepts that the Nazi regime's own propaganda had, intentionally or not, obfuscated. It constituted a dramatic example of applied "scientific antisemitism."

Stuckart and Globke based their presentation in large part on the work of Hans F. K. Günther. They opened their introductory essay with a meditation on the concepts of "race" and Volk. In many Nazi texts and speeches, these terms had been employed more or less interchangeably (and historians of the Third Reich have usually treated the terms as synonyms in the Nazi parlance.) Stuckart and Globke, however, insisted on distinguishing between the two concepts, both of which were the "products of research in the modern natural sciences," particularly in biology and anthropology.[78] Although the notion of Volk may have originated as a "historical-cultural" concept, its meaning had evolved as it became clear that the characteristics of a Volk were determined largely by its racial composition. There were "Germanic, Romantic, and Slavic languages," Stuckart and Globke asserted, "but no Germanic, Romantic, or Slavic races."[79] Where one can speak of a "German Volk, but no German race," there was also, "strictly speaking, no Jewish race." The Jews, like the Germans, were a Volk comprising a "mixture of races" that was commonly, but misleadingly, referred to as the "Jewish race." Whereas the German Volk consisted by and large of a combination of European races, the Jewish Volk was constituted primarily by a mixture of races whose origins lay outside of Europe.[80]

Citing Günther's *Racial Characteristics of the Jewish People,* Stuckart and Globke described the Jewish *Volk* as a mixture of the Near Eastern and Oriental races. "The Jewish problem," they argued, stemmed from the fact that the Jewish and German peoples were different by both "blood" and "their most internal essence."[81] Tensions between the two peoples were the inevitable result of their close contact, especially inasmuch as the Jews in Germany did not live in a "closed settlement" or as a "national minority" but were distributed intimately among the German population.[82] Echoing Hitler's frequent criticisms of traditional antisemitism, Stuckart and Globke noted that those who in previous decades had attempted to address the Jewish question through "mixing and intellectual convergence" had lacked a "racial consciousness."[83] The assimilation of the Jews into German society had only made things worse. The Nuremberg laws would promote the "only possible solution," namely, "dissimilation."[84] The German *Volk* simply wished to keep its "blood and its culture pure," Stuckart and Globke observed, "much like [what] the Jews have desired for themselves since the days of the Prophet Ezra."[85]

The reference to Ezra echoed a belief that had been expressed by Günther and other racist antisemites. For centuries Jews had cultivated, through their laws and rituals, racial purity among themselves. If Jewish law recognized the importance of maintaining racial purity, then how could anyone blame the Nazi regime for attempting to halt the mixing of the Jewish and German peoples? The purpose of Stuckart and Globke's essay on Volk and race was to rationalize the Nuremberg laws, at the core of which lay the idea of racial separation. The new laws, they claimed, would bring about a "clear separation based on blood between Jewry and Germandom," thereby providing a "modus vivendi" that would be "just" for both peoples.[86] The laws not only would prevent the "penetration of further Jewish blood into the body of the German *Volk*" but would also gradually eliminate the "mixed race," or *Mischling,* problem that had been the result of decades of Jewish assimilation. This would be accomplished through a set of rules, sometimes quite complex, governing marriage (hence reproduction) among persons in the various racial categories.

Although the Stuckart-Globke essay was intended as a justification for legislation rather than a work of scholarship, it provides a clear example of how some prominent members of the Nazi regime perceived a need to rationalize policy on a foundation of "scientific antisemitism." The legal commentary would have served its practical purpose well even without an ideological introduction. But the inner logic of the legislation, as Stuckart and Globke saw it, could be laid out more persuasively within the context of the racial theory on which it was based. They wished to present an explanation of Nazi thinking about race that went a good deal deeper than the regime's "emotional" propaganda. They invoked Hans F. K. Günther to validate their distinction between *Volk* and race, their allusion to the multitude of ur-races that formed the bases of modern-day peoples, and their explanation of why Jews sometimes had blond hair and blue eyes. Yet by citing Günther, Stuckart and Globke were relying on the authority of a race expert whose work was behind the times methodologically. The German field of race science was already moving well beyond him.

Modernizing Racial Theory: Baur-Fischer-Lenz, Otmar von Verschuer

During the Third Reich, the racial origins and characteristics of the Jews were a major preoccupation for several of Germany's leading specialists in racial anthropology and human genetics. Among them were two of the three authors of the most widely read and cited German genetics text in the Weimar and Nazi periods, *The Study of Human Heredity (Menschliche Erblehre)*. This book, commonly referred to as the "Baur-Fischer-Lenz," after its authors Erwin Baur, Eugen Fischer, and Fritz Lenz, first appeared in 1921, with revised editions following every few years. The 1936 fourth revised edition was the only edition to be published in the Nazi era;[87] a fifth edition that was in preparation and scheduled for publication around 1940 never appeared.[88]

All three authors were pioneers in the scientific study of genetics. Erwin Baur's academic background and interests lay primarily in the area of botany. In 1928 he helped to found and became director of a new Kaiser Wilhelm Institute devoted to research on plant cultivation. He died in 1933, before he could play much of a role in the Nazi period. His co-authors, however, thrived professionally after 1933. Eugen Fischer had received his academic training in anatomy but then became increasingly interested in anthropology.[89] In 1913, after an extended visit to German Southwest Africa, he published his now notorious study of the "Rehoboth bastards," which examined the applicability of Mendel's laws of heredity to humans and warned of the dangers of racial mixing between Europeans and Africans. In 1927 Fischer accepted a professorship for anthropology at the University of Berlin, and at the same time was named director of the newly founded Kaiser Wilhelm Institute for Anthropology, Human Heredity, and Eugenics. Fischer remained in this position until his retirement in 1942, and was thus a central figure in the German establishment dedicated to research on heredity during the Nazi era.

The same could be said for Fritz Lenz. Trained as a pathologist, and closely connected with the German eugenics movement, in 1933 Lenz accepted a position as leader of the Race Hygiene office in the Institute directed by Fischer. After World War II, Lenz was able to continue his academic career with a professorship at the University of Göttingen, from which he retired in 1955. His egregious antisemitic assertions in the 1936 edition of Baur-Fischer-Lenz were not enough to disqualify him from a prestigious academic position in the postwar Federal Republic. Neither was his involvement with Fischer's Kaiser Wilhelm Institute, which lent its expertise to Nazi eugenic and antisemitic policies in a variety of ways.

In the 1936 edition of the Baur-Fischer-Lenz, Eugen Fischer's section entitled "The Normal Physical Hereditary of Humans" had relatively little to say about Jews. Citing innovative American research on the fingerprints of various national groups, Fischer noted that Jews exhibited much different patterns from those of most European peoples, thus adding yet another marker of Jewish physiological otherness.[90] Aside from this and a few more minor passages, Jews were not a major theme in Fischer's section. Perhaps this was because Fischer had earlier run into some trouble with the Nazi party's Racial-Political Office, headed by Walter Gross, when he had spoken about Jewish racial characteristics primarily in terms of difference rather than inferiority.[91] But while the substance and tone of Fischer's work might not have satisfied certain hardcore racists, Fischer was hardly a political dissident. His entry into the Nazi party in 1940 received the personal support of Heinrich Himmler. And although his section in Baur-Fischer-Lenz avoided the question of Jewish racial origins, Fischer did address the issue extensively elsewhere.

In July 1938, Fischer delivered a lecture entitled "The Racial Origins and Ancient Racial History of the Hebrews" at a conference convened in Munich by the Research Department for the Jewish Question of the Institute for History of the New Germany, the leading sponsor of scholarly antisemitism. The participation by Fischer, the director of a branch of the Kaiser Wilhelm Society and one of Germany's most respected scientists, undoubtedly enhanced the legitimacy and stature of the Institute. Fischer's lecture was then published in the Institute's journal, *Forschungen zur Judenfrage*.[92] Previous conferences and issues of the *Forschungen* had concentrated mainly on Jewish history and religion, so Fischer's contribution from the perspective of a natural scientist represented somewhat of a departure. Fischer commenced his lecture with some general observations about how humans began as a unitary race, then dispersed geographically and subdivided into genetically disparate groups as the result of gene mutation and natural selection. The Jews emerged as a genetically distinct group in ancient Palestine, with the "Oriental race as its basis, the Mediterranean race as an admixture, the Near Eastern race as a second basis, crossed from time to time by Nordic elements." He emphasized that the racial formation of the Jews had been finalized in ancient times and had remained fairly stable ever since. Whereas Hans F. K. Günther had posited greater fluidity in the racial composition of the Jews through the Middle Ages, and cautioned against using the term "race" to describe the Jews of modern times, Fischer argued that Jewish inbreeding had "harmonized" the originally disparate racial elements into a new race rather early on. Physiological diversity among Jews could easily be explained by reference to Mendel's laws concerning dominant and recessive genes (just as Fischer had explained such diversity among the "Rehoboth bastards" he had studied over two decades earlier). What was important was that dominant genes determined the psychological character of the Jews in general, a character to which Fischer ascribed passion, hatred, and cruelty (inherited from the Oriental race) and cleverness, cunning, and a thirst for power (inherited from the Near Eastern race). The Jews, Fischer concluded, were "alien to us Europeans" by virtue of their ancient racial composition, something that "we sense instinctually to this very day."

Fischer's 1938 comments were similar to Fritz Lenz's observations about Jews in his section of the 1936 Baur-Fischer-Lenz. Arguing that the definition of a race ought not to depend too much on morphological characteristics, Lenz believed that one could rightly call the Jews a "psychological race," despite heterogeneity in outward appearance.[93] In explaining the "peculiar nature" of the Jews, Lenz laid much of his emphasis on breeding and selection over the course of millennia. The Jewish propensity for commerce, for example, was reinforced over time because Jews who possessed this aptitude in abundance were best able to thrive, establish large families, and pass the relevant genetic disposition down to the next generation.[94] A supposed "Jewish aversion to war" Lenz saw as the genetic inheritance of a race whose militarily gifted members had been annihilated by the Greek and Roman conquerors of ancient Israel.[95] Similar patterns of selection helped to explain the high frequency of superior intelligence among Jews as well as their low level of natural competence in farming, to which Lenz attributed alleged Zionist agricultural frustrations in Palestine.[96] When Jews bore physical and behavioral similarities to the people around them, selection was still at work, in this case through the phenomenon known as "mimicry." Jews who resembled their host *Völker* stood a better chance of succeeding and reproducing, Lenz contended, much as butterflies are bred by nature to blend into their environment.[97] Lenz's contribution at times departed from its tone of scientific description, exhibiting instead an undisguised hostility to Jews. In a particularly sharp passage, Lenz described the Jews as parasites who had learned that it was contrary to their interests to destroy their hosts, their sources of sustenance. Instead the Jews promoted only partial "decomposition" in order to perpetuate the parasitic relationship.[98]

Another scholar associated with the Kaiser Wilhelm Institute for Anthropology, Human Heredity, and Eugenics who lectured and published on the "Jewish question" was Otmar von Verschuer. From 1927 to 1935, Verschuer's base was the Department of Anthropology at Fischer's Institute in Berlin. He moved to Frankfurt in 1935 to head up his own Institute for Hereditary Biology and Racial Hygiene, where he mentored, among others, Josef Mengele. Upon Eugen Fischer's retirement, Verschuer returned to the Kaiser Wilhelm Institute in Berlin as the new director. His reputation as a scientist derived primarily from research on genetic predisposition for diseases, and a method closely associated with him was the use of human twins as subjects of study. Verschuer would continue his academic career after the end of the Nazi regime, serving as professor and director of the Institute for Human Genetics at the University of Münster from 1951 until his retirement in 1964, and filling many academic positions in the field of human genetics with his students.[99]

In 1937 and 1938, during his time in Frankfurt, Verschuer delivered lectures at the conferences sponsored by the Jewish Research Department of the Institute for History of the New Germany, both of which were later published in the *Forschungen zur Judenfrage*.[100] Verschuer's contribution had been intended to infuse a small modicum of hard science into proceedings otherwise dominated by historians and other scholars of the humanities. Both of Verschuer's lectures focused primarily on methodological questions relevant to understanding the "racial biology" of the Jews. They took stock of the then current state of biological knowledge about the Jews, and outlined an agenda for future scientific research employing cutting-edge methods. In Verschuer's opinion, future research would ideally focus not so much on the racial origins of the Jews as on the degree to which they had become genetically mixed with their "host peoples" in Europe, particularly the Germans. In his 1937 lecture, Verschuer advocated the close study of so-called mixed marriages between Jews and Germans. The preferred method of such a "genetic and anthropological investigation" would involve "precise measurement of the physiological and psychological characteristics of the racially different parents, of the children produced by these mixed marriages, and of further progeny."[101] Verschuer pointed to Eugen Fischer's 1913 study of the "Rehoboth bastards" as a potential model, and noted that similar studies of racial mixing had been published in the intervening years by British and American researchers, including Melville Herskovits. In the case of Jews and Germans, Verschuer noted, research would benefit from the massive documentation that the Nazi regime had been collecting about the personal ancestry of mixed-race persons for the purpose of implementing the Nuremberg laws. This documentation included applications submitted by *Mischlinge* for permission to marry, which contained potentially useful impressionistic observations recorded by government officials about the prospective partners and their families.

In his 1938 lecture, Verschuer placed more of an emphasis on biomedical research, specifically pathology. A literature on disease patterns within discrete population groups had been growing since the turn of the century, and had burgeoned in the 1920s. Many such studies pertaining to Jews had been conducted by Jewish scholars, but Nazi scholars now appropriated their findings and integrated them into an antisemitic framework. A literature that sprang from a serious scientific and humanitarian desire to understand genetic predisposition for disease thus intersected with exclusionist discourses about race and eugenics.

In 1937 Verschuer became coeditor of a new journal devoted largely to studying the connection between race and disease, *Advances in Hereditary Pathology, Racial Hygiene, and Adjacent Fields* (*Fortschritte der Erbpathologie, Rassenhygiene und ihrer Grenzgebiete*). Verschuer's editorial collaborator on the journal, Johannes Schottky, was a physician and high-level official in the office of Reich Peasant Leader Walter Darré, one of the more hard-line racists in the Nazi leadership. In 1937 Schottky brought out a large anthology, *Race and Disease*, which contained essays by established professors of medicine who intended to summarize the state of knowledge about racial dispositions to a whole host of illnesses, including tropical diseases, skin conditions, diseases of the eyes, and toothaches. The chapters on mental illness, "feeble-mindedness," and "psychopathic" conditions, especially important in the context of the ongoing Nazi eugenic sterilization program, were contributed by Schottky himself. His interest in demonstrating Jewish genetic predispositions for neurotic or psychopathic behavior, as well as for more purely physiological diseases such as diabetes, was not humanitarian but rather was intended to underscore genetic differences between Jews and Germans, and to identify in medical terms the threat posed to Germans by racial mixing with Jews. The majority of studies cited by Schottky and his coauthors had been conducted in the 1920s, and many were by Jewish researchers. Before 1933, Jewish and non-Jewish researchers alike had concluded that schizophrenia, manic-depression, and other psychological conditions were more common among Jews than among other groups, and it was easy for Nazi scientists to put an antisemitic spin on these data.[102]

In his 1938 lecture, Verschuer acknowledged the contributions in Schottky's volume but also hinted at the inadequacies of the existing research. Jewish predispositions for diseases had been established primarily through statistical comparisons between Jews and other populations. While Verschuer found these data convincing, he remained frustrated by their inability to explain the biological mechanisms that underlay them. He noted that Jews possessed a higher resistance to tuberculosis than did the non-Jewish population in Europe. Picking up on a theme emphasized by Lenz in the Baur-Fischer-Lenz text, Verschuer believed that this could be explained as the result of natural selection. Tuberculosis spreads most easily in cities, and for centuries Jews had been the most urbanized people in Europe. Modern-day Jews had therefore been selected to withstand tuberculosis, as periodic outbreaks of the disease had killed off ancestors with low resistance.[103] This Darwinian argument, however, did not provide Verschuer with insight into the genetic or biochemical basis of Jewish resistance to tuberculosis, which could potentially be applied to a vaccine or cure.

Several years later, during the war, Verschuer secured Jewish blood samples from Auschwitz with the cooperation of his protégé Josef Mengele, who was stationed there as a physician.[104] After the war, Verschuer admitted that for his research on the heritability of specific blood proteins (Serum-Eiweisskörper) and their connection to tuberculosis he had required blood samples from "people of various geographic origins," and that he had received several deliveries of 20 to 30 samples from Mengele in Auschwitz.[105] This statement was disingenuous, as the samples had more to do with race than with geography. Verschuer was more honest about the nature of his research needs at the actual time of his experiments in 1944. In a report to the German Research Foundation (Deutsche Forschungsgemeinschaft), which funded his tuberculosis research, Verschuer noted that the samples had come from "over 200 persons of the most diverse racial membership."[106] The actual fates of the Jewish and other inmates at Auschwitz whose blood was used in Verschuer's research are not known; most likely, the vast majority perished at Auschwitz. It has plausibly been suggested that, in the case of the Jewish inmates, Mengele drew the blood from the same people on whom he later experimented to determine possible differences in susceptibility to typhus between Ashkenazic and Sephardic Jews. In that experiment, all of the subjects eventually died.[107] Although many of the details of Verschuer's connection with Mengele and Auschwitz remain unclear, the case illustrates how closely intertwined "serious science" could become with the horrific crimes of the Third Reich.

Historians of science have sometimes distinguished between the serious "scientific" work and the "pseudoscientific" activities conducted by Verschuer, Fischer, Lenz, and similar figures who were active in the Nazi era.[108] Lectures and articles about the racial origins of the Jews, in this typology, constituted pseudoscience, but did not necessarily negate the legitimacy of the genuine science conducted concurrently by the same scholars. The distinction between science and pseudoscience is a reasonable one, but it did not exist in the minds of those scientists at the time. In his lectures in 1937 and 1938, when Verschuer emphasized to his audience the desirability of making the study of the Jewish question more scientific, it is unlikely that he imagined to himself that he was engaging in or promoting pseudoscience. In an unpublished autobiographical statement written after the war, Verschuer explained his participation at those antisemitic conferences: "The *völkisch* and racial separation between Germans and Jews appeared to me to be, for both parties, a necessary step toward the best solution to the difficulties that had arisen. I was determined to work out a basis for the solution to this question through my scientific activities."[109] The study of Jewish racial origins and the ensuing genetic differences between Jews and Germans was not a pseudoscience to him but rather a field of study that had been taken only so far by the methodologies of the past and now required modernization.

Eugen Fischer articulated essentially the same motivation in a long contribution, "Ancient World Jewry," to *Forschungen zur Judenfrage*,[110] which he prepared in collaboration with Gerhard Kittel, a prominent Protestant academic theologian.[111] The article was signed in April 1942, by which time the deportations, ghettoization, and slave labor conditions that had been imposed on Jews were common knowledge, even if news of the actual mass murders may not yet have reached Fischer and Kittel. The work was intended to demonstrate that a unified "world Jewry" had existed already in ancient times, and that modern-day "world Jewry" represented an unbroken racial continuity with its ancient ancestor. Then, as now, the goal of Jewry was to attain "power over the world."[112] Fischer's contribution to the piece consisted of a racial-anthropological assessment of 198 portraits found on Egyptian mummies dating from the second and third centuries C.E., among which he found individuals whose physiognomy suggested that they had been Jewish. He compared the portraits to photographs of modern-day Jews, emphasizing the commonality of features, and concluded that the mummy portraits indicated a clearly identifiable "physiognomy of the world Jew," one that "remains to this day."[113] Hans F. K. Günther had done this in his 1930 book on the Jewish race, but with just a handful of images.

Fischer's guesswork about the racial affiliation of ancient persons depicted in mummy portraiture drew on experience he had garnered as a racial assessor for the Nazi regime (about which he did not inform his readers). The sorting out of the German population into the various racial categories imposed by the Nazis was conducted on the basis of ancestry documentation. In cases where such documentation was incomplete or ambiguous, the German government, mainly through the Reich Office for Genealogical Research (*Reichsstelle für Sippenforschung*), could commission medical-anthropological examinations by academic race experts. Eugen Fischer's Kaiser Wilhelm Institute carried out about eight hundred such examinations. Fischer participated directly in sixty of these in a one-year period in 1935 and 1936, in addition to "hereditary health" examinations he conducted in connection with the eugenic sterilization program.[114] Among the factors considered by Fischer and his assistant Wolfgang Abel to determine racial affiliation were the shape and proportions of the head and face. Without access to living, three-dimensional human beings, a racial assessment was far more difficult, but Fischer employed the same methods and criteria to his study of the mummy portraits.

Fischer understood that he was on scientifically shaky ground here, and acknowledged a host of problems, such as the uncertain provenance and identification of the mummies, or the possibility that the accuracy of the images may have been distorted by ancient aesthetic conventions. "Nobody," he wrote, "can be more strongly and sincerely persuaded of the difficulties presented by the portraits, and the resulting deficiencies of the present study, than the author himself." But he defended himself against the potential charge of pseudoscience by presenting himself as a natural scientist who dared to cross over into a softer discipline, where conclusions might be tentative but must still be taken under consideration. Despite all of its deficiencies, he felt justified in that his study had to be "dared," and that it could serve as a "building block" toward a broader understanding of Jewry.[115]

Two Young Researchers: Walter Dornfeldt and Alexander Paul

During the Nazi period, forty-seven doctoral dissertations were completed under the auspices of the Kaiser Wilhelm Institute for Anthropology, the vast majority of which were supervised by Eugen Fischer and Fritz Lenz. Fischer, who had a professorial appointment at the University of Berlin, also supervised dissertations outside the institutional framework of his institute. Only a few of these dissertations dealt mainly or even substantially with Jews.[116] Two that did so were defended within a single week in December 1939. Both intended to subject the question of Jewish racial characteristics to rigorous investigation, employing both Jewish human subjects and government racial records as source materials.

On 21 December 1939, Walter Dornfeldt successfully defended his dissertation on the head shapes of eastern European Jewish parents and their children living in Berlin.[117] His supervisors were Eugen Fischer and Wolfgang Abel. Dornfeldt worked as a schoolteacher in Berlin, and had to research and write his dissertation while working full-time. The central issue in his dissertation was an old one in physical anthropology: the extent to which the shape of heads in discrete population groups was determined by heredity, on the one hand, and by environment, on the other. An established method for studying this question had been to compare head shapes and other physiological characteristics across generations within groups undergoing dramatic changes in environment. The degree to which heads underwent change was understood as an indication of the persistence or mutability of racial characteristics more generally. Among the most celebrated studies was that of Franz Boas, the American anthropologist of German Jewish origin, whose subjects had been Jewish, Italian, and other immigrants and their American-born children living in New York City. According to Boas's study, published in 1911, the heads of the American-born children had statistically measurable differences from those of their European-born parents, suggesting a significant environmental (as opposed to hereditary) influence on human development. Dornfeldt wanted to test Boas's conclusions, using as his subjects eastern European Jews who had moved to Berlin, primarily from Poland, between the late nineteenth century and the early 1930s.

Between 1932 and 1934, Dornfeldt took the head measurements of 2,252 Jews (broken down as 456 male parents, 447 female parents, 627 male children, and 722 female children). Dornfeldt, himself a teacher, surveyed the children at several Berlin schools, as well as at a sports club operated by the Jewish community. In his dissertation he thanked the leaders of these institutions for their assistance, although it is unclear whether after 1933 they felt that they were under pressure to cooperate. Dornfeldt did report that many of the parents, whose head measurements he took during visits to their homes, were extremely distrustful and reluctant to cooperate with him. Over time, Dornfeldt wrote, he learned that it was best to avoid conducting such visits on the Jewish Sabbath and other holidays.[118] Working as a full-time schoolteacher, Dornfeldt took several years more to complete and defend the dissertation.

Dornfeldt's conclusions confirmed the observations of Boas, but only to a point. In Berlin, as in New York, the heads of locally born Jewish children were less round than those of their parents. Environmental influences were undoubtedly at work. Among the possible factors were climate and the socioeconomic conditions of daily life. Dornfeldt identified nutrition as an especially important factor, suggesting that dietary changes from one generation to the next might affect glandular secretions that, in turn, could influence growth of the head during childhood. Such factors had their limits, however. "It should be emphasized," Dornfeldt wrote, "that it is not a matter of a change in the race, but only of a shift of the phenotype within the hereditary, racially determined range of reactions." Within every race, the shape of the head exhibits a certain "plasticity," he argued, the limits of which are set by heredity.[119] Dornfeldt thus carefully distanced himself from those who, like Boas, would place too heavy an emphasis on environmental factors. His conclusions ultimately validated the National Socialist regime's hereditarian view of human nature, even as they avoided the explicit expressions of antisemitism.

Alexander Paul's dissertation, in contrast to Dornfeldt's, was fiercely antisemitic in both content and tone. Paul's study, titled "Jewish-German Blood Mixing: A Social-Biological Investigation," was supervised by Eugen Fischer and Hans F. K. Günther, and successfully defended at the University of Berlin on 27 November 1939.[120] Paul acknowledged Günther as his main inspiration. The study would not have been possible without the cooperation of the Interior Ministry, which placed at Paul's disposal documentation it had systematically collected about Mischlinge. In 1937 Otmar von Verschuer had identified government racial records as a potential source for innovative research into Jewish-German "mixed marriages" and the racial qualities of their progeny. In the same year, the Interior Ministry commissioned the anthropologist Gisela Lemme to organize such records for scientific research purposes. Care of the documents was given over to Paul at the beginning of 1938.[121] Paul's study was published in 1940 by the ministry in a series on "People's Health" (Volksgesundheit). One reviewer judged the published dissertation to be "an extraordinarily valuable contribution to the scientific understanding of the problem of racial mixing as well as to practical racial policy."[122] Another reviewer pointed to the "great importance" of Paul's dissertation, which would serve as a "model" for future research in the field.[123]

Paul worked through the files of 1,785 adult "*Mischlinge* of the first degree," that is, half-Jews. The 1939 German census counted 72,738 persons in this racial category.[124] Unlike Dornfeldt, Paul did not have direct contact with his subjects in the field but depended entirely on the information collected by the Ministry of the Interior, which included data on family ancestry, marital status, education, occupation, medical history, and criminal record. These records pertained not only to the *Mischlinge* themselves but also to their parents. Paul's intention was to create a profile of the Germans and Jews who had entered into mixed marriages (or had produced illegitimate children) and of the children who had been produced by this "Jewish-German blood mixing."

Presented in the context of Germany's escalating campaign to rid the country of Jews, Paul's conclusions confirmed the worst fears of antisemites who had been warning against the biological dangers posed by the mixing of races. Paul found that the Germans who had paired with Jewish partners were well below average in terms of social background, occupation, and "hereditary health." Only 41.2 percent of the German partners had come from the middle and upper classes, and only 33.6 percent of the German women. Moreover, 14.1 percent of the German partners could be classified as having "low hereditary value" based on their economic, criminal, or medical histories. A "lack of racial instinct," Paul concluded, had led these Germans to take Jewish partners.[125] In contrast, he reported, the Jewish partners represented an above-average selection from the overall Jewish population. Paul's main conclusion concerned the racial worth of the offspring. He contended that the mixed-race offspring were even worse off than their below-average German parents. Like other Nazi scholars, Paul believed that all *Mischlinge* suffered from psychological and physical "disharmonies" that gave rise to a host of pathologies.[126] Paul classified a full 22 percent of the *Mischlinge* in his sample as having "low hereditary value." Among *Mischlinge* born out of wedlock, this percentage climbed to over 30, and among those who themselves had produced children out of wedlock, the percentage reached almost 40. Examined in retrospect, the statistical tables and other accoutrements of empirical rigor in Paul's dissertation did little to camouflage the highly subjective and ideological nature of the criteria used to assign "low hereditary value." Among the characteristics or transgressions cited by Paul as indicators of "low hereditary value" were homosexuality, sexual promiscuity, "notorious drinking," document falsification, abortion, begging, and desertion.[127] Such behaviors routinely passed as objective assessments of human worth in Nazi Germany. For Paul, their manifestations among *Mischlinge* validated the wisdom of the prohibition of sex between Jews and Germans, as the Nuremberg laws had done. But he was worried that illegal sex and reproduction among *Mischlinge* and between *Mischlinge* and Germans in the future might perpetuate the Jewish contamination of the German gene pool into the future.[128] It was precisely this concern that later motivated some Nazi officials to advocate the inclusion of half-Jews in the "Final Solution."[129]

Wartime Racial Anthropology and the Jews

The coming of World War II radicalized Nazi policy toward Jews, escalating it from persecution, to ghettoization, and ultimately to murder. The war and accompanying genocide shoved aside many of the few remaining moral inhibitions against using Jews as the subjects for scientific research. Many of the experiments, conducted primarily in concentration camps, sought to test human reactions to high pressure, cold water, or the application to the skin of certain chemical agents. The results were intended to have military and pharmaceutical applications. Other experiments investigated technical methods for mass sterilization of human beings. Many of the camp inmates selected as subjects for these experiments were Jewish, although the research was not related to a pursuit of knowledge about Jewish genetic or racial characteristics.[130] Rather, an ideology of racial hostility toward Jews rationalized their use as human subjects, making them subjects of convenience rather than subjects of necessity. Research conducted by Otmar von Verschuer on Jewish blood proteins and the heritability of resistance to tuberculosis was an exception to this general pattern.

The coming of war presented Nazi scholars with attractive opportunities for anthropological research on Jews. The Museum of Natural History in Vienna, which housed one of Europe's most extensive anthropological collections, moved aggressively to take advantage.[131] Scholars working for the museum's Anthropology Department undertook extensive measurement and photography of prisoners in Austria and the Reich Protectorate of Bohemia and Moravia. In all, their survey encompassed seven thousand live subjects; the number of Jews among them is not known.

Among the very first prisoners encompassed by the survey were 440 stateless Jewish men of Polish background whom the Gestapo had rounded up in September 1939 and interned for three weeks in the Vienna soccer stadium. The research team from the Museum of Natural History spent several days in the stadium, taking personal data, body measurements, and photographs of the prisoners. The prisoners were then shipped to the Buchenwald concentration camp, and almost all of them perished there before the end of the war.[132] The Anthropology Department also planned to conduct a survey of Sephardic Jews in Holland. Although scholars from the Museum made a preliminary trip to Amsterdam for that purpose in June 1941, we have no evidence that they followed through on the study.

As it collected measurements of living Jews, the museum also sought to expand its existing research collection of Jewish skulls and skeletons. These would yield anatomical data believed to be useful for tracing Jewish racial development. The Anthropology Department already included 19 Jewish skulls that it had bought or received as gifts before World War I. The demolition of the Währinger cemetery in Vienna in 1942 and 1943 offered a golden opportunity to add to the museum's collection. The museum planned to exhume 252 Jewish bodies from their graves. Some of the exhumations were carried out, but it is not known how many skeletons and skulls were taken by the anthropologists.[133] Another source from which the museum received skulls was the laboratory of the anatomist Hermann Voss at the University of Posen. In 1942 Voss sold 29 Jewish skulls (and 15 Polish ones) to the Vienna museum. Voss himself had received them from concentration camps in Poland, according to an arrangement he had made with the Gestapo. After the war Voss held a professorship at the University of Jena in the German Democratic Republic, and was the coauthor of the so-called Voss-Herrlinger, a widely used anatomy textbook.[134]

The Museum of Natural History was not the only Viennese institution that conducted anthropological research on Jews. In 1942, the Anthropological Institute of the University of Vienna sent an anthropological research team to study Jews in Tarnow, a city about 45 miles east of Cracow in Nazi-occupied Poland. The Viennese scientists collaborated with German colleagues from the Cracow-based Institute for German Work in the East, an organ of the German occupation authority. Notably, several of the key personnel involved in the study were women for whom the war seemingly opened up new academic career opportunities. They included Dora Kahlich-Koenner, Marianne Pevny, and Elfriede Flieth-mann, who authored the published report. With logistical assistance from the Reich Security Main Office, the anthropologists photographed and took physical measurements of 578 Jews in Tarnow between 23 March and 2 April 1942. In addition to the usual data about body type, head shape, eye color, and other physiological characteristics, they also collected information regarding education, occupation, medical history, military service, religious orientation, and other biographical details. In her published report on the data, Elfriede Fliethmann noted that the Jews of Tarnow seemed to exhibit quite different racial characteristics from those of Vienna, although she was reluctant to posit definitive conclusions until a more rigorous analysis could be undertaken. By the time Fliethmann's report appeared in print, many of the Jews her team had examined had been murdered. Starting in June 1942, just weeks after the anthropologists had concluded their work, thousands of Jews from Tarnow were deported to the extermination camp at Belzec, where they were gassed. The agency that was primarily responsible for these mass murders was the Reich Security Main Office, to which Fliethmann had expressed gratitude for its "friendly intervention" in facilitating the anthropological research in Tarnow.[135]

What may well have been the single most gruesome research project about Jews pursued in Germany during the Nazi years was the creation of an anatomical and anthropological research collection of Jewish skeletons at the Reich University of Strasbourg, in German-occupied Alsace.[136] The collection was a joint project of August Hirt, a professor of anatomy at Strasbourg, and Bruno Beger, an anthropologist employed by the Ahnenerbe, the scientific research office of the SS. Hirt described the idea for the project to Heinrich Himmler in a proposal, dated February 1942, titled "Impounding of Skulls of Jewish-Bolshevist Commissars for Scientific Research."[137] "Comprehensive collections of skulls are available for almost all races and peoples," Hirt explained, but for Jews the existing collections are too small to allow for systematic research. Fortunately, however, "the war in the East now offers us the opportunity to remedy this shortage." The skulls of Jewish-Bolshevist commissars would constitute a valuable scientific document. Hirt proposed to Himmler that an arrangement be worked out with the Wehrmacht whereby captured Jewish commissars from the Soviet army would be kept alive and turned over to the custody of the SS. (Hirt obviously knew about the "commissar order," which stipulated that such persons be executed.) A medical student or intern would then take a series of photographs and anthropological measurements of the captured Jews, in addition to personal and ancestral information. Hirt's proposal proceeded further to describe how the Jews would be killed in a manner that would not damage their heads, and how the heads would then be removed and conserved. Equipped with the photographs, measurements, and finally the skulls themselves, Hirt concluded, he would be able to conduct "comparative anatomical research" on questions of "racial affiliation," "pathological symptoms of the skull structure," the "shape and size of the brain," and "much more."

Collecting skulls and bones was certainly a normal part of research in physical anthropology in the first half of the twentieth century. Many universities in the United States, for example, established such collections for research on American Indians. In those cases, however, the bones were dug up from Indian burial sites, an activity whose unethical nature has only recently come to be acknowledged by the institutions involved.[138] We can only speculate as to why Nazi scientists like August Hirt and Bruno Beger would not have been satisfied with a systematic program for plundering Jewish graves, which would have been easy in Nazi-occupied Europe, and which would have yielded anthropologically valuable centuries-old specimens. It was advantageous from their point of view to study the subjects first, while still alive, and then to preserve the bodies under controlled conditions, much as the procedure would have been with laboratory research using animals.

Himmler approved the plan, but it did not proceed according to the original proposal. Instead of receiving captured Jews from the Eastern Front, Hirt and Beger turned their attention to Auschwitz. Beger selected 115 inmates from the camp, including 79 Jewish men, 30 Jewish women, 2 Poles, and 4 Central Asians.[139] Helping Beger to choose the subjects was another racial anthropologist connected with the SS-Ahnenerbe, Hans Helmut Fleischhacker, who in the 1930s had worked at the Bavarian State Anthropological Collection in Munich, where he likely gained experience in the preparation and preservation of skeletons.[140] Beger's interest in the Central Asians stemmed from his previous participation in an Ahnenerbe-sponsored anthropological expedition to Tibet. We do not know what specific criteria Beger and Fleischhacker employed in choosing their Jewish subjects, but years later Beger told investigators that his assignment had been to secure samples of "as many varieties of Jewry as possible."[141] The anthropological training of both men would have made it probable that they sought a geographically and ancestrally heterogeneous sample. The human subjects were transferred at the end of July 1943 to the concentration camp Natzweiler in eastern France, where they were killed with poison gas. The bodies were then taken to the University at Strasbourg.

Hirt skeletalized the bodies only gradually, as first he wanted to take "hominid castings" from the preserved corpses. By September 1944, as the American army approached Strasbourg, eighty of the corpses were still intact. Hirt began to worry that the collection would fall into the hands of the Americans, who might well piece together the origin of the corpses. One way of obscuring the identity of the bodies would be to complete the process of skeletalization, but Hirt was reluctant to proceed in this manner lest it prevent him from taking further castings, thus resulting in a "great scientific loss for this unique collection."[142] Wolfram Sievers, head of the Ahnenerbe, nonetheless ordered Hirt to destroy the collection. Hirt did so, but was not entirely successful. Remnants of the collection fell into American hands, as did damning correspondence between Hirt and the Ahnenerbe.

Hirt committed suicide in June 1945. In the famous "Doctors Trial" conducted by the Americans in 1946–1947, the skeleton project was cited as evidence against Wolfram Sievers. Beger and Fleischhacker survived the war and were interned by the Americans for a time, but were not placed on trial. Beger found work as a business clerk, while Fleischhacker took a position as assistant professor at the Institute for Hereditary Science at the University of Frankfurt. Both were investigated during the 1960s by the German prosecutor Fritz Bauer for their roles in the skeleton project. They were indicted in 1968, and placed on trial in Frankfurt in 1970, together with Wolf-Dietrich Wolff, the SS officer who actually gassed the victims at Natzweiler. Fleischhacker was acquitted on grounds that the prosecution could not demonstrate that he had been aware of the ultimate purpose of the anthropological examinations and selections he had conducted at Auschwitz. Beger was convicted for aiding and abetting murder, and was sentenced to three years in prison. The Frankfurt court acknowledged Wolff's direct responsibility for the murders, but dropped the charges against him because of a technicality: by the time the verdict on Wolff came to be handed down, the statute of limitations for accessory to murder had expired.[143]

Only a dozen years separated Günther's *Racial Characteristics of the Jewish People* from August Hirt's reliance on mass murder as a research method. Whereas antisemitic racist scholarship had at first been intended to provide an intellectual foundation for the forced separation of Germans and Jews, it culminated in the reduction of Jews to a status no better than that of expendable laboratory animals. Nazi race scientists cheapened the value of Jewish life through their persistent demonization of the Jews, and thus did much to determine the deadly trajectory not only of their own scholarship but of Nazi anti-Jewish policy in general. Their disgraceful contribution to bigotry, social exclusion, and murder was the result of a search for knowledge that was driven by personal ambition, perverted by ideology, devoid of ethical reflection, and carried out at the behest and with the financial and institutional support of a regime that enjoyed substantial popularity among the German people.

3

The Blood and Sins of Their Fathers

Religion

Whereas defining Jews primarily in racial terms marked a relatively recent development in the history of antisemitism, derogating the Jewish religion had a very long tradition in Christian Europe, arguably dating back as far as the composition of the New Testament Gospels in the first century C.E. Even as antisemitism took on cultural, economic, and racial layers over the subsequent two millennia, religious anti-Judaism remained at the foundation of, and accounted in large part for the persistence of, popular anti-Jewish sentiment into modern times in many parts of Europe. While Nazi antisemitism was undoubtedly racist, rather than religious, at its core, it was sufficiently flexible to incorporate traditional religious bigotry into its critique of the Jews. In *Mein Kampf*, a book saturated with racial theory, Hitler claimed that in pursuing his antisemitic agenda he was "acting in accordance with the will of the Almighty Creator" and "fighting for the work of the Lord."[1]

Before the Nazi seizure of power, German scholarly discussions about the Jewish religion had taken place in several distinct but overlapping intellectual spheres. Chief among these was the German Jewish community itself, where serious research and writing continued well after 1933. Among the prominent German Jewish scholars whose work on the Jewish religion appeared during the Nazi era were Leo Baeck, Martin Buber, Elias Auerbach, Ismar Elbogen, and Simon Dubnow.[2] Overlapping somewhat with the world of Jewish scholarship was another sphere, the academic field of comparative religion, which understood religion as a social, historical, and psychological phenomenon, and which did not, at least officially, privilege Christianity over other traditions. This academic enterprise had enjoyed an efflorescence in the Weimar Republic, with perhaps its most representative embodiment being the multivolume encyclopedia *Religion Past and Present (Die Religion in Geschichte und Gegenwart)*. Many of the articles on Judaism were contributed by Jewish scholars, and the overall spirit of the work was tolerant and capacious.

A third sphere was the field that has been called "*Völkisch* religious studies."[3] Its center of attention was the pre-Christian pagan religion of the ancient Indo-Germanic tribes. Scholarship on this subject was often closely linked to the modern neopagan movement, which regarded Christianity as a foreign import and sought to return Germans to their allegedly more authentic pagan roots.[4] Limited in both size and influence at German universities during the Weimar Republic, the field benefited from Nazi political support and expanded considerably after 1933. It proved especially amenable to the SS, which financed relevant research through the Ahnenerbe.[5] The leading scholar in the field, Jakob Hauer, a professor of "Indology, Comparative Religious History, and Aryan Ideology" at Tübingen, had also been a key figure in the neopagan German Faith Movement (*Deutsche Glaubensbewegung*). While "*Völkisch* religious studies" and its practitioners tended strongly toward racial antisemitism, the field devoted little effort to the actual study of Jews and Judaism. With respect to religion, the neopagan position tended to lump Judaism and Christianity together as semitically tainted creeds that were alien to the German *Volk*.[6]

The last sphere, and the one that produced the most notable body of antisemitic religious scholarship, was that of Protestant Bible studies, which operated at the intersection where the academic fields of theology and ancient Semitic languages crossed. This academic milieu became an important locus of antisemitic research after 1933. The scholars working in these fields, whose primary interest lay in understanding the origins and early development of Christianity, studied the Jewish religion, ancient Jewish languages, and Jewish religious and legal texts. They possessed knowledge and skills that otherwise were not common outside the Jewish community. Bible studies in Germany (and elsewhere) had long been dominated by Christian scholars who had been motivated by the belief that Judaism was an obsolete faith that had been superseded by Christianity. The advent of Nazi rule provoked some of these scholars to reformulate their religion-based Christian antipathy to Judaism so as to make it consistent with a modern, racist sensibility.

The very close connection between antisemitic scholarship in the Third Reich and pastoral work in Nazi Germany, particularly in the case of the Protestant church, has been compellingly documented.[7] In 1939, several regional Protestant churches created the Institute for the Study and Eradication of Jewish Influence on German Religious Life, in Eisenach, near Jena. The Institute was closely linked to the German Christian movement, the racist, pro-Nazi wing of German Protestantism, and affiliated de facto with the Faculty of Theology at the University of Jena. The academic director of the Institute, Walter Grundmann, a professor of New Testament at Jena, had joined the Nazi party in 1930 and had been an important figure in the German Christian movement. In his own scholarship and in the work of his Institute, Grundmann sought to undermine the notion that Christianity had derived from Judaism, and to promote the theory that Jesus had been an anti-Jewish Aryan.[8] The Institute sponsored publications highlighting the degenerate nature of Judaism at the time of Jesus, and depicting the aggressive nature of the Jews throughout history. Among the more notable products of the Institute, one aimed at church pastors and parishioners, was a de-Judaized edition of the New Testament, which eliminated terms derived from Hebrew and avoided reference to Jesus' descent from King David. After the collapse of the Third Reich, the guiding spirit of the Institute, Walter Grundmann, continued his career in the Protestant church in East Germany, serving in a variety of academic and ecclesiastical positions.[9]

Among the Nazi scholars who produced detailed scholarship on the religious history and faith of the Jews, two were academic relatives of Grundmann. Gerhard Kittel, professor of New Testament at the University of Tübingen, had been Grundmann's doctoral mentor. Karl Georg Kuhn had also been a student of Kittel, and through much of the Third Reich taught alongside Kittel at Tübingen. Scholars of formidable talent and erudition, Kittel and Kuhn were the two most prominent religion scholars active in Nazi Jewish studies. Both marshaled their considerable talent and knowledge for the purpose of integrating an understanding of the Jewish religion into Nazi views on the Jewish race.

Merging Christian Anti-Judaism and Nazi Antisemitism: Gerhard Kittel

If there is a single tragic figure in the history of Nazi anti-Jewish scholarship, it is Gerhard Kittel. A prominent, established professor and scholar well before 1933, and a person who exhibited no notable animus against Jews well into the mature phase of his career, Kittel did not seem like a probable candidate to evolve into a racist antisemite. Yet by the end of the Third Reich, Kittel had left behind a significant body of racist antisemitic scholarship. His writings combined theological Christian supersessionism, longstanding anti-Jewish stereotypes, and Nazi-style racism. He was a scholar of undeniably great ability, whose legacy included important works on the New Testament that remained influential after 1945, and whose students and devotees remained active in German academic theology. The multivolume *Theological Dictionary of the New Testament (Theologisches Wörterbuch zum neuen Testament)*, which was published during the Nazi era under Kittel's editorial direction, endures to this day as an important reference work. After 1945, German theologians long remained in denial about Kittel's actions and writings during the Nazi era. The silence was broken hesitatingly only in the late 1970s;[10] and it took a complete outsider, the American scholar Robert P. Ericksen, to document the egregious nature of Kittel's record of antisemitism in a book published in 1985, a full forty years after the end of the Third Reich.[11]

The son of Rudolf Kittel, a prominent Old Testament scholar who became the rector of the University of Leipzig, Gerhard Kittel focused his scholarship on the New Testament and on Judaism during the early phase of Christianity. He spent most of his professorial career at the University of Tübingen, where he held the chair in New Testament studies and trained many students, among them Grundmann and Kuhn. Kittel's publications during the 1920s were not marked by antisemitic bias. To the contrary, some of his writings expressed admiration for Judaism, called attention to the Jewishness of Jesus, and emphasized the rootedness of Christianity in the ethical and moral core of Judaism.[12] To be sure, like most Christian theologians of his time, Kittel regarded Christianity as a superior religion to Judaism and as its proper successor, but nothing that Kittel said or wrote before 1933 anticipated the depth and intensity of the antisemitism contained in his later writings. Kittel's abrupt emergence as a Nazi scholar is therefore difficult to explain.[13] It seems as though he underwent an ideological metamorphosis once the Nazi regime had placed the "Jewish question" on the public agenda. As a scholar of Kittel's standing did not need to become politically active in order to protect his professorship, his writings and statements probably reflected a genuine (and perhaps arrogant) desire to bring his expertise to bear on a major issue of national policy.

Kittel joined the Nazi party in May 1933, hardly a necessary step for an established university professor. A public lecture entitled "The Jewish Question" that he delivered the following month in Tübingen later became the first in a series of increasingly racist anti-Jewish publications. Many of these appeared in the *Forschungen zur Judenfrage* published by Walter Frank's Reich Institute. In fact, Kittel appeared in the *Forschungen* more frequently than any other author. His antisemitic lectures and publications continued into 1944, well past the point that most German Jews had been deported, and well past the point when he had received a first-hand report from his son about the mass killings of Jews in the east.[14] As the war came to an end, Kittel was arrested and then imprisoned for seventeen months by French occupation authorities. He died in 1948.

Kittel's Nazi-era writings on the Jewish question dealt in large part with the racial origins of modern Jews and, by extension, with the relationship of the modern Jewish race to the Jews of the Old Testament. They also examined the dispersion of the Jews in ancient and early medieval times, intermarriage between Jews and non-Jews through the ages, the nature of the Talmud and its relationship to Jewish behavior, and, finally, the nature of modern, secular, assimilated Jewry. Through an accumulation of lectures and articles, Kittel promoted what he saw as a cohesive picture of Jewry from its ancient beginnings to the present. The Jewish race of modern times, he argued, is not identical with the Israelites of the Old Testament but represents a later racial formation. Through this argument Kittel intended to disassociate Judaism from the Old Testament, which he wanted to salvage for Christianity. Kittel claimed that modern Jewry traced its racial and religious roots not so much to the Old Testament period as to the postexilic period, that is, the period after the return from the Babylonian exile in the sixth century B.C.E. For about a thousand years after the close of the Old Testament period, the Jews spread out in their Diaspora, underwent racial mixing with other peoples, and eventually adopted the Talmud as the basis of their society. Thus the Jews who were locked into the ghettos in medieval Europe were racially and religiously quite different from the ancient Israelites. When the Jews emerged from the ghettos in the nineteenth century, however, they were basically the same race that had entered the ghetto centuries earlier. This modern Jewish race, according to Kittel, was fundamentally alien to the peoples around them, including the Germans. They were different in both appearance and behavior. The religious differences between Judaism and Christianity were not merely theological, they were ethical as well. Whereas Christianity had inherited the ethical core of Old Testament Judaism, rabbinic Judaism operated according to the Talmud, which sanctioned corruption, dishonesty, materialism, and antipathy toward non-Jews. This last accusation was hardly new in the annals of Christian anti-Judaism, but Kittel was innovative in anchoring theological and religious differences in the divergent racial developments of Jewish and non-Jewish Germans.

Kittel made his first major Nazi-era statement on these matters in a speech delivered in Tübingen in May 1933. Titled simply "The Jewish Question," the speech was later published as a 78-page booklet.[15] Although this contribution preceded Kittel's turn to a more archaeologically grounded, scientific form of antisemitism, it already contained the basic elements of a synthesis between racism and religious anti-Judaism. Kittel described the Jews as an "alien" people (*Fremdling*), racially as well as religiously distinct from their host peoples.[16] This fundamental incompatibility was made worse, in Kittel's view, by the degenerate attitudes of modern, secular, assimilated Jews. In Germany these were the Jews who promoted materialism, financial corruption, cosmopolitanism, secularism, and political radicalism. The Jewish question, he suggested, was to a large extent a "problem of decadence."[17] As a rhetorical device, Kittel suggested four possible approaches for dealing with the Jews: extermination, Zionism, assimilation, and guest status.[18] Historical experience had proven the first three to be unfeasible. Kittel dismissed the option of extermination on practical rather than moral grounds. Not able to imagine what would actually come to pass less than a decade later, he observed that both the Spanish Inquisition and the pogroms of Russia had demonstrated the futility of this solution.[19] Kittel cited several reasons why Zionism was doomed to failure, chief among them the inability of the Jews to establish and maintain a self-sufficient state.[20] As for assimilation, this, Kittel pointed out, was not the solution to the Jewish question but rather one of its chief causes.[21] By the process of elimination, Kittel arrived at the granting of guest status as the preferred solution to the "Jewish question."

Kittel recommended that the widely used term "German citizens of the Jewish faith" be recast as "Jews living in Germany." The question of citizenship would have to be "solved by the jurists," who would need to devise some kind of special system of laws that would define the abbreviated rights of Germany's permanent Jewish guests.[22] Among these rights would be the freedom to practice Judaism openly and uninhibited by the state. The more orthodox the form of Judaism practiced the better, Kittel argued. When compared to modern, secular Jews, he reasoned, Orthodox Jews were less likely to produce cultural "decadence," and were more easily demarcated from the non-Jewish population.[23] Kittel did not specify how the Jews would be expected to earn a living, but he did stipulate the exclusion of Jews from several important professions. "The Jew," he wrote, "precisely because he is a guest, must relinquish major influence in endeavors related to the life of the German people and state, German culture, and German education."[24] More concretely, Kittel noted, Jews should not be allowed to serve as newspaper editors, university professors, or teachers, except within their own circumscribed racial and religious community. The timing of these suggestions could not have been coincidental. In April 1933, just weeks before Kittel's speech in Tübingen, the Nazi government had issued a law banning Jews from positions in the civil service, including in the education field. Nazi activists had long been insisting upon the elimination of Jewish writers and editors from the German press. Their demands came to fruition in October 1933 with the promulgation of the Reich Editors Law, which established Aryan ancestry as a condition for employment as an editor.[25] Kittel contributed his lecture and booklet on "The Jewish Question" at a time when the exclusion of Jews from German professions was not merely the subject of a hypothetical discussion but a work-in-progress. In later years, the Nazi regime implemented similar purges in the fields of medicine and law, both of which, in Kittel's characterization, had been "over flooded" by greedy, unscrupulous Jewish practitioners.[26]

Consistent as well with the persistent demands of the Nazi movement was Kittel's plea for a prohibition on marriage between Jews and non-Jews, something that was realized in the Nuremberg laws of late 1935. Kittel's self-proclaimed Christian perspective left plenty of room for rhetoric about miscegenation and the supposed problems posed by persons of mixed-race backgrounds. In "The Jewish Question" he bemoaned the existence of hundreds of thousands of Jewish *Mischlinge*, who, he added, "contribute in many ways to unbridled Jewish influence."[27] Kittel's assertion reflected an apparent ignorance of the fact that a very large percentage of the *Mischlinge* did not identify or affiliate as Jews. But Kittel was less worried about the existing *Mischlinge* than about future miscegenation. The existing *Mischlinge,* numerous as they were, could eventually be absorbed into an Aryan and Christian Germany, provided that further mixed marriages could be prevented. In the absence of drastic measures against mixed marriage, however, Kittel believed the problem would fester. Mixed marriages, Kittel concluded, when not "radically prohibited," ought at the very least to be strongly discouraged by forcing the Jewish partner "and all of his progeny" to belong to the Jewish community and thereby suffer all the disadvantages of "guest status."[28]

Kittel hoped that Jews, living in the legal and demographic ghetto imposed by their "guest status," would jettison their decadent, secular ways and return to their traditional religion, customs, and rituals. They would then represent "authentic Jewry," and their presence in Germany would serve as a "symbol of the restless and homeless" wandering Jew, the sign of God's punishment.[29] Kittel also advocated the corollary of this medieval Christian position: Jews should be encouraged and permitted to convert to Christianity. Kittel proposed the classification "Jewish Christian" (*Judenchrist*) to denote persons of Jewish race but Christian faith. But he insisted that the religious conversion did not affect one's race. "Baptism," Kittel noted, "does not affect the Jewishness of the Jew." Similarly, "becoming a Christian does not mean becoming a German."[30] The Jewish Christians, of whom Kittel did not expect there would be a large number, should have their own church, and be fully accepted as "Christian brothers." On the other hand, this "brotherhood of Christians doesn't have the slightest bit to do with the political position of the Jew as an alien."[31]

Kittel's vision for the future of Germany's Jews may well strike a post-Holocaust reader as somewhat bizarre. After the war, Kittel drafted a self-defense in which he characterized "The Jewish Question" as a moderate statement. In this postwar apologia, Kittel depicted himself as a moral Christian who sought some kind of middle position between Jewish decadence on the one hand and vulgar Nazi racism on the other.[32] The apologia seriously understated the racism of the "The Jewish Question" (as well as his other Nazi-era writings), although Kittel's claim to relative moderation was not entirely devoid of substance. His willingness to accept baptized Jews as Christians did, indeed, distinguish him from the more fanatical racists who dominated the German Christian movement, the pro-Nazi wing of the Protestant church that subscribed to a more racially determined notion of religion and rejected the baptism of Jews on principle.[33] Kittel's suggestion that the Jews be granted "guest status," while despicable from a liberal perspective, did not entail the co-erced emigration of the Jews, as many Nazis advocated. Nor did Kittel engage in the common Nazi practice of using Zionism as a fig leaf to dis-guise his desire to be rid of the Jews. As for the "Jewish Christians," Kit-tel did not invoke international comparisons, but his scheme for their future in a racially segregated church did not differ all that profoundly from the situation of African Americans in the American South. On the other hand, what Kittel advocated for the rest of the Jews amounted to something a good deal worse than a simple return to the preemancipation era, for the logic of race ruled out any possibility of ultimate acceptance as the result of conversion or assimilation. Whatever disagreements he may have had with other Nazis, Kittel lent his authority and prestige to the Third Reich's antisemitic program from almost the very beginning of Nazi rule.

Unlike "The Jewish Question," which was overtly political in sub-stance and tone, Kittel's contributions to *Forschungen zur Judenfrage* were intended as scholarship. They were written in a sober academic style, packed densely with displays of the author's erudition, and sup-plemented by numerous footnotes to primary and secondary sources in several languages. The sources included works by both Jewish and non-Jewish authors. Over time, as Kittel's argumentation grew more racialist, he tended to make increasing use of archaeological materials. The stri-dent Christianity of "The Jewish Question" was absent from Kittel's writings in the *Forschungen,* and only in a few passages does Kittel's self-identification as a Christian become manifest. His emphasis shifted in-creasingly from a religious to a racial logic.

Kittel's first article in the *Forschungen* was entitled "The Origins of Jewry and the Origins of the Jewish Question,"[34] and established the main themes, avenues of inquiry, and rhetorical patterns for his future contributions to the series. It combined an impressive command of texts with a relentless and undisguised antipathy toward the Jewish people and religion. Kittel introduced his piece with the proposition that the Jewish "people, race, and religion" have posed an enduring problem to other peoples;[35] he concluded with a note of congratulation to Hitler for his "radical determination" to address the problem "on an entirely new basis."[36] In the 20 pages in between, Kittel mobilized texts from sources in German, English, French, Greek, and Hebrew, quoted from the Old

Testament, Jewish Midrash, the Talmud, and the work of Josephus, and cited the writings of modern scholars such as Theodor Mommsen, Adolf Harnack, and Ismar Elbogen. He used articles from the *Jewish Quarterly Review* and invoked the recent findings of a Yale University–sponsored archaeological expedition at Dura on the Euphrates.[37] For his insights on the Jews as a race, Kittel relied heavily on Hans F. K. Günther's *Racial Characteristics of the Jewish People*.[38] One of his key sources for Jewish texts was the Strack-Billerbeck commentary on the New Testament, which was based largely on Talmudic and Midrashic sources. Many Jewish scholars had responded positively to the publication of the Strack-Billerbeck, which appeared in four volumes during the 1920s, because of its emphasis on the Jewishness of Jesus, and because its coauthor, the Orientalist and theologian Hermann Strack, had been an ardent foe of antisemitism (even though he had proselytized to Jews).[39] By citing Strack-Billerbeck in support of an antisemitic argument, Kittel thoroughly inverted the intentions of its authors.

It was in this article that Kittel introduced his theory of a significant break between Old Testament and postexilic Judaism, a critical idea that he would develop further in his later contributions. Kittel traced the origins of the Jewish diaspora to the Babylonian exile of the sixth century B.C.E. The extensive racial mixing of Jews with other peoples began at that moment, and intensified in subsequent centuries as Jews migrated to many parts of the ancient empires of the Near East.[40] As a result of the destruction of the Jerusalem Temple in 70 C.E., the Talmud became the key cohesive force in Judaism. Repeating an old and persistent anti-Jewish stereotype, Kittel characterized the rabbinic Judaism based on the Talmud as excessively legalistic, in contrast to the much more spiritual and ethical religion of Christianity. Kittel reiterated the longstanding accusation that the Talmud sanctioned abusive conduct by Jews toward non-Jews, substantiating his claims with references to the Strack-Billerbeck text.[41] He laid great emphasis on a supposed Jewish "will to power," which he interpreted as a perversion of the original Jewish idea of selection by God. Among the Jews, Kittel explained, loss of homeland, dispersion, and oppression at the hands of others distorted the notion of divine selection into a form of megalomania. The Jews, Kittel concluded, considered themselves chosen by God to rule over others as a "People of World Domination" (*Volk der Weltherrschaft*) and regarded non-Jews as an "anti-God" who ought to be "exterminated."[42]

After this article appeared in 1936, Kittel published five further pieces in the *Forschungen zur Judenfrage* during the Third Reich, in each case exploring in greater depth issues he had raised in the initial contribution. In a piece entitled "Marriage with Non-Jews in Ancient Jewry," published in 1937, he began to delve more deeply into the question of Jewish racial composition.[43] He wanted to demonstrate that Jews often circumvented the prohibition on exogamy imposed by Ezra and Nehemiah. One of the questions at the core of his inquiry—the status under Jewish law of gentiles who married Jews—was not, in and of itself, an unreasonable one. The antisemitic line of interpretation was, nonetheless, conspicuous throughout the piece. Wherever they wandered and lived in the ancient world, Kittel argued, Jews had employed intermarriage as a means for racial proliferation. Talmudic casuistry had made it possible for the Jews to evade the ban on intermarriage, and to integrate non-Jews into the community. The result was a racial mix. The advent of the ghetto, however, imposed centuries of inbreeding on the Jews, so that the people who emerged from the ghettos in modern times constituted what Hans F. K. Günther had called a "race of the second order." Thus the threat posed by Jewish exogamy persisted into the present day. In the Germany of 1937, where the supposed dangers of race mixing had been made a national obsession, and where marriages between Jews and Aryans had been banned, Kittel's argument amounted to a clear endorsement of official policy. At the end of his article, Kittel went so far as to claim that the prohibition of intermarriage would prove beneficial to the Jews, who would be allowed to return to a more authentic condition.

In 1940, Kittel published a short piece in the *Forschungen* about ancient terra cotta figures that had been excavated by archaeologists in Trier.[44] He speculated that the hook-nosed appearance of some of the figures were antisemitic caricatures. His method was clearly influenced by the tautological reasoning found in the writings of Günther. Modern Jews, Kittel assumed, are marked by their hook noses, hence ancient images of hook-nosed faces must be those of Jews. On the basis of this supposition, Kittel could interpret the ancient images as evidence of the physiognomic continuity of the Jewish race from ancient times to the present. From this specious basis he concluded that the caricatures themselves reflected the racial consciousness of ancient antisemites, who ridiculed Jews on the basis of physical appearance rather than religion. Kittel employed the same warped methodology in the very long article entitled "Ancient World Jewry" that he published together with Eugen Fischer in the 1943 issue of the *Forschungen*.[45] This 225-page article constituted the entire volume of the journal. It featured a lengthy, profusely illustrated analysis of the racial characteristics of persons found in images from ancient Palestine, Assyria, Egypt, Greece, and the Roman Empire. Kittel wrote most of the article, although Fischer's expertise in race science was intended to endow the piece with scientific authority. The heavy use of archaeological evidence and the partnership with Eugen Fischer reflected Kittel's desire to push his Jewish research in a more interdisciplinary and scientific direction. He and Fischer saw it as "the fruit of a genuine collaboration between the humanities and the natural sciences."[46]

The year 1943 also saw the publication of Kittel's most pronouncedly antisemitic article, "The Treatment of Non-Jews According to the Talmud."[47] It appeared in the first issue of the *Archive for Jewish Questions*, the organ of the "Antisemitic Action," an initiative sponsored by the German Ministry of Propaganda under Joseph Goebbels. The point of Kittel's article was hardly novel. Jews, he asserted, harbor a deeply rooted, "fundamental hatred of non-Jews," a hatred that is sanctioned and encouraged in the Talmud. But while not new, the argument was now pushed to an extreme that was uncharacteristic of Kittel. He declared that the Talmud bestowed upon Jews "full freedom to kill" non-Jews.[48] Kittel derived this conclusion from a tortured and ahistorical analysis of a passage found in the tractate Sanhedrin, a part of the Talmud that deals with the adjudication and punishment of crimes. Much of Sanhedrin consists of hypothetical discussions about draconian punishments that Jewish communities never actually put into practice.[49] Chapter 9 of the tractate records rabbinic arguments about the applicability of capital punishment in cases of murder. In his article, Kittel extracted three sentences out of the complex rabbinic discussions, asserting that they equated the killing of a non-Jew to the killing of an animal.[50]

Kittel's article in the *Archive* was something different from the ideologically biased scholarship he had published in the *Forschungen*. The Propaganda Minstry's purpose was not to promote scholarship but rather to generate support for the Nazi regime's anti-Jewish policies within Germany and abroad.[51] Kittel's contribution, therefore, amounted to direct participation in the regime's antisemitic propaganda effort at a time when the "Final Solution" was already quite well advanced. Whether or not he

Manipulates Talmud

justification

knew about the mass murders, he most certainly knew that the Jews of Germany and of other countries had been deprived of their property, deported from their homelands, crowded into ghettos, and subjected to forced labor, all of which was fairly common knowledge.[52] Kittel thus accused Jews of the murderous dehumanization of others precisely at the moment that this treatment was being applied to them. His willful distortion of Jewish texts provided intellectual cover for genocide.

Antisemitic Exegesis of the Talmud: Karl Georg Kuhn

Gerhard Kittel's dishonest manipulation of passages from the Talmud represented nothing new in the history of antisemitism. This technique had an old pedigree in Christian Europe, as the Talmud had made a convenient target for anti-Jewish polemics. A vast compendium of Jewish learning, the Talmud—specifically the Babylonian Talmud—contains two and a half million words on almost six thousand folio pages. It consists for the most part of the written record of arguments carried on in the rabbinical academies of Mesopotamia during the third, fourth, and fifth centuries C.E. The rabbis debated law, beliefs, customs, and history, with the ultimate goal of creating a comprehensive framework for Jewish life outside of Israel. The text constitutes an extraordinarily complex dialectic of arguments and counterarguments, many of which were posed speculatively, hypothetically, and hyperbolically, not to be taken literally. The vastness, depth, and complexity of the text has led many scholars to apply the description "Sea of the Talmud" to the sprawling work.[53] Many have regarded this quality of the Talmud in a positive light. Gerhard Kittel, writing in 1926, before his turn to antisemitism, celebrated the Talmud as "a giant sack into which was stuffed everything which Judaism had stored up in terms of memories and traditions, so that its contents are the most colorful and joyful confusion and juxtaposition that one can imagine."[54]

These very qualities, however, could easily lend themselves to misunderstanding among those not well versed in the Talmud, as well as to intentional misrepresentation by anti-Jewish polemicists. Critics derided the Talmud as the inspiration for all kinds of alleged Jewish misconduct, including blasphemy against Christian doctrine, the ritual murder of Christian children, and dishonesty in business dealings with non-Jews. During the Middle Ages the Talmud was repeatedly banned, confiscated, and burned on the urging of the Catholic Church. The hostility toward the work persisted through the Reformation and into modern times. Among those writing in German, the most notable anti-Talmudic polemicists were Johannes Pfefferkorn, a converted Jew who published several tracts in the early sixteenth century; Johann Eisenmenger, whose *Judaism Unmasked (Entdecktes Judentum)*, published in 1699, became a classic of its genre; and August Rohling, whose book *The Talmud Jew,* published in 1871, borrowed heavily from Eisenmenger. Theodor Fritsch reproduced the same arguments in his popular *Handbook of the Jewish Question.*[55] The genre also included attacks on the Shulchan Aruch, a distillation of Talmudic opinions intended to be a user-friendly reference work for practicing Jews. The most aggressive such assault was published in 1929 by Erich Bischoff, a disciple of Theodor Fritsch.[56]

The basic method of these works was to present passages from the "Sea of the Talmud" out of their original textual or historical contexts. They seized upon utterances of ancient rabbis that originated as tactical debating maneuvers and misrepresented them as statements of Jewish doctrine. Similarly, they pointed to unflattering Talmudic characterizations of Gentiles as proof of Jewish disdain for non-Jews, ignoring the circumstances of persecution and oppression that gave rise to such rabbinical polemics. They selected only those Talmudic passages that cast Jews in a negative light, and omitted contradictory passages that might have softened the harsh portrait.

This tradition of anti-Talmudic polemic continued in the Third Reich, embodied most conspicuously in propaganda tracts intended for dissemination to a broad readership. Facile attacks on the Talmud saturated Nazi newspapers, most notably the obsessively antisemitic *Stürmer.*[57] Less dripping in venom, but no less misrepresentative of the spirit of the Talmudic texts, were the articles and brochures of Johannes Pohl, a trained Bible scholar who helped organize the looting of Jewish libraries in Nazi-occupied Europe during World War II.[58] Several book-length compilations of Talmudic passages appeared during the Nazi era as well. These included Walter Fasolt's book *The Foundations of the Talmud: A Non-Jewish Perspective,* which was published in 1935 and then went through multiple editions; it was a malicious polemic by a propagandist whose other Nazi-era publications included *Papal Domination,* a fierce attack on the Catholic Church.[59] Both of these books were brought out by the Pötsch publishing house in Breslau, which specialized in sensationalist hate literature aimed at mass audiences. Another product of the same publisher was Gerhard Utikal's book *Jewish Ritual Murder,* which purported to demonstrate the veracity of this antisemitic accusation to the nonscholarly reader in a manner that was "simple and clear" and "easy to understand."[60]

Among the works by antisemitic scholars in the Third Reich, the most ambitious attempt to explain the meaning and content of the Talmud was undertaken by Karl Georg Kuhn, a colleague of Gerhard Kittel at the University of Tübingen.[61] Born in 1906, Kuhn studied Protestant theology and semitic languages in Breslau, where he also attended classes at the famous Jewish Theological Seminar. As a protégé of Kittel, he pursued graduate studies at Tübingen in Semitic languages, New Testament studies, and Iranian philogogy, receiving his doctorate in 1931. He joined the Nazi party in 1932. Kuhn remained at Tübingen, completing his advanced research certification (*Habilitation*) in Semitic languages in 1934. Between 1935 and 1940 he offered courses at Tübingen regularly under the auspices of the theology faculty. He contributed to Kittel's *Theological Dictionary of the New Testament,* translated a volume of Midrash into German, and published a book on the Psalms. Like Kittel, he also became involved with the Jewish Research Department of the Institute for History of the New Germany and its organ, *Forschungen zur Judenfrage.* Kuhn came to be widely regarded as one the most able German experts on the Jewish religion, on the basis of his powerful intellect, his knowledge of ancient Jewish languages, and his familiarity with Jewish texts.[62]

Kuhn's teaching at Tübingen included lecture courses and seminars entitled "Rabbinic Texts" (in collaboration with Kittel), "The Jews of the Ancient World," "The Talmud," "The Attitude of Jews to Non-Jews in the Talmud and Shulchan Aruch," "Zionism," and the "History of the Jewish Question and Attempted Solutions to It."[63] The subjects of Kuhn's courses between 1935 and 1940 were closely tied to his publications. For example, his course "The Talmud: Origins and Nature of Jewish-Babylonian Literature," offered in the winter semester of 1935–1936, addressed the same topic as a 1936 contribution to *Forschungen zur Judenfrage,* while his course "The Attitude of Jews to Non-Jews in the Talmud and Shulchan Aruch," taught in the winter semester of 1937–1938, focused on the same subject as an article he published in the *Forschungen zur Judenfrage* in 1938. Although former students of Kuhn later testified that the courses had emphasized politically neutral, objective scholarship that was not antisemitic, it is very difficult to believe in light of the pronounced antisemitic content of Kuhn's contemporaneously published articles on the same subjects.

Kuhn's antisemitic writings of the Nazi era tapped into the basic methodology of earlier anti-Talmudists. They were marked by a willful, or ideologically determined, disregard for literary and historical context and a tendentious interpretation of Talmudic passages selected mainly for their expressions of anti-Gentile sentiment.[64] But Kuhn was very conscious of his academic credentials and did what he could to distance himself from the more vulgar anti-Talmudic polemics. Never once did he cite Eisenmenger, Rohling, or Fritsch. He relied instead on academically respected sources, such as the Strack-Billerbeck commentary, and on Jewish texts themselves. Kuhn's assault on the Talmud was a good deal more complex and sophisticated than that of his more popularly oriented predecessors. Rather than simply critique the teachings contained in the Talmud, Kuhn subjected the entire structure of Talmudic reasoning to attack. To be sure, Kuhn's representation of Talmudic hermeneutics was as misleading as his description of Talmudic teachings, but no other antisemitic scholar in Nazi Germany could approach the subject with such professed authority.

A good illustration of Kuhn's zeal to maintain a safe scholarly distance from the mongers of mere propaganda can be seen in his review of Hermann Schroer's *Blood and Money in Jewry*. Schroer's book, which appeared in 1936, consisted primarily of a reprinting of part of Heinrich Loewe's 1836 edition of the Shulchan Aruch.[65] Loewe, a Jewish convert to Christianity, had published the work to help non-Jews understand Jewish law and ritual. Schroer, a Wuppertal-based attorney, supplemented Loewe's introduction with one of his own, in which he described the Shulchan Aruch as a synthesis of "bastardized late-Roman law" and "Jewish money law" and as the embodiment of "Jewish-materialist legal thinking." Schroer supplemented the original text with annotations that underscored the ostensible racial basis of Jewish rituals and practices in order to expose the "destructive forces of racially alien legal thinking."[66]

Kuhn assessed Schroer's book in the *Historische Zeitschrift*, Germany's most venerable academic historical journal.[67] Kuhn disparaged both the original Loewe translation as well as the Schroer republication of a hundred years later. The Loewe translation, Kuhn noted, was a poor one, having been originally produced under "entirely different ideological conditions" from those of the present day. As for the Schroer edition, Kuhn declared the work "scientifically worthless." Schroer, a lawyer by profession, could not even read Hebrew, and his entire familiarity with the subject seemed to have been based on the translated document itself and a small amount of additional secondary literature. "It will not do," Kuhn pronounced, "when one takes a more than hundred-year-old translation by a baptized Jew, equips it with a lively antisemitic title and an equally lively antisemitic introduction, and then thinks that by publishing it he is doing a service to National Socialism." To the contrary, the publication of such an amateurish work only "discredits our scholarship in the new Germany." Instead, scholars need to "go to the sources."

Kuhn claimed to have done precisely that for the three articles he contributed to the *Forschungen zur Judenfrage*. The first of these, published in 1936 and entitled "The Origin of Talmudic Thought," was based on a lecture delivered at the inaugural meeting of the Jewish Research Department of the Reich Institute.[68] In contrast to Gerhard Kittel's contribution in the same issue of the *Forschungen,* Kuhn's article examined the nature of the Jews not in racial terms but in cultural and intellectual ones. Nevertheless, it resonated with familiar stereotypes about the Talmud and traditional Judaism.

The Talmud, according to Kuhn, embodied a unique thought process, the understanding of which was necessary for an understanding of the very essence of Judaism. Kuhn dissented from the widely held Christian view that rabbinic Judaism represented a perversion of the Old Testament tradition. The dominant Christian position, even among liberal Protestant theologians, was that Christianity had taken over the positive qualities of ancient Judaism, such as a passionate devotion to God and a concern for justice, while Judaism, after 70 C.E., had devolved into a casuistic formalism that ultimately reached its apotheosis in the Talmud. Kuhn dissented from the notion that there had been a fundamental break between biblical and rabbinic Judaism. "The history of the Jews," he maintained, "must be understood as a continuous whole." He saw the Talmud not as the product of the "spiritual ossification of genuine Jewry" but rather as Judaism's "most inevitable manifestation." A spiritually empty, legalistic, textual literalism, Kuhn contended, had been the essence of Judaism from the very beginning.[69]

As a modern, scientific student of the Bible, Kuhn characterized the Torah not as a divine revelation but as a textual montage consisting of multiple narrative strands that had undergone human redaction. He dated the actual beginning of Judaism to the year 458 B.C.E., when Ezra declared the Torah the binding "law of God." Ezra imposed on Judaism the dogma that the Torah was not merely a reflection of a divine moral and ethical wisdom but also "letter for letter" the actual word of God. Thus, Kuhn argued, Judaism was founded as a religion in which the "word of God had to be fulfilled with the most precise exactitude." Fulfilling the 613 laws of the Torah became "the decisive, exclusive religious mission of Jewry."[70] The "entire internal development of Jewry up until Talmudism," Kuhn contended, was presaged by the sanctification of the actual text of the Torah. In order that its commandments be fulfilled, "every single sentence, every single word" of the Torah had to be studied and understood. Because the Torah was the literal word of God, Jews could not acknowledge that it might contain contradictions, assuming instead that imperfect human intelligence had not yet deduced God's meaning.[71]

As Jewish society could not function properly if every person were allowed to interpret Torah for himself, Kuhn reasoned, inherent to the nature of Judaism was the need for a cadre of scholars who would perform this task for the community. These were the scribes and the rabbis. Moreover, the 613 laws of the Torah were often vague, and did not cover every eventuality, so they had to be supplemented by what came to be known as the oral law. The job of the scribes, and later the rabbis, was to deduce these laws from the text of the Torah. The divine authenticity of these laws rested on the claim that God gave the oral law to Moses on Mount Sinai together with the written Torah. The Talmud is the oral law written down for the purpose of making it available for future generations.[72]

Jewish hermeneutics, Kuhn continued, arose out of the theologically inherent need of Judaism to anchor newly created oral laws in the Torah. Kuhn pointed to the special role played by the Pharisees, the first-century Jewish sect that is presented in an especially negative light in the New Testament. In response to criticism from the Sadducees, who rejected all embellishments to the written Torah, the Pharisees developed ever more elaborate ways to anchor new laws in the scripture. These debates gave rise to the method known as Midrash, which Jews have traditionally seen as a source of intellectual creativity, but which Kuhn characterized as an insincere form of cleverness. Kuhn sarcastically observed that Rabbi Akiva, who was active in the early second century C.E., had raised the disingenuous method to a new level of "virtuosity."[73] He omitted any mention of Akiva's dictum "Thou shalt love thy neighbor as thyself."

Rooted in Midrash, Talmudic exegesis, Kuhn argued, was a fundamentally dishonest intellectual process. Rather than analyzing a text in order to discover what might logically follow from it, Midrash did the exact opposite, seeking to establish a textual basis for a predetermined legal outcome. Midrash operated according to mechanical principles of reasoning that resulted in "purely formalistic thinking" that was divorced from the concrete reality of the issue. The questionable methods, according to Kuhn, included deducing from particular cases to general principles, invoking tenuous analogies, and engaging in clever word play. Once a new law was accepted according to these methods, it became the basis for further exegetical invention. The entire Midrashic and Talmudic enterprise, encapsulated in the Hebrew term *pilpul,* Kuhn condemned as "intellectual gymnastics," a form of "purely formalistic game-playing" that had little or nothing to do with the obvious meaning of the written law.[74] Thus, while Talmudic exegesis was performed in the name of upholding God's law, its actual purpose was to justify circumventing that law. To support this claim, Kuhn described how Orthodox Jews get around limitations on traveling on the Sabbath.[75]

Kuhn compounded this stereotype of Talmudic legalism with a further stereotype, that of the Jews as a loquacious, argumentative people. In explaining why the Talmudic text consists in large part of dialogues among rabbis, he drew a contrast between the verbal dialectic that produced Talmudic scholarship and the more contemplative method of non-Jewish scholars who think and write in the "quiet solitude of the study."[76] "Generation upon generation of Jews" have received their intellectual training in this tradition, which, in Kuhn's opinion, explained why among Jews there are always a hundred arguments in favor of and a hundred against something. Unlike Christianity, which is focused on a single, large, meaningful idea, Judaism and Jews have from the very beginning been obsessed with "formalistic-logical virtuosity."[77]

The core substance of Kuhn's critique would not have been unfamiliar to Protestant critics of Judaism, and even Reform or secular Jews might have recognized in it some elements of their own frustrations with the Talmudic tradition. Its antisemitism lay mainly in its skewed, caricatured representation of rabbinic Judaism. Kuhn recognized in the Talmud only a legal dialectic, ignoring altogether its value to the Jewish people as a source of wisdom, ethics, history, and folklore. His emphasis on the issue of scriptural authenticity led him to ignore the psychological dimension of adherence to Jewish law, which helped preserve a sense of Jewish identity in foreign and often hostile environments. Kuhn depicted Judaism as a monolithic entity, failing to acknowledge that Talmudic legalism had coexisted, often in a tense relationship, with the Jewish prophetic tradition, and with spiritual movements such as Karaism, mysticism, and Hasidism. Perhaps most egregiously, Kuhn did not mention modern Reform Judaism, the dominant form of faith among German Jews of his day, and one which did not consider scripturally based laws binding. None of these essential elements of modern Judaism found a place in Kuhn's intellectual agenda, the purpose of which was to demonstrate an unbroken continuity of Jewish religious and cultural development from the ancient world to modern times.

Kuhn added a further wrinkle to his notion of unbroken development in his contribution to the 1937 issue of the *Forschungen*, an article entitled "World Jewry in Antiquity."[78] He described ancient Jewry as a heterogeneous entity in terms of religion, social structure, language, customs, and race. He differentiated between two main branches of Jewry, the Palestinian Jews and the Jews of the Greco-Roman Diaspora. Palestinian Jewry constituted a territorially based nation with a common religion, which was normal for that age and region. Diaspora Jewry, in contrast, consisted of Jews in what for the time was an abnormal situation, that of a geographically dispersed minority. The Jews of the Diaspora exhibited dramatically different characteristics from those of Palestinian Jews and, in Kuhn's opinion, could be properly regarded as the first manifestation of a "world Jewry" that continued into modern times.[79]

Ancient Palestinian Jewry, according to Kuhn, possessed a "healthy national structure," based as it was on agriculture and a rural peasantry.[80] Notwithstanding occasional conflicts with immediately neighboring peoples, these Jews largely kept to themselves and were not perceived by others in the region as the source of a "Jewish problem." A sign of their national health was their ability to resist assimilation into Greek and Roman culture.[81] Diaspora Jewry, on the other hand, was predominantly urban and involved in commercial, financial, and intellectual activities, all of which rendered it culturally and sociologically unhealthy.[82] One result of this unhealthy state was a strong tendency toward assimilation into host cultures, although not to the point of religious conversion.[83] These Diaspora Jews attracted resentment by virtue of their group insularity, their wealth, and their refusal to give up their religion.[84]

Of these two fundamentally different types of Jewries, only the Diaspora version survived, and became the basis for later Jewry, while the Palestinian type disappeared from history.[85] There was a parallel between Kuhn's depiction of Diaspora Jewry and that often promoted in Zionist circles. Both views shared the belief that a people can only be "normal" if they possess a territory of their own and till the land. Some of Kuhn's Nazi contemporaries, such as Hans F. K. Günther, subscribed to this view as well, and at least claimed to support a program of Jewish settlement in Palestine. Kuhn, however, unlike Kittel, who rejected Zionism as unworkable, never issued an opinion on that subject.

In 1938 Kuhn published his third article in *Forschungen,* entitled "The Origin and Essence of the Talmudic Attitude toward Non-Jews."[86] Of his three contributions to the journal, this was the longest, most heavily documented, and most virulent. Kuhn's portrayal of the Talmud was not as a corrupted form of ancient Judaism but as a vessel of its very essence. Although Kuhn acknowledged passages in both the Torah and the Talmud urging hospitality toward strangers, he depicted Judaism as being intrinsically hostile toward other peoples and religions. He saw this hostility rooted in the Jewish doctrine of divine selection, and in the rivalries between the ancient Israelites and the neighbors and conquerors with whom they came into contact. Jews, who regarded themselves as holy, as God's people, developed a gradually intensifying disdain for others. This development, Kuhn contended, was reflected in the evolution of the Hebrew term *goyim* from its origin as a simple reference to "the other nations" into the much more derisive term for "heathens."[87] For Kuhn, Jewish xenophobia was reinforced by the discourses surrounding the prohibition against exogamy, in which non-Jews were depicted as idolaters, criminals, and fornicators.[88] The catastrophic destruction of the Jerusalem temple by the Romans in 70 C.E. further intensified the "tenacious anger and excessive hatred of the definitively subjugated people against their foreign overlords and against everything alien." Jewish attitudes toward non-Jews were now characterized by "an unconstrained mistrust and a powerful craving for small acts of revenge."[89]

This psychology of a vanquished people, in Kuhn's judgment, formed the basis for Talmudic statements on Jewish relations with non-Jews. While Christianity had achieved "the apex of religious development" through its preaching of "universal love of man," the Talmud had simply magnified the already existing xenophobia of the Jews.[90] What was more, the Talmud encouraged Jews to believe that they would always be hated by the goyim, a point illustrated by Kuhn in page after page of Talmudic excerpts.[91] The Talmud, he wrote, discouraged friendships and cordial interactions with non-Jews, and encouraged Jews to cheat them. The Talmud even absolved the guilt of Jews who had killed non-Jews. Here Kuhn exploited the same passage from Sanhedrin that Kittel would later use in his 1943 article for the Propaganda Ministry.[92] Kuhn cited the passages directly out of Talmudic tractates, and also relied on the Strack-Billerbeck commentary. The cynicism here is especially striking, as Kuhn was a sophisticated scholar who most certainly understood the hypothetical and polemical nature of the Talmudic passages he was turning against the Jews. In the end, Kuhn rejected any notion that the Talmudic bias against non-Jews had influenced only Orthodox Jews. The Talmud, he concluded, had profoundly shaped "the character of all of Jewry" and had contributed much to "making Jewry what it is."[93] With this declaration, Kuhn summarily dismissed the richness and complexity of the Talmud and the enormous range of Jewish attitudes toward it.

Kuhn's three articles in the *Forschungen* had all focused chronologically on the periods of Second Temple and early rabbinic Judaism, and had all been written with a relatively limited readership in mind. In 1939, however, he reached out to a much broader audience with a fifty-one-page booklet entitled "The Jewish Question as a World-Historical Problem."[94] This publication contained a revised version of lectures he had delivered twice in the weeks following the November 1938 "Kristallnacht" pogrom, first at Walter Frank's Reich Institute in Berlin, and then at the University of Berlin before an overflow audience of 2,500 listeners.[95]

Kuhn began by claiming for himself and for his discipline of "Semitics" (*Semitistik*) an especially important role in Jewish research. With their command of languages such as Hebrew and Aramaic, such scholars enjoyed direct access to the Jewish Bible, the Mishnah, the Talmud, the Kabala, and other Jewish texts through which the "essence of Jewry" could best be understood.[96] This comment was an implied criticism of historians who approached the Jewish question primarily through the study of

German and Christian texts. Kuhn proceeded from this assertion of intellectual authority to a sweeping analysis of the history of the "Jewish question" on a global scale. From ancient times to the present, in pagan, Christian, and Islamic societies, wherever Jews have lived, they have been perceived as a problem. The fundamental reason for the existence of a "Jewish question" must therefore lie in the "basic structure," "essence," and "existential form" of Jewry itself.[97] Kuhn reiterated his claim that the Jews—all Jews, and not only the Talmudically conscious Orthodox— were guided by a "morality of *völkisch* struggle" against other peoples.[98] Relying on a tortured interpretation of Maimonides, Kuhn told his listeners and readers that Jews used commerce as a "method of combat" to compensate for their minority status.[99] He made this assertion at precisely the moment that the German government was implementing a rapid, coerced "Aryanization" of Jewish property.

It was also in this piece that Kuhn made the leap from religiocultural to racist antisemitism. Despite having been a member of the Nazi party since 1932 and a protégé of the increasingly racist Gerhard Kittel, Kuhn had so far resisted crossing this line in his scholarship. While it is difficult to tell whether he underwent a genuine intellectual conversion, professional opportunism almost certainly played a role. Still in his early thirties, Kuhn's position at Tübingen was that of a nonpermanent instructor. Aspiring to a coveted professorship, Kuhn probably wanted to reassure the regime that his scholarship was in line with Nazi racial doctrine. Whatever the reason for his change of mind, Kuhn was no longer content to predicate his explanation for Jewish behavior on religious and cultural factors. The Talmud and Judaism, he observed, could not by themselves explain why the Jews had maintained their cohesion over so many centuries and throughout their vast geographic dispersion. An even more fundamental cause had to be identified. Citing the work of Eugen Fischer, Kuhn attributed Jewish behaviors to "hereditary biological predispositions" and the "racial substance" of the Jews.[100] He closed his article with praise for the Third Reich's decisive measures against the Jews, noting that the Jews were now simply "reaping what they have sown for the past 150 years."[101] This was an especially foreboding statement in view of the massive pogrom that had been perpetrated upon the Jews of Germany in November 1938, just a few weeks before Kuhn's first lecture.

Kuhn served in the German army from 1940 to 1944. During his service he received a furlough to research and write a memorandum about the racial origins of the Karaites.[102] A religious sect originating in the eighth century, the Karaites perceived themselves as the successors of the ancient Sadducees, defending the sanctity of the Jewish Bible while rejecting the authority of the oral law as embodied in the Talmud. For centuries they considered themselves to be Jews, and were regarded by the rabbinic establishment as a schismatic but nonetheless Jewish sect. The two communities became increasingly alienated from one another, however, and by the early twentieth century, Karaites and Jews had come to be generally regarded as distinct peoples. In modern times, the chief centers of Karaite settlement were in Lithuania, Poland, and the Crimea. Modern Karaite leaders persistently claimed that their people had descended mainly from medieval Turko-Mongol converts who had not been of Jewish origin. In January 1939, the German Ministry of the Interior sustained this theory, ruling that the tiny Karaite community inside Germany would not be classified racially as Jews. But the question of Karaite racial origins arose once again after the Nazi conquest of eastern Europe. Einsatzgruppen commanders and occupation officials on the ground required clarification from Berlin about how to handle the Karaites. The Reich Ministry for the Occupied Eastern Territories, a part of Alfred Rosenberg's administrative empire, solicited professional opinions from several German scholars, Karl Georg Kuhn among them, and from Jewish scholars as well.[103] In the end, the ministry confirmed the earlier opinion of the Interior Ministry, and the Karaites were not included in the "Final Solution."

The memorandum submitted by Kuhn supported the Karaites' own contention that they were Jews in neither religious nor racial terms.[104] After the war, Kuhn used the memorandum for exculpatory purposes, claiming that he had designed it to help save the Karaites from racial persecution. Yet there had been nothing in his memorandum that was inconsistent with widely held views about Karaite racial origins. Neither the German Interior Ministry, Jewish scholars, nor the Karaites themselves had regarded the Karaites as Jews, and Kuhn's memorandum was but one among a number of expert opinions solicited by the German government that came to the same conclusion. Maintaining that the anti-Talmudic Karaites were not Jews was entirely consistent with Kuhn's previous writings, and can hardly be construed as an act of resistance against Nazi racial policy.

Upon his decommissioning from the Wehrmacht in 1944, Kuhn returned to Tübingen to teach in the final semester before the war came to an end. His two courses were titled "The Talmud: Introduction to Its Origin and Content," and "Readings in Talmudic Texts."[105] In July 1945 the French occupation authorities in southwest Germany suspended him from the faculty. Over the next several years, Kuhn successfully fought for his political rehabilitation and received a series of academic appointments culminating in a prestigious professorial chair at the University of Heidelberg. The arguments contained in Kuhn's own postwar apologia, the defenses of him submitted by his academic colleagues, and the rationale behind the decisions of two denazification committees all paint a revealing and disturbing picture of how Kuhn's brand of learned antisemitism was perceived by his contemporaries.

Kuhn went through two denazification proceedings in 1948.[106] The first was conducted by the regular denazification board for the community of Stuttgart-Feuerbach. For Kuhn's case, the board consisted of a bank employee, an electrical mechanic, a chemist, and a retiree. The second proceeding was conducted by a special board, consisting of academics, set up specifically to denazify the faculty of the University of Tübingen. Both boards classified Kuhn as "exonerated," employing identical evidence and reasoning. Kuhn presented himself as an apolitical scholar who had struggled to inject a modicum of sober objectivity into the discourse on the Jewish question. He convinced the Tübingen board that his decision to join the Nazi party in 1932 had been more personal than political, a reaction, he claimed, to the breakup of his engagement after his fiancée had become a communist. He produced correspondence he had carried on with Jewish scholars in the mid-1930s, which the Stuttgart board accepted as evidence of Kuhn's "resistance against National Socialist tyranny." Kuhn secured recommendations from former students, who persuaded the Tübingen board that Kuhn "had never propagated National Socialist teaching," and that Kuhn's "purely objective and scientific introduction to the world of Rabbinic Judaism significantly contributed to immunizing his students against rampant antisemitic slogans." The Tübingen board was impressed by a letter from the university's postwar rector, according to whom Kuhn had "remained a pure scholar, having carefully refrained from the slightest bias toward antisemitism." Both boards praised Kuhn for helping to save the Karaites from extinction. Neither board acknowledged the logical corollary to this conclusion, that Kuhn had participated in the racial definition of the Jews after the "Final Solution" had begun.

Neither board concluded that any of Kuhn's Nazi-era writings or lectures presented cause for concern. The Stuttgart board, which relied on outside evaluations of Kuhn's writings, felt satisfied that they were not antisemitic because they did not reflect "the spirit of *Der Stürmer.*" The Tübingen board conducted its own inspection of the publications, and agreed with this assessment. By documenting a strong Talmudic prohibition against sexual intercourse with non-Jews, the board concluded, Kuhn's scholarship had discredited *Stürmer's* charge that the Talmud encouraged Jewish men to rape Christian women. The Tübingen board also cited Kuhn's scathing review of Schroer's *Blood and Money in Jewry* as evidence of his scholarly objectivity and aloofness from antisemitism. When Kuhn had published this review in 1937, his main purpose had been to protect the intellectual respectability of scholarly antisemitism. Now, over a decade later, Kuhn and his defenders disingenuously, and successfully, invoked the review as evidence of his lack of antisemitism altogether.

Regarding Kuhn's three contributions to the *Forschungen zur Judenfrage,* the Tübingen board was impressed by the "purely objective-scientific attitude of the author." Kuhn, the board concluded, had intended only to ensure that the journal included at least some "objective scholarship based on solid study of the sources." As for Kuhn's booklet *The Jewish Question as a World-Historical Problem,* the Tübingen board saw only a "specialized scholarly treatment" in which "no antisemitic tendencies could be recognized."

These interpretations of Kuhn's writings and actions during the Nazi era rested in part on the willful mendacity of Kuhn and his apologists, and in part on the mystique exercised by scholarship on nonacademics. In comparison to the vulgar antisemitism that was so common in the Third Reich, Kuhn's writings seemed moderate and reasonable to the laypersons on the Stuttgart board. While it would be very difficult to believe that the Tübingen denazification board, composed of professors, genuinely recognized no antisemitism at all in Kuhn's writings, it may have considered Kuhn's sentiments as within the acceptable limits of the Christian anti-Jewish tradition.

With his exoneration secured, Kuhn received a temporary appointment to the chair in New Testament studies at the University of Göttingen in 1949. In requesting permission for Kuhn's appointment from the Cultural Ministry of the state of Lower Saxony, the dean of the Theolog-

ical Faculty at Göttingen omitted any mention of Kuhn's antisemitic publications, restricting himself instead to a discussion of Kuhn's Midrash
translation and his book on the Psalms. The dean identified Kuhn as
"among the few Christian scholars presently in Germany who possess expertise in rabbinics."[107] During his five years at Göttingen, Kuhn also
taught New Testament at the University of Mainz and served as theological examiner for the Evangelical-Lutheran church in Hannover. In 1954
Kuhn received a permanent appointment to a New Testament chair at
Heidelberg. The Heidelberg faculty considered Kuhn "a pioneer of modern, critical, and sharply focused religious-historical methodology"
and a "leading representative of rabbinics." Kuhn was also sought after
because he had garnered expertise in the Dead Sea Scrolls, which had
recently been discovered at Qumran. The documentation accompanying the appointment once more omitted Kuhn's problematic Nazi-era
record, noting only that Kuhn had been briefly suspended from teaching
after 1945, a matter that had since been "officially resolved" and therefore required no further discussion.[108] Kuhn taught at Heidelberg until
1971, achieving prominence as one of Germany's leading experts on the
Dead Sea Scrolls and their significance for understanding early Christianity.

During his post-1945 career, Kuhn did not remain entirely silent
about his early mistakes. In 1951 he did something that was highly unusual for a West German ex-Nazi who had published antisemitic statements before 1945: he issued a public "retraction" and apology. Writing
in the journal *Evangelische Theologie,* Kuhn repudiated "in every respect" his 1939 booklet *The Jews as a World-Historical Problem* and apol-
ogized for his "blindness" in not having recognized that "Hitler's Jewish
policies" would lead inevitably into "the abyss of horror."[109] The retraction, however admirable, was quite limited, applying only to the single
booklet from 1939. It did not refer to Kuhn's articles in the *Forschungen.*
Years later, in 1968, Rolf Seeliger, who published a series of short book-
lets exposing the pre-1945 records of West German university professors, demanded that Kuhn also repudiate the *Forschungen* pieces. Kuhn
refused, defending them as "historical accounts of ancient Judaism" that
were "based on appropriate quotations from and citations to the sources
of antiquity."[110]

Kuhn retired from the University of Heidelberg in 1971, and was hon-
ored with a *Festschrift* by his friends, students, and colleagues.[111] Unlike

most such volumes, Kuhn's *Festschrift* included no biographical portrait of the honoree, and no bibliography of his publications. Although the entry for Kuhn in the German academic *Who's Who* omitted his anti-semitic articles in *Forschungen zur Judenfrage*,[112] there is no record that Kuhn ever publicly repudiated them.

The case of Karl Georg Kuhn exemplifies the willingness of postwar Germans to excuse, rationalize, or disregard the involvement of promi-nent individuals in the Nazi campaign against the Jews, especially those whose antisemitic actions had been bureaucratic or rhetorical. Owing to the fact that antisemitic statements had not been illegal in Germany be-fore 1945, Kuhn and others like him suffered few consequences for their demonization of the Jews, unlike Germans of lower social standing who had been petty perpetrators in anti-Jewish violence. A shroud of academic "respectability" obfuscated the virulent substance of Kuhn's antisemitism, making it appear moderate, even unobjectionable, to the academic and government officials in the Federal Republic who ap-pointed him to an important professorship at one of Germany's most prestigious universities. Kuhn's continued defense of the academic legit-imacy of his *Forschungen* articles, three decades after they were pub-lished, demonstrated a remarkable disregard for truth and decency. His dishonesty was compounded by the disinclination of his colleagues and students to acknowledge that there was a problem; by remaining silent, they tolerated the antisemitism of Kuhn's articles. If Kuhn's Nazi-era ca-reer illustrated the perversion of scholarship by antisemitic ideology, his postwar career reflected the failure of many in the German academic world to honestly confront the persistence of antisemitism in their own ranks and to hold their peers accountable for violating the integrity of their profession.

4

Dissimilation through Scholarship

Historians were especially active in the effort to create Nazi Jewish studies. They were instrumental in the founding of antisemitic research institutes and journals, and, in purely quantitative terms, contributed more published scholarship to the genre than the members of any other discipline. The central task they set for themselves was to create a historical "pedigree" for Nazi antisemitism.[1] They sought to justify Nazism's racial approach to the "Jewish question" by identifying its antecedents in previous centuries. For these historians, racism embodied the culmination of the historical development of antisemitism. The wisdom of Nazi racism, they argued, could be validated through comparisons with the religious, cultural, and economic antisemitism of earlier times. Lacking insight into the racial basis of human behavior, misguided Christians had attempted to convert or assimilate the Jews. Nazi historians emphasized the futility and dangers inherent in such attempts to contravene nature. They also set out to refute the claims of Jewish historiography, which they believed represented a racial perspective hostile to Germans.

When the Nazis came to power in Germany in 1933, expertise in the history of the Jews and of Jewish-Christian relations was, indeed, in short supply. Prior to 1933, historical scholarship about these subjects had been carried out in large part by Jews themselves. The number of non-Jewish historians to whom the Nazi regime could turn for ideologically correct scholarship on the history of the "Jewish question" was minuscule, and the leaders in the field of Jewish research after 1933 often emphasized the importance of training a new generation of such scholars.

Indeed, even after the advent of Nazi rule, Jewish scholars continued to produce the majority of historical studies of Jews that appeared in Germany. They published their work with Jewish publishers, who were allowed to operate well after 1933. Such intellectual and publishing activity among German Jews was consistent with a Nazi policy that promoted the separation of Jews from German society. Despite the emigration of many scholars, and despite having to operate under the watchful eye of the Gestapo, Jewish academic institutions in Germany carried their work forward after 1933. Three rabbinical seminars—two in Berlin and one in Breslau—remained open until November 1938. The Academy for the Science of Judaism in Berlin (Hochschule für die Wissenschaft des Judentums), the single most important center of Jewish learning in Germany, employed a faculty of twenty-two scholars in 1938. The Nazi regime severely curtailed the activities of Jewish cultural and intellectual institutions after the November 1938 "Kristallnacht" pogrom, although the *Hochschule* in Berlin was allowed to function until 1942.[2]

The continued preeminence of Jews in German Jewish historiography was reflected in annual bibliographies of historical scholarship published by the Prussian State Library in Berlin.[3] The joint issue for 1933 and 1934 listed two dozen dissertations, books, and major journal articles. Only one of the items on the list had been written in an antisemitic vein. The others had been authored by Jewish scholars, and in many cases published in respected Jewish scholarly periodicals, such as the *Journal of the History of Jews in Germany, Jewish Family Research,* and the *Monthly Journal of the Society for the Promotion of the Science of Judaism.* The pattern for the 1935 issue was similar: of the 26 items catalogued, 4 were antisemitic works. The 1936 issue listed 26 items, 7 of which could be considered antisemitic. The 1936 issue also featured a special bibliographical essay on the historiography of the "Jewish question." The 1937 issue, which was the last to appear, reflected both the burgeoning of Nazi antisemitic historical scholarship and the erosion of Jewish scholarship produced in Germany. Nine of the 27 items were the products of Nazi anti-Jewish scholarship, whereas only a dozen were books and articles by Jewish authors published with Jewish presses or in Jewish journals.

The antisemitic historians of Nazi Germany did not ignore the scholarship of their Jewish counterparts but in fact paid quite close attention to it. One of their central ideological tenets was the belief that new scholarship was needed to correct the errors of Jewish historiography, which had interpreted Jewish history and Jewish-Christian relations in a manner that was inherently biased toward a Jewish perspective and hostile to a German one. At the ceremonial opening of the Research Department for the Jewish Question in Munich in November 1936, Professor Karl Alexander von Müller of the University of Munich congratulated his students for breaking a longstanding "taboo" against writing Jewish history from something other than a "pro-Jewish standpoint."[4] A conservative nationalist historian who joined the Nazi party in 1933, Müller edited the venerable *Historische Zeitschrift* during much of the Third Reich. Several prominent antisemitic historians, including both Walter Frank and Wilhelm Grau, received their doctorates under his tutelage in the 1920s and early 1930s.[5] Walter Frank, head of the Reich Institute, developed Müller's position further in his own remarks at the November 1936 ceremony. A historiography on the Jewish question, that was Germanic rather than Jewish oriented, Frank asserted, amounted to a "research journey into unknown territory." "Only one side of the Jewish problem has been addressed, the Jewish side; almost all books on the Jewish question have been written by Jews; at German universities, dissertations on the Jewish question have been submitted almost entirely by Jews; the historical journals have selected only Jews as editors for matters Jewish."[6]

Frank was not incorrect in pointing out that Jewish historical scholarship had been a largely Jewish affair. His disingenuousness lay in his characterization of this reality as the result of a Jewish drive for intellectual hegemony over popular understanding of the Jewish question. Jewish historiography, Frank argued, had been motivated by a desire to justify the emancipation of the Jews and the subsequent assimilation of Jews into German society. Jewish scholarship, he continued, had presented itself as objective and scientific, but this had been a sham. Jewish "scientific objectivity," he held, had really represented the "subordination of the will to understanding to the actual power relationships of the liberal age."[7] Only because Jewish assimilation had come to be widely accepted by German intellectuals *a priori* as a positive development did Jewish scholarship take on a deceptive aura of objectivity.

Wilhelm Grau, whom Frank placed in charge of the Reich Institute's Research Department for the Jewish Question, had developed the same arguments in rather more depth in an article published a year earlier, in

1935. Grau referred to several non-Jewish scholars who had managed to defy the Jewish monopoly on Jewish history. These had included Otto Stobbe, who in the 1860s had published important work on the legal position of Jews in the Middle Ages; Herbert Meyer, who had contributed a study of property in Jewish law; and Werner Sombart, the well-known political economist who had written about the Jewish propensity for capitalism. But these were exceptional cases, Grau lamented, and he expressed a grudging admiration for the immense output of Jewish scholars such as Abraham Geiger, Ismar Elbogen, and Simon Dubnow, as well as for the *Encyclopedia Judaica* and similar collective projects. When one considered the quantity and quality of this work, Grau observed, "it should not be surprising that the world's picture of the Jewish question is entirely shaped by Jews." Unfortunately, Grau concluded, non-Jewish scholars have often reinforced the Jewish perspective because they have had no choice but to draw on Jewish scholarship for information.[8]

The claim that Jewish scholarship about Jewish life and history was inherently biased was a basic assumption of Nazi Jewish research, one that was often stated explicitly in books and articles. It derived from two key pillars of Nazi ideology, romantic nationalism and racialism, both of which posited the inevitable subjectivity of knowledge and perception. Because many Nazi-era historians depended heavily on Jewish scholarship as sources, they faced the dilemma of how one might exploit Jewish knowledge while correcting for its subjective, pro-Jewish bias. An additional challenge, which was rarely acknowledged, was that of how one could claim objectivity for oneself and one's own group while simultaneously positing the impossibility of objectivity for others. Anxious to be taken seriously as scholars, many Nazi Jewish researchers presented their work as the product of rigorous scholarship, or *Wissenschaft*. They asserted that their conclusions conformed to Nazi ideology not because they were biased but because Nazi ideology happened to represent the truth. Walter Frank underscored this assertion in his 1936 speech when he referred to Nazi scholarship as an example of "politics and science becoming a vitally self-fulfilling unity."[9]

Assessed in retrospect, however, the kind of scholarship championed by Frank was a grand enterprise in tautological argumentation, the goal of which was to demonstrate the validity of the Nazi interpretation of the Jewish question. At the core of this interpretation was, of course, the notion that the Jews constituted a distinct *Volk* in racial terms, one whose biologically determined characteristics rendered them incompatible with, and hostile to, the European peoples among whom they lived. While it was self-evident that such scholarship would be critical of the Jews, many of the chief targets of these works were liberal Gentiles, who had championed Jewish emancipation. Gentile antisemites who had understood the Jewish question in religious or economic, rather than racial, terms, and had therefore held that assimilation offered the best solution, were attacked as well. The Jews, according to this Nazi view, had achieved economic, political, and cultural influence in modern times in large part because of the actions of misguided or ignorant Gentiles, who in many cases shoved Jewish emancipation down the throats of the overwhelmingly antisemitic common people.

The Munich School

The methodologies and arguments of Nazi historical writing on the "Jewish question" were exemplified in the works of three historians who had received their doctorates in Munich under Karl Alexander von Müller: Walter Frank, Wilhelm Grau, and Klaus Schickert. Walter Frank was a prolific author who wrote in a popular, accessible, narrative style. The driven, disciplined Frank was only twenty-three years old when he finished his doctorate, and only thirty when he became director of the Institute for History of the New Germany. He had been attracted to right-wing politics since the age of sixteen and had begun to move in Nazi circles in Munich in 1925, although, as a gesture of intellectual independence, he never actually joined the party.[10] As it later turned out, this independent streak exacerbated Frank's disadvantage in the personal, ideological, and institutional struggle with Alfred Rosenberg, the Nazi party ideologue. Although Frank's early career had been promoted by Rosenberg, his attacks on Rosenberg's writings as simplistic and "unscientific" escalated to a series of crises that ultimately cost Frank his institute, his positions, and his friendships.[11] In the end, Frank took his own life in May 1945.

Frank's most scholarly work was his biography of the preacher Adolf Stoecker, an important antisemitic figure of late nineteenth-century Germany.[12] Stoecker had been the court pastor to the imperial family in Berlin and the central figure in the Christian socialist movement, which associated Jews with exploitative practices in modern capitalism. Frank was the first scholar to enjoy access to Stoecker's private papers, which included manuscripts of sermons and speeches. The work had originated as Frank's doctoral dissertation, completed under von Müller in 1928, and initially only a small number of copies were printed. Frank later claimed to have delivered one to Hitler personally.[13] In 1935 Frank published a second edition, this time with a major publisher, a sign of changing political times. The book was thoroughly antisemitic in both tone and interpretation, yet it proved itself a useful source of information for legitimate historians in the United States, Britain, and Israel decades later.[14]

Frank's study added a racial dimension to the explanation for Stoecker's success as an antisemitic organizer. Previous interpretations of Stoecker's career had tended to attribute the preacher's popularity mainly to his attacks on large-scale capitalism, which appealed to German artisans and small business owners who were struggling to stay afloat in a rapidly modernizing economy. Frank agreed that the social and economic conflicts of the German Empire had to be taken into account. The Jews, he claimed, had been an element of the "capitalist liberal bourgeoisie" that had been involved in an increasingly sharp conflict against an alliance of "old Prussian conservative" agrarians and the lower middle class.[15] But Frank argued against simply subordinating the "Jewish question" to the "social question," as previous studies of Stoecker, in his estimation, had done. Stoecker's career demonstrated the special resonance effected by antisemitism in the realm of mass politics. The perception not of class struggle but of "racial difference," Frank concluded, drew many supporters to Stoecker, even though Stoecker himself did not employ an explicitly racial definition of the Jews.[16]

In 1933 Frank published a second book, *Nationalism and Democracy in the French Third Republic*.[17] Frank based this formidable tome of well over six hundred pages on research he had conducted in Paris between 1928 and 1930. Much of it dealt with the origins of modern French antisemitism. Much as he had done in the study of Stoecker, Frank characterized the Jews as an important element of an exploitative capitalist plutocracy. And much as he depicted Stoecker as a courageous patriot who had been willing to stand up to the plutocracy and expose its Jewish face, Frank portrayed Charles Maurras, the guiding spirit of the antisemitic and protofascist *Action Française*, as an admirable figure who sought to rescue the French from Jewish domination. The book's longest chapter, "Merchants and Soldiers," chronicled the Dreyfus Affair and was published simultaneously as a book in its own right, geared to a wide, nonacademic readership.[18] In it, Frank

Dreyfus [handwritten marginalia]

argued that Dreyfus's guilt or innocence was really beside the point. What really mattered was that the widespread opposition to Dreyfus in many sectors of French society reflected the instinctive aversion of Frenchmen for Jews, an aversion grounded in racial difference. According to Frank, race had always been the basis for antisemitism in Europe, but in the absence of consciousness about race, antisemitic sentiment had manifested itself in the form of religious antipathy, economic resentment, or, as in the Dreyfus Affair, suspicion of treachery. For him it was only Jewish financial machinations and Jewish influence over the press that enabled the Jews to win Dreyfus's freedom in the end. All of Frank's research was cloaked and unified in the antisemitic conviction of Jewish racial identity and guilt.

The historical publications of Wilhelm Grau contained similar arguments about the innate antisemitism of non-Jewish Europeans.[19] As a student, Grau had been associated not with the Nazis but with the nationalistic, antisemitic Catholic right. This Catholic orientation came to be reflected in some of his early work, which attempted to merge traditional religious anti-Judaism with modern, racial antisemitism. Grau directed the Research Department for the Jewish Question in Frank's Institute from its founding in 1936 until a personal break with Frank in 1938. From July 1940 to October 1942, under the patronage of Alfred Rosenberg, Grau administered the Institute for Research on the Jewish Question in Frankfurt, as well as the Jewish library that was associated with it. In 1942, still only thirty-two years old, Grau entered the Wehrmacht. He survived the war and later started a small publishing house.

Grau's dissertation, published as a book in 1934, was titled *Antisemitism in the Late Middle Ages: The End of the Jewish Community of Regensburg, 1450–1519*.[20] Its purpose was to explain the expulsion of the Jews from that city in 1519, the catalyzing event for which had been a ritual murder trial. Grau differentiated between two important issues: one was the "factual guilt or innocence of the Jews"; the other was "the psychological and subjective disposition" of the Christian population. With regard to the historical veracity of ritual murder, Grau claimed to be agnostic. Christian historians, he argued, had made the mistake of taking all accusations and confessions at face value, while Jewish apologists had committed the error of assuming that all confessions were made under the duress of torture. Positioning himself as the objective scholar, Grau posed a series of questions to both sides. Of the Jewish apologists he asked whether Jewish prohibitions against using blood for ritual purposes meant that this, in fact, never happened. Did not the Jews from time to time engage in secretive, superstitious rituals? Did not hostility to Christianity at times attain great intensity? Are confessions made under torture necessarily always false? Grau then turned around to pose questions to the accusers. Did not medieval Christians harbor major illusions about Jewish religious practice? Were not superstitious fantasies common among Christians of that era? Shouldn't we be suspicious of confessions extracted through torture? Isn't it possible that the bones produced at the trial had been misidentified?

None of these questions, according to Grau, were likely to be answered with any degree of confidence. Instead he would examine the social and psychological reasons why the Christians of Regensburg believed in the reality of Jewish ritual murder, and why, in their sixteenth-century Christian worldview, the accusation made perfect sense. Grau employed what for his day was a progressive historical methodology, re-creating social reality on the ground at the local level, and asking the reader to understand events from the subjective perspective of those who experienced it. Grau examined the popular Christian piety of the early sixteenth century, and explained how Christian hostility toward Jews in Regensburg had been fueled by well-documented Jewish unscrupulousness in money-lending, pawnbroking, and other business practices. He presented the Christians of Regensburg as impoverished and desperate, suffering genuinely from material exploitation at the hands of Jews, and operating in a religious cosmos in which Jewish ritual murder seemed credible. Underlying all of this he found the same racially based instinctive revulsion toward Jews that Frank had.

What is especially striking is Grau's emphasis on understanding the subjective reality of ordinary people while downplaying the importance, or even relevance, of getting at a more objective reality. This methodology allowed Grau to distance himself from some of the more preposterous accusations of medieval anti-Judaism, but without having to actually refute them. His view of history from the ground up typified an historical methodology known as "people's history" (*Volksgeschichte*) as it developed in the Third Reich. An outgrowth of the populist, blood-and-soil tendencies in Nazi ideology, "people's history" represented a departure from the traditional "great man—great ideas" emphasis of German his-

torical scholarship, providing instead an appreciation, usually highly ro-
manticized, of the common folk.[21]

One further aspect of Wilhelm Grau's book about Regensburg de-
serves mention. Grau had a complicated relationship with Raphael
Straus, a Jewish scholar who was recognized as the leading expert on the
Jewish community of Regensburg in the late Middle Ages. Grau be-
friended Straus while he, Grau, was writing his doctoral dissertation at
the University of Munich in the early 1930s, under the supervision of
von Müller. Straus helped Grau with his project, even granting Grau access to a still unpublished collection of documents. In the published version of Grau's dissertation, which appeared in 1934, *after* the Nazis had
come to power, Grau thanked Straus for his assistance. In 1935, Straus
published a review of Grau's book in the *Journal of the History of Jews in
Germany,* an important Jewish periodical that the Nazi regime had not
yet banned. Straus's review was extremely negative, taking Grau to task
for factual errors and tendentious interpretation in the book's treatment
of Jewish religion and society. After enumerating a long sequence of such
problems in Grau's work, Straus observed "how difficult it must be for a
non-Jew to find his way around in Jewish history." Grau was allowed to
publish a response to Straus's review in the same (Jewish) journal. In his
response, Grau insisted that the history of the "Jewish question" should
not be the preserve of Jewish scholars, and that Straus and other Jews
should be confident that "Aryan" scholars like himself would approach
the subject with "German scientific rigor and German thoroughness"
("deutsche Wissenschaftlichkeit und deutsche Gründlichkeit").[22] Four
years later, in 1939, Grau published a second edition of his book about
Regensburg; the acknowledgment of Straus's support was gone.

Grau's writings often emphasized the contrast between the healthy
racial instincts of the antisemitic common folk on the one hand and
the racially treacherous, pro-Jewish, Enlightenment liberalism of the political elite on the other. While his book on Regensburg purported to
illustrate how the common folk could prevail, he intended a second
book, on the German humanist Wilhelm von Humboldt, to show how
even admirable figures from the German past could be implicated in the
emancipation of the Jews and all of its negative consequences. Grau published *Wilhelm von Humboldt and the Problem of the Jew* in 1935, the year
in which Germans observed the one-hundredth anniversary of Humboldt's death.[23] Grau resented the way the commemoration of Hum-

boldt's life had been "uncritical and unhistorical," as though "liberalism itself were celebrating its resurrection." Grau did not mean to demonize Humboldt but rather, he wrote in his preface, simply to recognize one of Humboldt's major failures. Because of his activism on behalf of Jews, Grau contended, Humboldt should not be regarded as "unambiguously great."[24]

Grau's central question was why Humboldt had labored so vociferously in support of Jewish emancipation, first within Prussia, in a memorandum drafted in 1809, and later more universally in Europe, at the Congress of Vienna, where Humboldt accompanied the Prussian delegation. Existing biographical studies of Humboldt, Grau alleged, had neglected to address this question adequately—further evidence, in his opinion, that "liberal scholarship" had "closed its eyes to the problem of the Jews."[25] Grau ascribed Humboldt's actions to personal experiences. Very early in his life, Humboldt had had a "disposition for things Jewish" instilled in him by his teachers, who themselves had been drawn from a "circle of friends" around Mendelssohn.[26] As a teenager Humboldt was then seduced by the charms of Henriette Herz, an intellectually accomplished and personally compelling woman in whose Berlin salon Jews had come into contact with reform-minded members of the Prussian elite. Grau paid a good deal of attention to the poisonous influence of Herz and other Jewish women. Humboldt's relationship with Herz endured over many years and passed through several phases, one of which was "passionate love."[27] There were other Jewish women in Humboldt's life as well, among them Dorothea Veit-Mendelssohn and Rachel Levin. These personal relationships with Jews exposed Humboldt to "optimistic rationalism," "intellectual Epicureanism," and other tendencies that contributed to a "weakening of the racial instinct."[28] As described by Grau, Humboldt came off seeming less an autonomous human being than a marionette whom the Jews, exploiting the sexuality of their women, had brainwashed from early on.

The Humboldt study was Grau's last major publication. In the mid- to late 1930s, he concentrated his energies on administrative duties in Frank's Institute, on short articles and reviews, and on editorial responsibilities for the *Historische Zeitschrift*. Although the central themes of Grau's writing underwent no significant evolution, the virulence of his rhetoric grew over time. The radicalization of Grau's antisemitism had a personal dimension, as it was one of his ways of asserting himself against

Walter Frank, as well as of appealing to the sensibilities of Alfred Rosenberg, his new boss as of 1941.[29] But the increasingly aggressive tone of Grau's writings and lectures was also consistent with the general intensification of the Nazi regime's rhetoric and actions toward the Jews. This was reflected in a lecture delivered by Grau at the ceremonial opening of the Institute for Research on the Jewish Question, to the directorship of which he had been appointed by Rosenberg. The March 1941 conference took place at a time when German officials were struggling to decide the long-term fate of the Jews under their control. Grau's contribution was entitled "Historical Attempts at Solutions to the Jewish Question." He reviewed the succession of strategies pursued in Europe over the centuries: ghettoization, emancipation, assimilation, emigration to America, and Zionism. All of these options had led—or, he predicted with regard to America, would soon lead—to failure or disaster. Without specifying exactly what scenario he had in mind, Grau concluded that the only solution was for the Jews to disappear. "Europe," he asserted, is "richer in its historical understanding of the Jewish question" than it had been in the past, "more experienced with the destructive activity of the Jews," and "more determined than ever once and for all in this century to achieve a definitive solution of this problem on European territory." Without question, Grau concluded, the end of the twentieth century would "no longer see Israel, because it will have disappeared from Europe." When Grau spoke these words in March 1941, mass killings of Jews in Nazi-occupied Europe had not yet begun. In 1943, however, when Rosenberg's Institute published the speech as a brochure intended for mass distribution, millions of Jews from across Europe had already been killed.[30] Grau's scholarship helped achieve a lethal legacy.

Klaus Schickert was a third student of Karl Alexander von Müller whose scholarship examined Jewish assimilation in a racialist framework. Schickert's dissertation, published as a book in 1937, was entitled *The Jewish Question in Hungary*.[31] The book was the first entry in a series published by the Reich Ministry of Propaganda, "The Jews among the Peoples: Studies on the Jewish Question in the Contemporary World," the purpose of which was to promote research on "the origins and growth of critical opposition against alien Jewish elements among all peoples," as well as on the "attempt of Jewry to eliminate its millennia-old conflict with its host peoples." This would be accomplished through the publication of "precise scholarship."[32]

Ironically enough, Schickert acknowledged receiving help from Jewish colleagues in Bratislava and Budapest, whose assistance was given despite "full knowledge of the existing racial antagonisms."[33] Schickert conceived his study as an attempt to revise the "highly developed Jewish historiography" that had emerged in Hungary, mainly through the efforts of the Israelite-Hungarian Literary Society. In Schickert's eyes, the "Judeocentric" historiography of the society had constructed an assimilationist narrative that corresponded to Jewish "propaganda goals." This Jewish perspective overstated the length of time Jews had been present in Hungary, and exaggerated the amity of Jewish-Magyar relations, said to have been disrupted ostensibly only as a result of external interference. The Jewish view posited the "age of assimilation" as the "logical culmination of a general development of humanity" and regarded Hungarian antisemitism as a disruption of this general "upward development." Schickert countered with an argument that saw Hungarian antisemitism as the "awakening of the defensive capacities of the country against the consequences of Jewish assimilation."[34]

The entire framework of Schickert's study was racial. The background section on Jewish history, for example, began with the "racial foundations" of Jewry. Schickert cited the work of Ignaz Einhorn, a Jewish scholar who in 1851 had published a book about Jewish participation in the revolution of 1848 in Hungary. Einhorn had pointed to "common Asiatic ancestry" and "linguistic similarities between Hungarian and Hebrew." Relying on the racial categories of Hans F. K. Günther, Schickert noted that Magyars, unlike Jews, consisted primarily of eastern Baltic, Dinaric, and Caucasian elements. Racial overlapping between Magyars and Jews was very minor, and to the extent that it did exist, might well have explained the Judeophilia of a small segment of the Magyar population.[35]

Schickert then chronicled the takeover of the Hungarian economy by Jews between 1867 and 1918. Schickert did not consider it important to engage the question, posed earlier in the century by Werner Sombart, of whether the Jews were the originators of capitalism or merely its effective exploiters, which he considered to be beside the point. Sombart's concept of the "commercialization of economic life" was less important for Schickert's purposes than the phenomenon of "Jewish parasitism."[36] As the Jews insinuated themselves into influential positions in the Hungarian economy, Schickert claimed, Hungarian society passively submitted. There was no resistance to growing Jewish power until the antisemitic wave of the 1880s. During that era, the Jews enjoyed the protection of the Magyar political elite, which, according to Schickert, was deluded by liberal ideas of progress and anxious to enjoy the financial advantages of cooperating with Jews. In Schickert's view, one key reason for the failure of Hungarian antisemitism was the absence of a powerful personality—a Hitler-like figure—who could galvanize and unite the many antisemitic groups.[37] Another was the high percentage of Jews in influential professions, which Schickert presumed was destructive for the Hungarian nation. Citing the familiar allegations of economic exploitation, erosion of morals, promotion of urbanization, and materialism, Schickert assumed that these unfortunate trends had been brought about by the Jews and the willingness of Magyar elites to indulge them.[38]

In 1942 Schickert succeeded Wilhelm Grau as director of Alfred Rosenberg's Institute for Research on the Jewish Question. A year later he published a second edition of his book, to which he added a new sixty-page chapter, "The Road to Solving the Jewish Question," which included a detailed chronicle of the unfolding anti-Jewish measures in Hungary since 1938.[39] Here Schickert's historical writing merged directly into his antisemitic politics. He was satisfied that the antisemitic movement in Hungary had finally begun to make important headway. But he regretted that the Jews still seemed to have their protectors in Hungary. Indeed, the reluctance of the Hungarian government to cooperate with the Germans on the matter of deporting Hungarian Jews had become a sore point in Nazi antisemitic circles, and Schickert's book reflected this disappointment. Schickert's chronicle ended in November 1942, at which time, Schickert claimed, the Jews of Hungary still "felt very secure, and dreamt of a reinstatement of their power."[40] Ultimately, in 1944, after Hungary attempted to withdraw from the war, Germany invaded Hungary and deported several hundred thousand Hungarian Jews, many of whom died in Auschwitz.

Challenging Jewish Historical Scholarship

Aside from their own publications, Wilhem Grau and Walter Frank, in succession, edited a special section on Jewish research for the *Historische Zeitschrift* (HZ), Germany's most venerable historical journal. In 1935, the distinguished historian and democrat Friedrich Meinecke was forced to resign the editorship of the *HZ*, giving way to Karl Alexander von

Müller, who was more sympathetic to the Nazi regime. In turn, Müller invited his ex-student Grau to contribute and edit reviews and historiographical essays for a section of the journal entitled "History of the Jewish Question." Frank took over editing the section in 1940;[41] he was then succeeded in 1942 by the Austrian scholar Ludwig Bittner. These essays became a regular fixture in the *HZ*, which otherwise published little in the way of overtly antisemitic scholarship during the Third Reich. The content of the *HZ* can thus be seen as an echo of the broader struggle within the German historical profession during the Nazi era. While ideologically motivated Nazis or fellow-travelers, such as von Müller and his students, endeavored to Nazify historical scholarship, historians of a more traditional bent avoided such pronounced politicization, notwithstanding their implicit endorsements of German nationalism or their personal feeling toward Nazism or Jews.[42]

In the very first issue of the *HZ* edited by von Müller, Grau supplied an introduction to the new section.[43] He underscored the previous suppression of honest scholarly assessment of the Jewish question. The very fact, he wrote, "that these pages might be perceived as unusual at first sight is indeed the most compelling reason for their existence."[44] Between 1936 and 1943, ten issues of the *HZ* contained significant sections devoted to the Jewish question. The sections totaled 170 pages. Although this added up to only a small percentage of the journal's space, it did mean that the subject was present and conspicuous. The section was set apart in the table of contents of each issue. The contributions consisted of bibliographies, bibliographical essays, book reviews, conference reports, reports on dissertations in progress, and library and archive reports. Many, but by no means all, of the pieces were contributed by people drawn from the antisemitic circle around von Müller, Frank, and Grau.

In addition to reviewing the growing body of antisemitic scholarship, the section offered a Nazi perspective on recent Jewish scholarship, a good deal of which had been published in Germany in the mid-1930s. In his inaugural contribution, Grau reviewed a new study by the Jewish Zionist author Abraham Heller, *The Situation of the Jews in Russia from the March Revolution to the Present,* a monograph published under the auspices of the Society for the Promotion of the Science of Judaism.[45] Although the book, Grau conceded, was anti-Bolshevik, Grau accused Heller of "obfuscat[ing] the diabolical interrelationship between Jewry and Bolshevism."[46] Grau ridiculed Heller's argument that Bolsheviks of

Jewish origin who had repudiated their Judaism should not be regarded as Jews. Religious affiliation and social networks were irrelevant, Grau wrote, because "Jewish ancestry manifests itself beyond the laws of the Jewish religion."[47] Moreover, according to Grau, it was a mistake to assume, as many did, that Bolshevism was hostile to Judaism. He pointed out that the Soviet government had recognized Yiddish as a language.[48] When discussing pogroms in which innocent Jewish civilians were slaughtered, Grau sarcastically characterized the tragedy as "deeply regrettable." This fate, he explained, was to be expected, as the Jews had been closely allied with the Bolsheviks. "A historian who wants to deal with the truth," Grau admonished Heller, "can not represent Jewish suffering one-sidedly." The Jews were responsible for "a much more violent and deeper stream of blood," that of the Russian people.[49]

Grau reviewed another book by a Jewish author in a similar vein. In 1935, the distinguished historian Ismar Elbogen published in Berlin, his *History of the Jews of Germany,* which he intended to be a celebration and defense of German Jewry at a moment of rising peril.[50] Grau condemned the unabashed "Jewish standpoint" of a book in which, according to Grau, all Jews were praised, all antisemites were condemned, and the sincere motives of the antisemites were not given serious consideration. Grau dismissed as simplistic and apologetic a view in which "the Jews are pure innocents, heroes and martyrs," while "the antisemites are everywhere the guilty ones, the criminals, the haters, the jealous ones, the reactionaries, and the idiots."[51]

Another work of Elbogen that was subjected to scathing criticism in the *HZ* was a volume of the *Germania Judaica,* an ambitious multivolume collection of documents intended to cover the span of Jewish history in Germany. Elbogen was among the three editors of the collection, which was sponsored by the Society for the Promotion of the Science of Judaism. In 1934 the volume covering the period until 1238 was published.[52] Grau assigned the *HZ* review to Eugen Wohlhaupter, who taught on the law faculty of the University of Munich.[53] The review expressed grudging admiration for the work, but emphasized that the editors were mainly interested in "the fate of the Jews on German territory," while not the least bit interested in the Jewish question as a part of German history. The editors "could not and did not want to address the fate of Germans that was determined by the presence of Jews in German historical space."[54]

Competence, rather than perspective, lay at the heart of the *Historische Zeitschrift's* review of Salomon Wininger's *Jewish National Biography*.[55] By 1936, seven volumes of Wininger's ambitious reference work had appeared, encompassing the biographies of over 11,000 people. Grau assigned the review to Friedrich Wilhelm "Wilfried" Euler, who was the Third Reich's foremost expert on Jewish genealogy. Euler rejected the work as "unusable" for scholarly purposes. The main problem was that Wininger had omitted a great many persons who were Jewish by race if not by confession, while he had included as Jews many people who either were not Jewish or were only partially so. Euler appended a thirteen-page list of persons whom Wininger listed as Jews but who were really *Mischlinge* or non-Jews.

Euler, a member of the Nazi party since 1932, had been educated as a lawyer, but his strong interest in genealogy landed him a job with the Interior Ministry's "Reich Office for Genealogical Research" (*Reichsstelle für Sippenforschung*) soon after the Nazi seizure of power. He then moved to the Propaganda Ministry before finally landing at Grau's Research Department in Munich. Euler maintained massive files on Jewish genealogy, which served as the basis for several publications during the Nazi era.[56] In 1941, he published a lengthy article entitled "The Penetration of Jewish Blood into the English Upper Class."[57] Euler asked how modern Britain had come to be the "protecting power of Jewry" despite the relatively small size of the Jewish community there. Too much emphasis, he claimed, had been placed on Jewish economic and intellectual influence, and not enough on the penetration of the English aristocracy by Jewish blood. Well before the emancipation of the British Jews had taken place in the nineteenth century, Euler argued, baptized members of commercially and financially successful Jewish families had married into the English nobility. Virtually all of his 148-page article consisted of a catalog of Jewish conversions and subsequent marriages with non-Jews, starting in the fourteenth century. The evidence proved, Euler argued, that the English aristocracy had literally in its "blood substance" sealed a "marriage with Jewry."[58]

Euler's antisemitic publications of the Nazi era did not prevent him from translating his expertise into a post-1945 success. He founded and served for decades as director of the Institute for Historical Research on Leadership Classes in Bensheim, the foundation of which was his own extensive collection of genealogical materials. The Bensheim institute became an important resource for serious scholarship on the German social and business elite.[59] In 1990, Euler received the Distinguished Service Cross from the government of the Federal Republic of Germany in recognition of his contributions to the field of genealogy.[60] As with so many other scholars who had collaborated with the Nazi regime, Euler's contributions to antisemitic scholarship were swept under the rug.

Although Nazis and other European antisemites were keenly interested in Zionism, which they often greeted as an opportunity for the Jews to depart for Palestine, the subject received relatively little scholarly attention. One exception was the *Historische Zeitschrift*'s review essay about Adolf Böhm's book *The Zionist Movement until the World War*. The review was contributed by Rudolf Craemer, a member of the history faculty at the University of Königsberg and a former student of Hans Rothfels, the prominent nationalist historian who had lost his position at Königsberg and then gone into exile on account of his Jewish ancestry.[61] Craemer's most substantive contribution to Nazi historiography on the Jewish question was a 1941 article about Benjamin Disraeli in the *Forschungen zur Judenfrage*, which repeated the well-worn antisemitic belief that the baptized Disraeli had never really stopped acting like a Jew.[62] In his review of Böhm in the *Historische Zeitschrift*,[63] Craemer applauded Böhm's readiness to admit openly that his book was intended not as an objective work of scholarship but as a means for promoting Zionism among young Jews. Böhm's stated intention was to discuss the positive and constructive aspects of Zionism. Craemer purported to respect this sincerity, pointing out that it was "better to talk with national-Jewish Zionism than with the hidden racial interests of assimilationism." Craemer approved of Böhm's argument that Zionism had originated not simply as a response to antisemitism but also as a Jewish national awakening in response to the nationalisms of the late nineteenth century. Craemer saw this as a positive development, for only by pursuing their own independent existence as a people would the Jews cease being parasites among other peoples.[64] On the other hand, Craemer asserted, the manner in which the Zionist movement had gone about pursuing its goals demonstrated how the Zionists employ the same secretive, dishonest methods as assimilationist Jews, citing as examples the Balfour declaration and the seizure of Arab land in Palestine. In the end, although Craemer was encouraged by the rise of a Zionist mentality among Jews, which would promote the departure of Jews from Germany, he still represented Zionism within a broader antisemitic framework.

While the special review section on the Jewish question guaranteed consistent overt antisemitic content in the *Historische Zeitschrift,* only once did the journal publish a major research article on this theme. Published in 1937, the article addressed "The Breakthrough of the Jewish Spirit in German Constitutional and Church Law," focusing on the role of the prominent legal theorist Friedrich Julius Stahl.[65] The author, Johannes Heckel, was a professor at the University of Munich and one of Germany's foremost experts on church law.[66] Heckel's piece was, therefore, the only antisemitic contribution to the Nazi-era *Historische Zeitschrift* to have been written by a senior, well-established scholar with a university professorship. Heckel based his article on a lecture delivered at Walter Frank's Institute for History of the New Germany.

Heckel presented his subject, Friedrich Julius Stahl, as the personification of how German culture and society had become Judaized in the nineteenth century. Stahl, who lived from 1802 to 1861, had been born as Julius Golson, the son of an Orthodox Jewish merchant. He converted to Lutheranism in order to pursue a career in law. Unlike most baptized Jews, Stahl was a conservative who opposed the 1848 revolution and who circulated chiefly among Prussian conservatives, who were not known for their Judeophilia. Eventually Stahl distinguished himself as a leading conservative theorist in matters of citizenship and religion. For Heckel the central question was the extent to which Stahl's Jewishness persisted beyond his conversion, and the extent to which it infused his legal theory and teaching.

Heckel reiterated the basic Nazi racist assumption that religious conversion could not de-Judaize a Jew. To be sure, Heckel conceded, Stahl had opposed emancipation of Jews who had not converted. But in doing so Stahl had propagated the doctrine that there were two kinds of Jews, those who had converted and those who had not. Converts, in Stahl's opinion, should be considered German and be granted full rights. While this might have seemed like an anti-Jewish position in the nineteenth century, in retrospect, Heckel argued, it helped reinforce a religious, as opposed to racial, definition of Jewishness, and thus helped pave the way for the assimilation into German society of persons of the Jewish race.[67] Moreover, Heckel pointed out, Stahl had helped to promote a legal theory that placed an emphasis on a mechanistic obeisance to the law, giving little heed to the question of sincerity. This, too, according to Heckel, reflected an essentially Jewish way of looking at the law.[68] Thus did Stahl's life and career typify the dangers inherent to a misguided religious and cultural antisemitism.

Preparing the Future Generation

How successful were those activists who tried to place the Jewish question on the agenda of serious historical scholarship? Measured quantitatively, the genre remained relatively small within the German historical profession. On the other hand, evidence that the genre was growing and becoming ever more institutionalized can be found in doctoral dissertations submitted in the late 1930s and early 1940s. These included Josef Müller's study "The Development of Racial Antisemitism in the Closing Decades of the Nineteenth Century," submitted at the University of Marburg;[69] Irmgard Müller's "Investigation of the Penetration and the Influence of Jewish Journalists in the Munich Press, 1825–1835," completed in Munich;[70] Margarete Dierks's study "The Prussian Old Conservatives and the Jewish Question, 1810–1847," submitted in Rostock;[71] Hans Pieper's analysis "Jews in Münster during the Nineteenth Century (with Special Attention to Freemason Influence)," submitted in Münster;[72] and Eckhard Günther's study "Jewry in Franconia," submitted at Würzburg.[73]

While most of the dissertations dealt with the history of the Jewish question inside Germany, a few were more outward looking. Hans Schuster's survey "The Jewish Question in Rumania," submitted at the University of Leipzig, addressed a set of questions similar to those posed by Klaus Schickert for Hungary, but for a country in which the Jews had enjoyed less success in penetrating the political, economic, and cultural elite.[74] Waltraute Sixta focused her University of Vienna dissertation on the career of Josef Unger, a prominent Jewish jurist in Austria.[75] These dissertations constitute but a sample of the output of young historians who were being trained at universities all over Germany. As Karl Alexander von Müller observed at the opening of the Research Department for the Jewish Question in 1936, "The fruits of scholarship need time to grow."[76] A new body of antisemitic *Wissenschaft* would require time to emerge. In the event, the period between the Nazi seizure of power in 1933 and the mobilization of German society for war in the early 1940s left room for the development of only one academic generation. The ensuing collapse of the Third Reich forced a radical change of plan among young scholars who had trained for and anticipated careers as experts on the Jewish question. What is important to keep in mind is that historians in the Third Reich did indeed intend to make antisemitic Jewish studies a permanent feature of their discipline.

Josef Sommerfeldt was one of the young historians whom Müller had in mind. While pursuing his doctorate in German history at the university of Berlin, Sommerfeldt held a staff position as a "specialist for Jewish research" at the Institute for German Work in the East in Crakow.[77] There he edited and published a document, originally published in 1618 by the Polish astronomer Sebastian Miczyński, that described, in Miczyński's words, "the heavy insults and great illnesses caused to Poles by Jews."[78] Sommerfeldt's edition of this work contained translated excerpts from the original, supplemented by his own running commentary. Most of the grievances cataloged by Miczyński concerned Jewish economic exploitation of Poles. Sommerfeldt claimed that Jewish historians, most notably Ignaz Schippers, had themselves used Miczyński as a source. This underscored, in Sommerfeldt's estimation, the reliability of Miczyński.[79] Sommerfeldt wrote explicitly about the contemporary relevance of Miczyński's work: "What is precisely so true today as it was three hundred years ago is the fact that the Jew undermines the economic foundations of the peoples that harbor him, and ruins all sectors of society through selfish exploitation."[80] Sommerfeldt concluded his publication with an ominous observation. "The Jews," he wrote, "will be given the opportunity, in a territory designated for them, to demonstrate whether their racial characteristics suffice for the creation from their own energies of a sensible and healthy social and economic order." So far, "the Jewish people have not provided this evidence."[81] The book went to press in December 1940, at which time the Jews of Poland lived mainly in ghettos and performed forced labor under German supervision. Sommerfeldt did not spell out what fate should befall the Jews if this experiment were to fail.

Ultimatley Sommerfeldt completed his doctorate in June 1942 at the University of Berlin, with a dissertation entitled "The Jewish Question as Administrative Problem in South Prussia."[82] Based on Prussian archives, his study encompassed the period from the beginning of the reign of Frederick II of Prussia in 1740 to the reforms of the Napoleonic era, examining civil marriage, the dissolution of Jewish communal self-administration, education reform, economic regulation, and the end of the ghettos for Jews. According to Sommerfeldt, Prussian administrators of the period had recognized the existence of a Jewish problem, but did not understand its racial basis. Thus they pursued ill-conceived policies, acting on the "presumption that the cultural and social betterment of the Jews would be the prerequisite for their later political emancipation."[83] The Prussian state, anxious to exploit Jewish commercial acumen, tolerated Jewish dominance of certain commercial and financial activities, while trying to curb the inevitable side effects, such as usury. The common folk, motivated by a healthy racial instinct, opposed the breaking down of the ghetto walls, but the reformers, animated by an ill-advised Enlightenment liberalism, overcame popular resistance. The reformers were less successful in promoting Jewish entry into the artisanal trades, which was successfully opposed by the Christian guilds. Reformist attempts to encourage Jews to take up farming failed because of the Jewish aversion to physical labor. Sommerfeldt admitted that some nonracial factors were at work in the struggle over emancipation. The entrenched economic interests of the guilds and the nobility constituted obstacles to the reformers. But Sommerfeldt ascribed the greatest importance to the racial motivation mounted by ordinary people. In conclusion he noted: "Now that we are no longer working to integrate the Jews into the community of Europe, but rather striving for their removal from the territory of Europe, every attempted solution from around the year 1800 seems wrong and pointless."[84] Few examples so vividly illustrate how historical scholarship could be used to legitimize Nazi anti-Jewish policy. When Sommerfeldt submitted his dissertation in June 1942, the "Final Solution" was well under way.

Johannes Pohl and the Plunder of Jewish Libraries

If the training of young scholars like Josef Sommerfeldt reflected the Third Reich's intention to perpetuate and institutionalize antisemitic historical scholarship, a similar motive underlay efforts to develop research collections that were deemed essential to this field. Nazi scholars endeavored to inventory and publicize relevant library collections and to compile bibliographies that would be useful to historians. They were also prepared to collect research materials through the systematic plunder of Jewish libraries throughout German-occupied Europe.

Even without the theft of books from Jewish collections, public and university libraries in Germany offered a rich body of historical source materials. The extent of these materials was reflected in the formidable *Bibliography on the History of the Jewish Question,* published by Volkmar Eichstädt in 1938.[85] As a librarian at the Prussian State Library in Berlin, Eichstädt had taken on the task of compiling a comprehensive systematic bibliography that would serve as an essential research tool for future historical scholarship on the Jewish question. But Eichstädt was hardly an ideologically neutral librarian. During the Nazi period he published bibliographical essays on the Jewish question in the *Annual Reports on German History.*[86] His harsh assessments of scholarship recently published by Jews drew largely from the views of Wilhelm Grau, Wilfried Euler, and other antisemitic historians. Eichstädt celebrated the German challenge to the Jewish monopoly on the writing of Jewish history, but emphasized that this had only just begun. Moreover, he emphasized that "the history of antisemitism has not been written,"[87] a lacuna he hoped his bibliography would help to fill.

Eichstädt's 1938 bibliography on the history of the Jewish question covered the years 1750 to 1848 and was the first volume of a projected three-volume work, although no further volumes ever appeared. The aim of the bibliography was to encompass "published statements on the Jewish question in the German-speaking lands from the Enlightenment to the present." The publication of the work was sponsored by Walter Frank's Reich Institute for History of the New Germany. It included citations to books, pamphlets, and article from theological, political, and legal sources. The volume for 1750 to 1848 contained an impressive 3,016 entries, cited primarily from the collections of Eichstädt's own Berlin State Library. Eichstädt arranged the listings chronologically, using a star to denote works of definite Jewish authorship and a question mark to indicate those of possible Jewish authorship. To assist scholars in tracking down desirable items, Eichstädt crossreferenced the entries to the collections of forty-three major German and Austrian libraries. Notwithstanding the circumstances of its creation and the ideological perspective of its compiler, the bibliography was the result of rigorous and meticulous preparation. In fact, the volume proved so useful that it was reprinted in 1969.[88]

In 1939, Eichstädt delivered a lecture in Graz at the annual meeting of German librarians, which he later published in the *Forschungen zur Judenfrage,* entitled "Writings on the Jewish Question in German Libraries."[89]

Eichstädt sought to explain how German libraries would be able to support the future expansion of historical research on the Jewish question. "Priceless materials found nowhere else" but in German libraries would enable historians to investigate the crucial questions: "How did the German people think about the Jews through the ages? How did they perceive Jews in their outward appearance as well as in their inner essence? How did they laugh at and tease Jews? How did they tolerate Jews, suffer under them, fight them?"

Eichstädt estimated that the literature on the Jewish question in German libraries extended to over 10,000 titles.[90] This included antisemitic pamphlets that survived in very small numbers. Few historians, however, were aware of this massive resource, for knowledge of its existence had been suppressed by the dominance of a liberal/Jewish perspective in scholarship. Eichstädt pointed specifically to the collections of the Prussian State Library in Berlin, the German National Library (Deutsche Bücherei) in Leipzig, and the city library of Frankfurt. He looked forward to the end of the war, when collections in regions recently conquered by Germany could be assessed for their value for historical research on the Jewish question, the most important of which were located in Strasbourg, Prague, Warsaw, and Cracow.[91] As a worthwhile long-term goal for German librarianship, Eichstädt recommended a massive program of genealogical research in order to establish the Jewish or part-Jewish authorship of all books published in the German language. This information, he hoped, would one day be listed on every library catalog card.[92]

The collection in Frankfurt was an especially notable one. The city library had housed a fine collection of Hebraica and Judaica since the nineteenth century. The Jewish librarian Aron Freiman had been in charge of it from 1897 until 1933, when he was fired as a result of the Nazi civil service law, which purged Jews from government employment. Freiman was not replaced, and the collection lay dormant until 1939, when the city of Frankfurt arranged to transfer the collection to the Nazi party university under the aegis of Alfred Rosenberg, who was already planning to create a Jewish research institute. When the Institute for Research on the Jewish Question opened in 1941, the Frankfurt collection served as its library. At this time the collection included about three hundred thousand volumes, including items that had been transferred from the private collections of Jews who had emigrated or been deported

Rosenberg library

growth by theft

from Germany. Although Rosenberg and his staff (which now included Wilhelm Grau) regarded this as a satisfactory starting point, they harbored grandiose ambitions for the future of the library. The collection was to be developed into the largest and most important depository in the world for Jewish research, and this would be accomplished primarily by means of theft.[93]

Beginning in early 1940, Hitler issued several orders that authorized Alfred Rosenberg to organize systematic programs of cultural plunder across Nazi-occupied Europe.[94] The acquisition of materials for a research collection on the Jewish question was just a part of a much broader venture in premeditated, organized looting of books, archives, and works of art. The theft was carried out by teams of German scholars working under the institutional umbrella of the Rosenberg Staff for Special Tasks (Einsatzstab Reichsleiter Rosenberg). Between 1940 and 1944, materials stolen from private and communal Jewish collections flowed into Frankfurt from, among other locations, Paris, Amsterdam, Riga, Vilnius, Minsk, Kiev, Salonika, Belgrade, and the Crimea.

Johannes Pohl was the German scholar who was most instrumental in the plundering of the Jewish communities.[95] A native of Cologne, Pohl took his degree in Catholic theology from the University of Bonn in 1926, and then entered the priesthood. While serving as a young vicar in the Ruhr district, he completed his doctorate at Bonn in Old Testament studies with a dissertation on messianism and the prophet Ezekiel. In 1929 the church arranged for the promising scholar to spend two and a half years studying languages at the Papal Bible Institute in Rome. Then in October 1932, Pohl received a fellowship to study biblical archaeology in Jerusalem, where he lived until May 1934. While in Jerusalem, Pohl completed a second doctorate under the auspices of the Papal Bible Institute; his dissertation dealt with family and society in ancient Israel as described in the books of the Prophets. After his return to Germany in 1934, Pohl left the priesthood in order to marry. Now in need of a job, he was fortunate to receive an appointment as curator for Hebraica and Judaica in the Oriental Collection at the Prussian State Library in Berlin. The position had been made possible by the recent dismissal of the Jewish librarian who had overseen the collection since 1921, Arthur Spanier.

While working in Berlin, Pohl published numerous antisemitic articles in lowbrow and middlebrow newspapers and magazines. Neither in his brief career as a priest nor in his earlier academic writings, including his two dissertations, had Pohl displayed any particular hostility toward Jews. We can surmise that his vicious Nazi-era antisemitism reflected either an opportunistic adjustment to his professional circumstances in Germany or the manifestation of a personal antisemitism that he had kept to himself well into his thirties. Whatever the motivation, his journalistic articles on the dangers of the Talmud and other ostensibly sinister aspects of Judaism multiplied in the late 1930s. In April 1941, Pohl moved to Frankfurt to become head of the Hebraica collection at Rosenberg's Institute. Within a couple of months he was off to Salonika on his first plundering expedition. More such trips followed, most notably to Vilnius in 1942, Belgrade in 1943, and Minsk in 1944.

Pohl presents a compelling figure among the German scholars who were active in Jewish research during the Nazi period. Through his academic preparation and travel experiences, Pohl had acquired unusual familiarity with the Jewish religion, the Jewish community in Palestine, and Jewish languages, including modern Hebrew. Yet during the 1930s, he failed to establish himself as an academic Jew expert. This was not for lack of trying. While working in the Prussian State Library he authored publications about Jews, which often appeared in places like *Der Stürmer* and the *National Socialist Party Correspondence*. These were mainly journalistic pieces that possessed an overtly propagandistic quality, hardly ever rising to the more intellectually ambitious level of, say, the work of Wilhelm Grau. At the same time, he applied for academic research grants several times, never succeeding, and he was refused permission to pursue the *Habilitation,* the German qualification required for appointment to a professorship. It has been suggested that Pohl, despite his educational résumé, simply possessed a mediocre intellect.[96] Equally plausible is that his activity as a propagandist warped his intellectual sensibility to the point where not even antisemitic scholars could take him seriously. Whatever the explanation, Pohl followed a low road to notoriety as a Jew expert in the Third Reich. His academic legacy is that of a dilettante and a thief.

The magnitude of the cultural larceny and spoliation perpetrated by Pohl and his colleagues was neatly summarized in a progress report drafted by Pohl for his superiors in July 1943.[97] Much of the plundered material had come from France. Some 40,000 volumes had been taken from the library of the *Alliance Israélite Universelle* in Paris, in addition to a newspaper clipping collection about the Dreyfus Affair and some valuable incunabula. A further 10,000 volumes, including much "worthwhile Talmud material," had been seized from the Parisian *École Rabbinique.* Other confiscations in Paris included 4,000 volumes, many in Russian, from the library of the *Fédération de Société des Juifs,* 20,000 volumes from the Jewish book dealer Lipschütz, and 28,000 volumes from the private collections of various members of the Rothschild family. The loot from the Rothschilds also encompassed 760 boxes of archival materials relating to the history of the Paris branch of the family bank. According to Pohl's report, 45,000 volumes had been obtained in Amsterdam, 25,000 of which had originated with the Sephardic community and would therefore prove especially useful. Similarly, 10,000 volumes had been acquired from Sephardic Jewish communities in Greece. Pohl included Germany in his survey as well, noting that one hundred thousand volumes had been turned over to the Frankfurt library by various German government offices. Pohl did not mention that these books had been taken from Jews upon their forced deportation from Germany.

The most fruitful looting, however, had taken place in eastern Europe. Pohl put his estimate of the number of volumes seized in Riga, Vilna (Vilnius), Minsk, Kiev, and other locations at 280,000. Many of the seized books, journals, newspapers, and other texts had not yet arrived in Frankfurt, Pohl noted, but lay packed away in boxes still awaiting shipment from several collection points. The total number of books received or expected in Frankfurt, according to Pohl, was 550,000. This figure, it should be emphasized, did not include additional materials seized by Pohl and his colleagues in the remaining months of 1943 and into 1944. Neither did it include archival collections that fell into the hands of the Rosenberg Special Task Staff, such as the Jewish collection from the central archive in Kiev, which encompassed five thousand files documenting Jewish affairs in Kiev from 1830 to 1936.[98] From his perspective as a librarian, Pohl was obviously pleased by the sheer size of his trophy. In the conclusion to his report, he boasted about its future academic significance, emphasizing the comprehensiveness of a collection that could be matched "neither in Europe nor anywhere else." After the collapse of the Third Reich, Allied prosecutors at the main Nuremberg trial used Pohl's report as evidence in their case against Alfred Rosenberg.

Pohl's report referred not to stolen or even confiscated goods but rather to materials that had simply been "secured" and then "transported" or "shipped" to Frankfurt from the occupied territories. Neither

[handwritten margin notes: destroyed books / destroyed a lot / They did not steal]

did Pohl note that he and his colleagues had destroyed a large portion of the Jewish collections that they had chosen not to confiscate. Fortunately, a record of how the plundering actually played itself out on the ground has been preserved in the diaries of two Jewish scholars in Vilna, a major center of Jewish learning where two of the most significant Jewish libraries were found. The most famous was YIVO (the Jewish Scientific Institute), one of the world's foremost institutions of Jewish research and scholarship, whose library contained an unparalleled collection of materials about East European Jewry.[99] Vilna was also home to the Strashun Library, a formidable scholarly collection of about 40,000 volumes. Herman Kruk, a librarian originally from Warsaw, had sought refuge in Vilna in late 1939, and in 1941 had organized a lending library for the population of the Vilna ghetto. Although he perished in 1944, Kruk left behind a detailed diary chronicling daily life in the ghetto.[100] Quite a few of the entries for the year 1942 describe the actions of Johannes Pohl and other German scholars who had come to plunder the libraries of Vilna. A second Jewish scholar who wrote down an account of these events was Zelig Kalmanovitch, one of the guiding lights of YIVO. Like Kruk, Kalmanovitch did not survive the war, but his experiences were preserved in his ghetto diary.[101] Tragically, before their deaths, both Kruk and Kalmanovitch had been forced by Pohl to assist in the plundering of the Vilna Jewish library collections.

The first team of German scholars arrived in Vilna at the beginning of February 1942. We do not know of whom this team consisted, but it did not include Pohl. The Germans went directly to the offices of the Jewish Council, demanding the names of the responsible individuals at the local Jewish libraries. They appointed Kruk as the official contact person on the Jewish side. Kruk then formed a so-called Paper Brigade of scholars, librarians, and other workers to help the Germans sort through the collections. At first there was the hope that cooperation with the Germans might help save the collections. The German team, after all, consisted of scholars, with whom, Kruk initially thought, some decent working arrangement might be possible. But the illusion of cooperation was shattered when Kruk learned that parts of the YIVO collection had disappeared.

Around the same time, in April 1942, Johannes Pohl arrived in Vilna. In his diary, Kruk referred to Pohl as "the Hebrew," a "soldier in Party uniform," who impressed Kruk as "polite and talkative" but also secretive about his position in Frankfurt and mission in Vilna. By late spring of 1942, the intentions of Pohl and the other Germans had become abundantly clear to Kruk and Kalmanovitch. Items in the Jewish libraries that were deemed useful for research or financially valuable by the Germans were to be transported out of Vilna, while the remainder would be turned into pulp. With no real alternative available, the Paper Brigade assisted in the process, at the very least buying extra time both for its members, who might otherwise have been assigned to far more dangerous kinds of labor, and for the books themselves. The work was agonizingly painful for the Jews, who well understood how their knowledge and expertise were being exploited to facilitate the looting.[102]

In addition to guiding the German looters through the contents and organization of the Vilna library collections, Jewish scholars were pressed into conducting research and translations. Although Pohl and other Germans trained in theology could read Hebrew, Yiddish—the primary everyday language of east European Jewry—was another matter entirely. When, for example, the Nazi scholars ran across a Yiddish-language book on the Jewish community of South Africa, they required a member of the YIVO staff to translate it for them.[103] An article published months later by Johannes Pohl entitled "The Yiddish Press in South Africa" plagiarized large sections of the translation.[104] For his part, Kalmanovitch was ordered to translate intercepted Yiddish correspondence, compile historical statistics about the Jewish community of Vilna, and prepare material about the treatment of Orthodox Jewry during the Soviet occupation of the region between 1939 and 1941.[105] He was also compelled to compile a bibliography on the Karaites in order to assist the Germans in deciding how to classify that group racially.[106]

For Zelig Kalmanovitch and his Jewish colleagues in Vilna, the destruction of books that the Germans did not want to take seemed to hurt as much as the theft itself. According to Kalmanovitch, during the summer of 1942 trucks arrived at YIVO three times a week to haul away mountains of books to the pulp factory. Members of the Paper Brigade risked their lives, he wrote, rescuing some of the volumes for storage in a secret *Geniza*, or depository.[107] But Kalmanovitch and his colleagues could neither save themselves nor prevent the thorough looting of YIVO. The Rosenberg team transferred about 20,000 books from YIVO to the Institute in Frankfurt. Most were lost when the Frankfurt Institute was destroyed in an Allied bombing raid in March 1944.[108] But at least not everything from YIVO had perished. In addition to what the Paper Brigade had secreted away, tons of books were discovered intact in Lithuanian paper mills after the Nazi retreat. In Frankfurt, the United States army recovered thousands of books that had been transported from Vilna. These volumes now form the Vilna Collection of the YIVO Institute in New York.[109] Herman Kruk, Zelig Kalmanovitch, and most of the other members of the Paper Brigade were murdered in Vilna or in nearby labor camps. Johannes Pohl, for his part, was never tried, and after the war he was able to take up activity as a Catholic journalist and an editor of the *Duden Rechtschreibung,* a widely used guide for writing in German.

The Nazi zeal for collecting books probably had as much to do with megalomaniacal acquisitiveness and institutional empire-building as with genuine intellectual curiosity about the Jews. For Johannes Pohl and Alfred Rosenberg, amassing the largest Judaica library in Europe was a means for securing bragging rights vis-à-vis competing Nazi antisemitic institutes, such as the Reich Institute for History of the New Germany. Rosenberg's Institute was not the only systematic plunderer of Jewish libraries. Massive looting was also carried on by the RSHA (Reich Security Main Office), the umbrella agency under which both the Gestapo and the Security Service (SD) were housed. Between 1939 and 1943, the RSHA seized hundreds of thousands of books from the collections of numerous Jewish organizations and educational institutions as these were closed down. Among these were the libraries of the Academy for the Science of Judaism, the Jewish-Theological Seminar of Breslau, the Central Association of Jews in Germany, and the Jewish communities of Berlin, Breslau, Hamburg, Königsberg, Munich, Warsaw, and Vienna.[110] The RSHA did not profess grandiose aspirations to scholarship but intended to use the books to gather practical information about Jewish communities throughout Europe and the world. Jewish scholars were coerced to organize and evaluate the looted collections. The vast majority of the books were destroyed in an Allied air raid on Berlin in November 1943.[111]

The Painful Legacy of Nazi Historical Scholarship

Beginning in the late 1990s, a wave of scholarship produced by young historians in Germany documented the depressing story of how members of their own academic discipline had collaborated with the Nazi regime. This collaboration took a variety of forms. Most often it involved the publication of historical writing that sought to legitimize aspects of Nazi ideology or policy. But sometimes it extended to direct participation in the formulation or implementation of official policy by scholars who served as expert consultants to the government or who worked directly for agencies of the Nazi government or party. Several of these historians, who were in their thirties during the Nazi era, were able to continue their academic careers in West Germany after 1945, in some cases occupying influential professorial chairs, from which they trained an entire generation of young historians who themselves went out to populate West German history departments. Why they were able to do so, why their Nazi-era activities were not denounced by their colleagues and students in West Germany, and whether their postwar scholarship bore some kind of Nazi imprint all became matters of heated controversy in the historical profession in Germany starting in 1998.[112]

Neither of the two figures at the center of the controversy—Werner Conze and Theodor Schieder—had been active in Jewish research during the Nazi era. They had, however, been connected with the closely related field of "eastern research" (*Ostforschung*), which encompassed the study of east-central and eastern Europe as well as Germany's historical relationship to those regions.[113] Scholars and institutions active in this field had supported the Nazi regime's expansionistic, colonial agenda in the east. They produced scholarship that was designed to validate German historical, cultural, and racial claims to the lands to the east and, perhaps more disturbingly, recommended drastic demographic measures to be carried out against both Poles and Jews. Between 1937 and 1940, Conze published several articles in which he pointed to "dejewification" as one possible option for addressing problems arising form the Jewish economic role in White Russia, Lithuania, and other parts of eastern Europe. The removal of the Jews, by means left unspecified by Conze, would be welcomed by the local peasantry, and would facilitate German hegemony in the region.[114] Schieder did not publish in this vein, but he drafted a memorandum in October 1939, recommending the "dejewification" of conquered territory as preparation for its colonization by German settlers.[115]

The later controversy over the careers of these scholars, it would be fair to say, had as much to do with the post-1945 successes of persons who had collaborated with Nazism as it did with their Nazi-era writings.

5

Pathologizing the Jew

Among the signal developments in Jewish scholarship during the first third of the twentieth century was the advent of Jewish sociology, an important dimension of which was the compilation and analysis of statistics.[1] Jewish scholars were attracted to such methodologies in their quest to understand the conditions of Jewish life and the nature of the relationship between Jews and non-Jews. Quantification featured prominently in studies of Jewish demography, economic behavior, family structure, and epidemiology. Scholars sought to establish with numerical precision where Jews lived, which occupations they practiced, how often they married Gentiles, how many children they produced, what kinds of crimes they committed, and what kinds of diseases they contracted. The scientific self-understanding attained through such studies, it was hoped, would lead to communal self-improvement. Data and conclusions were also marshaled by participants in the major internal Jewish debate between Zionists and integrationists. Could the Jews be successfully integrated into the societies in which they lived, or were they a distinctive people who required their own homeland? To what extent were the economic, demographic, and cultural patterns that distinguished them from their Gentile neighbors in Europe the result of essential Jewish characteristics, and to what extent were they distortions wrought by centuries of subaltern life in an inhospitable diaspora? It was difficult for Jewish scholars to be neutral when it came to such questions. One of the most comprehensive and impressive quantitative studies of Jewish society, *Sociology of the Jews*, was produced by Arthur Ruppin, a prominent Zionist who was eager to justify the necessity of a Jewish homeland. He

123

interpreted his statistical data as evidence of Jewish degeneration in the Diaspora.

Nazi social scientists also mobilized statistics in their research on the Jews. Employing data produced by official government census surveys, which the German government had collected in the process of implementing its system of racial classification and segregation, they invoked the persuasive power of statistics to mark the Jews as a pathological *Volk*, unfit for cohabitation with other peoples. They marshaled quantitative data to validate notions about the criminal nature of the Jews and the degenerative consequences of intermarriage between Aryans and Jews. In the process, they generated, compiled, and published statistical information that was useful to policy-makers on a practical level, showing, for example, where Jews lived, what occupations they held, and to what degree they were integrated into the local non-Jewish population through marriage. Nazi social scientists exploited the work of Jewish counterparts, like Ruppin, with whom they shared a belief in the explanatory power of statistics.

Counting the Jews: Friedrich Burgdörfer

Upon its accession to power in 1933, the Nazi regime was keen to collect data about the society it intended to revolutionize racially and demographically.[2] Nazi leaders possessed a very modern faith in the utility of demographic and economic statistics for addressing the problems facing Germany. Moreover, the envisaged racial reordering of German society would require a detailed survey of the population. The Weimar Republic had conducted a census in 1925 but had then postponed, for financial reasons, a subsequent survey scheduled for 1930. In April 1933, just ten weeks after Hitler's appointment as chancellor, the Nazi regime ordered that the census go forward. It was conducted on 16 June. Among the personal information gleaned from Germans was official religious affiliation. The census therefore identified and counted as Jews only persons who officially belonged to Jewish communities, or so-called *Glaubensjuden*. In this respect, the census did not reflect Nazi racial thinking, as it treated Jews as a religious community rather than as a group defined by ancestry. After the completion of the general census, the regime conducted a second, special survey of foreigners and Jews; again, a religious rather than racial definition was employed for the latter. The results of the Jewish census were published in 1936.[3]

Friedrich Burgdörfer was one of Germany's leading official statisticians. A protégé of Friedrich Zahn, one of the grand old men of the statistical sciences in Germany, Burgdörfer served during the Weimar Republic as director of the Department of Population and Cultural Statistics in the Reich Statistical Office, where he played an important role in designing both the 1925 and the 1933 census. He gravitated toward right-wing politics in the late 1920s, voicing his concern about "national death" (*Volkstod*) stemming from the low German birthrate, a demographic trend revealed by both census surveys. In a book published in 1932, *Volk without Youth* (*Volk ohne Jugend*), Burgdörfer attributed the low birthrate to what he called the "rationalization of sexual life," this being his negative characterization of birth control and abortion. During the Nazi regime, Burgdörfer served as a consultant to the Racial-Political Office of the Nazi party, among other agencies, and in 1939 was appointed to the presidency of the State Statistical Office of Bavaria. After World War II, Burgdörfer was forced out of this office on account of his Nazi-era activities and publications, although he continued to receive accolades from professional statisticians.[4]

In 1938, at the annual conference of the Jewish Research Department of the Reich Institute in Munich, Burgdörfer offered his analysis of the special Jewish census. Published later in the *Forschungen zur Judenfrage*, Burgdörfer's lecture was conceived as a "statistical contribution" to the understanding of "the biological, occupational, and social structure of Jewry in Germany."[5] Burgdörfer regretted that the census had encompassed Jews by religion rather than by race, explaining that the survey had been taken before the regime had had a chance to implement a system of official racial categories. Given the extent of Jewish intermarriage with "racial" Germans since the previous century, the number of *Mischlinge* was undoubtedly very significant, and thus the "Jewish question" quantitatively a good deal larger than would be suggested by simply counting the number of *Glaubensjuden*, as the 1933 survey had done. This deficiency, Burgdörfer claimed, would be rectified in the next census, scheduled for May 1939, in the planning of which he was instrumental. The 1939 census would be conducted according to a racial definition of Jewry, and would distinguish between full Jews, half-Jews, and quarter-Jews.[6]

But the 1933 Jewish special census, despite its problems, Burgdörfer maintained, shed important light on the Jews of Germany. In 1935,

Burgdörfer had been asked by Walter Gross, head of the Nazi party's Racial-Political Office, to calculate the total number of "racial" Jews and *Mischlinge,* based on available census data and other statistics. Burgdörfer took as his point of departure the roughly five hundred thousand *Glaubensjuden* counted by the 1933 census. He then factored in a number of other variables for which reliable statistics were available, in some cases dating back to the early nineteenth century. These variables included conversions from and to Judaism, formal resignations from the Jewish community, marriages between Jews and non-Jews, family size, emigration, and immigration. Some of the data on Jewish migration and conversion were drawn from Ruppin's *Sociology of the Jews.*[7] Burgdörfer estimated that in 1933 the German population had included, in addition to the 500,000 *Glaubensjuden* who had actually been counted, 50,000 "non-Mosaic full-Jews," 200,000 half-Jews, and 100,000 quarter-Jews, yielding an alarming grand total of 850,000. In 1938, after the German annexation of Austria, Burgdörfer came up with a figure of three hundred thousand to four hundred thousand full and part Jews for that territory. Even taking into account the accelerated departure of Jews from Germany since 1933, Burgdörfer concluded that over a million persons with Jewish ancestry lived within the borders of the expanded "Greater Germany" at the time of his 1938 lecture. Burgdörfer clearly intended to shock his listeners and readers with this number, suggesting that the magnitude of the "Jewish question" was, indeed, greater than many had understood. The results of the May 1939 census suggest, however, that Burgdörfer's estimate was a good deal too high.[8]

According to Burgdörfer, the 1933 census, analyzed together with earlier surveys, indicated several notable demographic characteristics among the Jews of Germany. The increasing concentration of Jews in cities and in commercial occupations had already been a widely recognized phenomenon, documented and discussed in works by Arthur Ruppin and other Jewish scholars. For his part, Burgdörfer massaged the numbers so as to sharpen the point even further. Thus, for example, he argued that because many Jews whose occupations had been classified by the census under "industry and artisanal trades" in actuality performed the kinds of work that were normally listed under "commerce," their numbers could be moved from the former category to the latter.[9] In doing so, Burgdörfer exaggerated the percentage of Jews engaged in commerce, not by fabricating data but through disingenuous manipula-

tion of the census results. Similarly, Burgdörfer underscored the alien nature of the Jews in Germany by lumping together foreign-born Jews,
who were mainly from Poland, with those who had been born in the regions that the German Empire had ceded to Poland in 1918.[10]

Burgdörfer maintained that the census figures proved that German
Jews had shirked their military responsibilities in World War I. Jews, so
went this staple of German antisemitism, had either dodged conscrip-
tion or avoided combat. In 1916, the German government had conducted
a study that refuted this accusation but had not published it, and the ca-
nard persisted in right-wing circles.[11] In the 1930's, Burgdörfer contended that the cowardice and treason of the Jews in the Great War was
reflected in their demographic structure, specifically in the relatively
small surplus of Jewish females for the war generation. The surplus of females, he observed, was considerably larger among non-Jewish Germans
for the cohorts born between 1878 and 1900, validating, in his opinion,
the claim that Jewish men had died at lower rates than other German
men in the war. Burgdörfer seemed unaware or unconcerned that the
data he himself presented actually contradicted this conclusion. A line
graph accompanying the article showed little or no difference between
the Jewish and non-Jewish female surplus for the annual cohorts most
directly affected by combat, those of the late 1890s. For older cohorts,
those born between 1878 and the late 1890s, there was, indeed, a smaller
surplus of females among Jews than non-Jews, but this was a result of
the surplus of males among Jewish immigrants to Germany from eastern
Europe before and after World War I, a fact that is itself conveyed in
Burgdörfer's statistical tables.[12]

Burgdörfer was most interested in the age structure of Jews in Germany, and in its demographic implications for the German *Volk*. For several decades leading up to 1933, he noted, birthrates in Germany had
been declining for Jews as well as for the population at large. The overall population was growing older. In Jewish circles, concerns about low
birthrates (in connection with intermarriage) had become common, and
Burgdörfer could cite as one of his sources the book *Decline of the Jews*
by the German Jewish scholar Felix Teilhaber.[13] Comparing Jewish and
non-Jewish birthrates in Prussia from 1823 to 1937, Burgdörfer pointed
out that the downward trend for Jewish birthrates generally ran a few
years ahead of that for the non-Jewish German population. He attributed
this not only to Jewish urbanization and upward social mobility but also

to the "rationalization of sexual life," that is, the use of birth control and family planning, which he ascribed to Jewish cultural influence. Referring to sex reformers such as Magnus Hirschfeld, and to Sigmund Freud and others who had theorized about sexuality, Burgdörfer concluded that it had been a "rootless, enlightened, urbanized, and all-subverting Jewry" that had supplied the leading "pioneers of population control." Had the Jews kept the "rationalization of sexuality" to themselves, he added, it would not have been a bad thing from the German point of view, for the Jewish birthrate would have declined while the German birthrate would have risen. However, he continued, they felt compelled to spread their gospel to the masses of the German people, exploiting their disproportionately large influence over German culture. Burgdörfer thought it was more than coincidental that the German birthrate had fallen in Vienna since 1933, when German Jewish advocates of abortion rights had taken up exile there.[14]

The Jewish Threat to Leipzig: Fritz Arlt

Among his many activities, Burgdörfer served as editor of a monograph series published by the *Archive of Population Science and Population Policy* (*Archiv für Bevölkerungswissenschaft und Bevölkerungspolitk*), a quantification-focused demographics journal that had commenced publication before the Nazi era. The fourth volume in the series edited by Burgdörfer appeared in 1938. The 47-page pamphlet was titled *Racial-Biological Investigation of the Jews in Leipzig*.[15] Its author, Fritz Arlt, a Nazi party member since 1932, had spent time in Leipzig as a doctoral student and as an official in the local Nazi party office, and had then moved to Breslau, where he served as chief of the Racial-Political Office of the Nazi party's Silesia district. His responsibilities in Breslau included maintaining a card catalog of "racial aliens," establishing the ancestry of persons who could not produce reliable genealogical documentation, coordinating racial propaganda, and overseeing "scientific and anthropological work."[16] During World War II, Arlt would become an important figure in the Third Reich's program of large-scale population transfer in eastern Europe.[17] Arlt's 1938 study of the Jews of Leipzig, despite its short length, and despite its militant antisemitic rhetoric, can be counted among the more detailed quantitative studies of Jewish communities published during the Nazi era.

Writing as a Nazi party official rather than as a university instructor, Arlt made no effort to restrain his antisemitic rhetoric, nor did he attempt to disguise the ideological assumptions of his study. Social science, he maintained, should be pursued in the political interest of the German people as defined by Nazi racial ideology. The task of scholars was "to investigate and clearly lay out the intrusion of the alien Jewish people into the German *Volk*, and its consequences."[18] Arlt saw no contradiction between ideology and scientific rigor, however, and he boasted of the unique qualities of his own study. "For the first time, the present study encompasses all the Jews of a major city, from infants to the elderly, from the unemployed on welfare to wealthy bankers."[19] Moreover, Arlt claimed, his was the first quantitative study of Jews to be based on statistics assembled using racial, as opposed to religious, categories. The study employed data gathered by the Nazi party Racial-Political Office in Saxony in 1936. It encompassed around 18,000 Jews in Saxony, about 11,000 of whom lived in Leipzig. More specifically, the study focused on 5,637 Jewish females and 5,450 Jewish males, 736 mixed marriages, and, finally, 308 female and 359 male half-Jews.[20] Arlt's study provided a demographic profile of the Leipzig Jewish community, giving emphasis to migration patterns, age structure, partner selection, and fertility. Arlt was especially interested in two questions: first, the geographic origins of the Jews of Leipzig; and second, the extent and implications of racial mixing between Jew and non-Jews.

A central theme in Arlt's study was the foreign-ness, and particularly eastern-ness, of German Jews. Arlt intended to undermine the notion that Jews had deep historical roots in Germany. He marshaled statistics to demonstrate that Leipzig's Jews represented a very recent biological transplantation of Polish Jewry onto German soil. Of the Jews living in Leipzig in 1936, 27 percent had been born in Poland, and a significant percentage of those born in Germany, including in Leipzig itself, were born to parents who had come from Poland. Analysis of birthplaces in Poland revealed a further important pattern, according to Arlt: "The Jews of Leipzig are a colony of Galician Jewry."[21] A highly disproportionate number of Leipzig's Jews had roots in the Polish region of Galicia, and in neighboring regions of southern Poland. "Leipzig Jewry," Arlt concluded, forebodingly, "is a part of the Galician-Jewish race-organism [Volkskörper], whose feelers stretch out to the Ukraine and the Black Sea, to White Russia and Moscow, to Warsaw, Lithuania, and the Baltic, to Ruthenia and Prague."[22] Terms such as "colonization" and the imagery of a "race-organism" extending its tentacles throughout Europe were intended to underscore not only the alien-ness of the Jews, but also their aggressive, exploitative, and grasping nature. Arlt developed this theme further in his discussion of Jewish occupational and residential patterns in Leipzig. The Jews who arrived from Poland in Leipzig, he argued, were overwhelmingly involved in trade. They avoided settling either in established working-class neighborhoods in the city or in agricultural areas on the city's outskirts. Instead, Jews gravitated toward the commercial districts and, once they had accumulated a sufficient amount of wealth, moved out to well-to-do residential quarters.[23] From the very beginning, then, the Galician-dominated Polish Jews who had come to Leipzig had sought to remain among themselves, pursue commerce, avoid physical labor, and profit from the toil of German workers.

Arlt seemed to have been unaware of the contradiction between his characterization of the Jewish "colony" in Leipzig as a self-segregated community on the one hand and his assertion of a Jewish penchant for so-called racial mixing on the other. Writing from the perspective of an official of the Nazi party's Racial-Political Office, Arlt was obsessed with the latter question. Much of his study focused on the frequency and biological consequences of marriages between Jews and Aryans, and with the phenomenon of "race defilement" (Rassenschande), that is, extramarital sex between Jews and Aryans.

According to the study, 736 mixed-marriage couples were present in Leipzig in 1936. One contemporary reviewer noted that this number of mixed marriages was probably a good deal lower than in communities of similar size in western Germany, where the Jewish population had become more thoroughly assimilated. The reviewer emphasized that the degree of racial mixing in Leipzig, worrisome as it was, was actually lower than in many other major German cities.[24] Arlt pointed out that more than half of mixed marriages in Leipzig stemmed from the years 1918 to 1932, a statistic interpreted by Arlt as confirmation that the racial contamination of the German people had accelerated during the short-lived Weimar Republic.[25] About two-thirds of the mixed marriages involved a Jewish husband and an Aryan wife. Arlt struggled to explain why Jewish men took Aryan partners at roughly twice the rate that Jewish women did. Ignoring the enormously complex cultural and situational factors relating to gender roles and expectations, Arlt cited the

influence of racial instinct, suggesting that "physiological and sexual differences between the Jewish woman and the German man" rendered
Jewish women less desirable as marriage partners.[26] Jewish men enjoyed
greater success in crossing the racial divide by virtue of their control of
wealth, Arlt maintained. He noted that 70 percent of Jewish men in
mixed marriages were businessmen whose pursuit of Aryan wives could
be attributed to an "aspiration to social and cultural respectability."[27]
Love and affection could not be accounted for in Arlt's race-conscious
social science.

In his section on "race defilement," Arlt examined data from 165 cases
that occurred in Leipzig in which the man was Jewish and the woman
Aryan. His description of this form of miscegenation invoked the most
negative stereotypes of sexually predatory Jewish men. Arlt's main point
was that the stereotype was, indeed, true: the statistics on mixed marriage proved that "the threat to German women from Jewish aliens is a
fact."[28] Unlike mixed marriage, which involved mainly affluent and
well-educated Jews, *Rassenschande* was not class specific but occurred
among Jews of all social classes. Moreover, in cases where the male was
Jewish and the female Aryan, the social background of the female partner was higher than average for German society as a whole. Arlt concluded from this fact that *Rassenschande* should not be understood as a
social-climbing phenomenon on the Aryan side but as something even
more ominous, namely a pathology among well-educated German women
who sought the exotic in male Jews. Age was an important factor as well.
Roughly two-thirds of the Aryan women involved with Jews belonged
to the 19–30 age group, while roughly two-thirds of the Jewish men belonged to the age groups over 31. Thus the vulnerability of Aryan
women to the sexual predations of Jewish men were greatest precisely at
the age when the women were most fertile. The danger posed by intermarriage was all the more acute, Arlt maintained, because, in demographic terms, the Jews of Leipzig were "biologically more healthy" than
the Aryan population. The Jewish community had a younger demographic structure than the non-Jewish population, even though emigration since 1933 has siphoned off a disproportionately high number of
younger Jews.[29]

It should be emphasized that in 1938, when Arlt published his study,
it was by no means yet a foregone conclusion that the Jewish community
of Leipzig would soon be approaching its end. A great many German

Jews had emigrated since 1933, but many had remained as well. Despite waves of occupational purges, Jews in Leipzig and elsewhere continued to own and operate businesses. Although it was the stated wish of the Nazi regime to encourage Jewish emigration, nobody could be certain how thoroughly this policy would be implemented in the end. A *juden-frei* Germany was by no means a certainty when Arlt collected his Leipzig data and published his study. It must, therefore, be understood as more than an academic exercise and, much in the way he intended it, as a work of applied social science, whose goal was to underscore the Jewish racial danger and promote the implementation of policies that would hasten the physical and biological separation of Jews and Aryans.

The Archive of Racial and Social Biology

The ideological orientation of Arlt's study characterized much of the empirical, quantitative social scientific research on Jewish communities in Germany. An outlet for some of this scholarship was the journal *Archive of Racial and Social Biology (Archiv für Rassen- und Gesellschaftsbiologie)*, which had been founded early in the twentieth century by Alfred Ploetz, a leading member of the German eugenics movement. In 1935 the journal published an article by Rudolf Euler, a medical researcher at the University of Marburg, entitled "The Question of Jewish Penetration of the Rural Districts of Electoral Hesse."[30] Euler's study was unusual inasmuch as it focused on Jewish communities in rural Germany. Although the vast majority of German Jews lived in cities—about one-third of the country's Jews resided in Berlin—the number of Jews in small towns in rural areas was not insignificant. Euler wanted to look at the phenomenon of mixed marriage in a single rural region. He chose Electoral Hesse (Kurhessen), a former principality located in central Germany, north of Frankfurt and east of the Rhine, including the city of Kassel and the university town of Marburg, where Euler was based. In 1833, Electoral Hesse, then governed by liberals, had granted full emancipation to its Jews, the first German principality to do so. In the Nazi period the largely rural region had a population of about 650,000, roughly 1 percent of which was Jewish.[31]

Euler's main purpose was to establish statistically the degree to which the physical presence of Jews in rural towns correlated to the frequency of mixed marriages. He used census data for individual communities, supplemented by materials placed at his disposal by local governments and party offices, which he received in part through the support of the Ministry of Propaganda.[32] Of the 1,069 distinct communities in Electoral Hesse, 175 contained at least one Jewish resident. Of these 175 communities, 128 could be classified as rural; indeed, 38 of them contained fewer than five hundred residents, and 59 contained between five hundred and one thousand. Factoring out the urban areas of Electoral Hesse, Euler calculated that Jews constituted seven-tenths of 1 percent of the rural population. Rather than being evenly distributed, the Jewish population was more concentrated in some rural areas than in others. In some of the rural communities, the number of Jews could sometimes be surprisingly high, as in Rhina, 162 of whose 498 residents were Jewish.[33]

Euler identified 68 mixed-marriage couples present in Electoral Hesse as of September 1934. Plotting the geographic distribution of the mixed marriages, Euler sought to determine whether the frequency of the mixed marriages was directly proportional to the percentage of Jews in a given community. His conclusion was that no such correlation existed. In fact, Euler pointed to many localities where there were few or no mixed marriages despite a significant Jewish presence. He highlighted the example of the county of Hünfeld, where there were no mixed marriages even though Jews constituted 1.9 percent of the population, the highest percentage of any rural county.[34] Euler explained this apparent anomaly by attributing to rural Germans a stronger attachment to their racial identity (*Volkstum*) than was the case among their cousins in the cities. Even though the farmers of Electoral Hesse came into frequent contact with Jews and conducted business with them, they had generally "rejected a community of blood with Jewry."[35] Euler's case study had, he claimed, statistically validated an important ideological tenet of Nazism: the rural folk who lived on and worked the land remained the most authentic vessel of the German race and German culture.

Jewish marriage and reproductive patterns were not the only issue to arise in Nazi antisemitic social science. Jewish economic activity and occupational structure also received a good deal of attention. In 1935 the *Archive of Racial and Social Biology* published a piece titled "Occupational Choices and Volk Character of the Jews" by Theodor Deneke, a Hamburg-based sociologist.[36] Deneke addressed himself to one of the central issues of the sociology of the Jews, that of explaining their disproportionately high representation in commercial occupations. Was this penchant for commerce a consequence of historical circumstances, or did it reflect something intrinsic to Jewish society, or to Judaism itself? The racialist essentialism of Nazism held that genetic factors were at work. Deneke desired to test this hypothesis empirically, specifically through the use of occupational statistics.

Deneke's project was a work of historical sociology that intended to track continuity and change in Jewish occupational patterns in one German city—Hamburg—across four generations, ending with the present one. Deneke would require data in which occupation was correlated to religion. In 1933 the German Reich had conducted an occupational census that took account of religious affiliation, but the data were not yet available when Deneke began work on his study. However, some useful data were readily accessible. An occupational census had been taken in 1925, and although it did not address religious affiliation in general, it did do so for Hamburg (and Bavaria). The previous national occupational census, that of 1907, contained data on religious affiliation for the entire German Reich. Data for the nineteenth century was far more fragmentary, however. Deneke therefore seized on the idea of generating his own data through a creative use of old Hamburg Address Books. These published volumes, which were common in the nineteenth century, listed the names, addresses, and occupations of all the city's residents. In order to encompass four generations, Deneke selected the Address Books for the years 1841, 1870, 1900, and 1930. The occupational structure of both Hamburg's Jewish and non-Jewish communities would be established for each of these years. But the Address Books did not specify religion, so Deneke faced the dilemma of deciding who was Jewish and who was not. His solution to this challenge was to work with samples from the Address Books. His Jewish sample consisted of entries with the names Cohen, Cohn, and Levy. Deneke considered it extremely unlikely that anyone with one of these names would be Gentile. Converts from Judaism who had these names, he argued, would likely have changed them upon leaving the Jewish community. For his non-Jewish sample, Deneke selected entries with the name Schultz. He maintained that Jews rarely had this family name, supporting this assertion by citing the names of Jewish soldiers from Hamburg who fell in World War I, which were compiled in a memorial book.

Deneke's comparison of the occupational structure of his samples led him to conclude that Jewish occupational preferences remained remarkably consistent over four generations, despite the fact that emancipation had made it possible for Jews to move into new lines of work. Commerce remained the predominant realm of activity for Jews, while manual labor and the artisanal trades continued to see only token Jewish participation. In Deneke's view, this demonstrated that Jews were predisposed by their very nature to engage in commerce, since the removal of legal barriers to their participation in other occupations made no significant difference in their occupational structure.

Two features of Deneke's study are especially striking. First is the conspicuous discrepancy between its empirical aspirations and its intellectual facileness. It generated and reproduced a wealth of statistical data, yet it proceeded from the absurd premise that the removal of vocational constraints delivered by Jewish emancipation should have led to an immediate and dramatic transformation of Jewish economic existence. Such a premise ignored entirely the influence of factors such as family tradition and the socialization of young Jews into the commercial middle class. Second, Deneke's main conclusion was not consistent with his own data. The statistics showed a steady migration of Hamburg's Jews away from commerce and toward other occupations, specifically the civil service and the academic professions, such as law and medicine. On the basis of Deneke's data, one could argue that the transformation of Jewish occupational structure in Hamburg was actually dramatic and rapid from 1841 to 1930, with the percentage of those involved in commerce declining from 77 to 54.[37] In spite of his own data, Deneke could see only what he wanted to see—that Jews always gravitated toward commerce.

Yet another quantitative study of German Jews that appeared in the *Archive of Racial and Social Biology* in 1940, an article entitled "Statistics on the Causes of Death in the Jewish population of Breslau in the Years 1928–1937," was contributed by Edeltraut Bienek, who had recently completed her doctorate at the Pathological Institute of the University of Breslau.[38] Accepting as a given that Jews and Germans belonged to distinct races, Bienek addressed the fundamental question of whether racial differences were reflected in statistical patterns of fatal illness. Limiting the study to a single city would help control for differences in climate, medical care, and hygiene between the two population groups. Bienek claimed that Jews and non-Jews in Breslau lived, aged, took ill, and died in almost identical circumstances, although she did take into account occupational and economic differences between the two populations. Bienek compiled her own data from death certificates placed at her disposal by the Statistical Office of the City of Breslau.[39] The death certificates indicated religious affiliation, which Bienek automatically (and in a manner not quite consistent with Nazi racial definitions) translated into racial affiliation.

In the empirical sense, Bienek's work was among the most ambitious of the quantitative studies of Jews undertaken in Nazi Germany. It encompassed 77,520 deaths that were recorded in Breslau over a ten-year period, 3,601 of which were of Jews. Keeping track of which cases were Jewish and which were not, Bienek inserted each fatality into a typology comprising 18 basic causes of death, ranging from disease to accident, to murder, and to suicide.[40] Among the results of her comparison of Jewish and non-Jewish deaths were that Jews experienced lower infant mortality than non-Jews, that tuberculosis was a good deal less common among Jews, and that diabetes was a good deal more common.[41] These findings were hardly dramatic or surprising, given their consistency with the assertions of earlier Jewish researchers such as Elias Auerbach, Maurice Fishberg, and Samuel Weissenberg, all of whom were cited by Bienek.[42] What was surprising was Bienek's ultimate conclusion that her statistics did not necessarily support the notion of a "racial disposition" for disease. She maintained that "external and social factors definitely played an essential role" in explaining the statistical differences between the causes of death for Jews and non-Jews.[43] Among what Bienek considered to be her most important findings was that, contrary to the assertions of previous research, Jews did not suffer from a significantly higher predisposition to cancer than non-Jews. Earlier studies by both Jewish and non-Jewish researchers, she maintained, had failed to note that Jews had longer than average life spans due to social and economic factors, and thus the cancer rate for all Jews was skewed upward by cancer cases among elderly Jews.[44] Bienek did allow for the possibility that racial difference could explain why intestinal cancer was relatively common among Jews, and why stomach cancer was uncommon among them, but even in these instances Bienek invoked a racial explanation only with a good deal of reluctance.[45]

Although Bienek framed her study using the politically correct racial bifurcation between Jews and Germans, her conclusions did not validate the widely held belief in a strong correlation between race and disease.

Nor did Bienek resort to the antisemitic rhetoric characteristic of other Nazi-era research about Jews, including that of Rudolf Euler and Theodor Deneke, who had published in the same journal. Indeed, Bienek's argument seemed to fly in the face of both the content and the tenor of the majority of Jewish research that appeared around the same time, the main point of which was the collective hereditary otherness of the Jews. That she could publish her article in a leading race science journal suggests that even in 1940 an ambitious scholar could carve out a largely nonideological space for research about Jews. Yet Bienek's was one of the very few Nazi-era studies of Germany's Jews that held its antisemitism in check.

The Jew as Lawbreaker: Antisemitic Criminology

In 1935, Kurt Daluege, one of the highest ranking police officials in Germany, observed that "the criminal element is represented particularly strongly among Jews." Statistics reflecting a high rate of Jewish criminality, he argued, served as a justification for the measures that the Nazi regime had taken against Jews. "In the final analysis," he maintained, anti-Jewish legislation was simply a "question of self-defense."[46] That Jews were predisposed to commit certain kinds of crimes was already an established belief by the time the Nazis came to power. The accusation focused on what today would be called "white-collar crime"—embezzlement, fraud, and other transgressions involving financial manipulation. It also frequently included transgressions against public morality. In the files about crimes committed by Jews kept by the Institute for Research on the Jewish Question, "racial defilement" constituted the single largest cluster of materials. Also included were files on Jewish responsibility for "crimes against morality" (*Sittlichkeitsverbrechen*), abortion, and prostitution.[47]

All of these accusations had become *idées fixes* of antisemitic discourse by the early twentieth century. But even among antisemitic writers, the sources of Jewish criminality remained a matter of dispute. Some attributed a Jewish propensity for certain crimes to the Jewish religion itself, as well as to other factors that could be classified as environmental. Others argued that heredity was at work. This disagreement, carried on within the broad framework of antisemitism, continued into the Nazi years. Nazi racial ideology undoubtedly created an intellectual and political climate that was more hospitable to hereditarian explanations of crime. The kind of criminological thinking that came to be known as "criminal biology" tended to emphasize hereditary, as opposed to sociological, factors in explaining involvement in crime. While it is true that some of the more nuanced scholars focused on the criminal tendencies of individuals and not entire peoples, and were in some cases reluctant to accept explanations that rested entirely on racial predispositions to criminality, racial arguments did become pervasive and unavoidable after 1933.[48]

Ironically enough, it was a Jew, the Italian criminologist Cesare Lombroso, who invented the concept of the "born criminal" in the 1870s. Lombroso argued for the existence of an innate predisposition to crime in individuals, but did not posit an association between that predisposition and entire races of people. While the thoroughly assimilated Lombroso clearly felt estranged from traditional Judaism, he took a strong position against racial antisemitism.[49] By the 1930s, Lombroso's work lay far in the past, and his rejection of racism found little resonance among scholars of criminal biology. Max Mikorey, a Munich psychiatrist and specialist in criminal psychology, proposed one rather creative way to acknowledge Lombroso's contribution to criminal biology while simultaneously rejecting his Jewish perspective. According to Mikorey, Lombroso had put forth his theory of the born criminal with the intention of weakening the authority of the state. The state's power to punish the criminal, Mikorey contended, was undermined when the criminal act was attributed to the innate nature rather than the free will of the criminal. This weakening of the state, Mikorey pointed out, was a central strategy employed by Jews in their attempts to seize power for themselves.[50] This distorted interpretation of Lombroso enabled Mikorey to use Lombroso's criminal biology for his own racist ends while, in effect, criminalizing Lombroso himself. After the war, Mikorey became the head physician at the neurological clinic of the University of Munich, as well as an administrator at the Red Cross medical center.[51]

Perhaps the most virulently racist interpretation of Jewish criminality was contained in the book *The Jew as Criminal (Der Jude als Verbrecher)*, published in 1937 by J. Keller and Hanns Andersen.[52] *The Jew as Criminal* was intended to be not a work of scholarship but a contribution in the popular nonfiction genre. Both authors had been active as writers of middlebrow Nazi propaganda, and neither held an academic appointment.[53] In over two hundred pages, the authors cataloged Jewish criminals and their misdeeds, devoting chapters to thieves, embezzlers, racketeers, card sharks, pimps, sex criminals, and murderers. The book's explanatory framework left no room for sociological or historical nuance. Jews, Keller and Andersen claimed, were "fundamentally and essentially criminal." "Born to crime," Jews possessed a "special predisposition to and ability for fraud, dirty dealing, dishonest gambling, usury, sexual transgressions of all kinds, pick pocketing, and treason." "The Jew," they continued, "is not merely the beneficiary of crime, but is also the boss and string puller of the criminal underworld." Jewish involvement in Bolshevism, they argued, should be understood as an additional form of criminal activity. All in all, Keller and Andersen concluded, the Jews constituted a criminal race that was nothing less than "the embodiment of evil."[54]

Although academic criminological publications usually avoided such rhetorical hyperbole, they often expressed in a more reasoned tone more or less the same facile racialism. A good example can be found in the work of Johann von Leers. An unusually prolific writer on many matters relating to Nazism, Leers, a trained jurist, had been a member of the Nazi party since 1929, and had played the role of Nazi campus activist at several universities. He served as a junior member of the faculty of law at the University of Berlin in the middle and late 1930s before receiving a professorship in history at Jena in 1940.[55] In October 1936, Leers took part in a conference in Berlin devoted to "Jewry in Legal Studies" (*Das Judentum in der Rechtswissenschaft*).[56] Most of the presentations dealt with ostensible domination by Jews over various branches of the legal profession. Leers's lecture, later published as a fifty-five-page article entitled "The Criminality of the Jews," focused on patterns of Jewish crimes from the sixteenth through the nineteenth centuries.[57] Leers's method was mainly anecdotal, yet he did mobilize data from Reich surveys of criminal statistics taken between 1892 and 1917. The statistics documented disproportionately high Jewish participation in several categories of nonviolent crime. According to the figures, in the last decade of the nineteenth century, Jews were 12 times more likely than non-Jews to be involved in usury; 11 times more likely to engage in theft of intellectual property; and 8.9 times as likely to declare fraudulent bankruptcy. Between 1903 and 1936, Leers pointed out, the frequency of Jewish participation in usury was 29 times that of non-Jews.[58] Leers chose not to include statistics on violent crime, such as murder, battery, and vandalism, which would have shown rates of criminality among Jews that were a good deal lower than those of non-Jews. The complete figures were not difficult to find,[59] and had been cited repeatedly over the years, mainly by Jewish authors seeking to refute antisemitic accusations.[60] Jews and their supporters had usually argued that patterns of criminality among Jews had simply reflected the occupational structure of Jewish society. It was only to be expected that Jews, whose involvement in business and finance was disproportionately high, would have a higher rate of involvement in financial crimes than non-Jews. Leers tried to turn this argument on its head. Jews, he asserted, gravitated toward precisely those occupations that provided an opportunity to enrich themselves through financial and commercial machinations.

Leers developed this argument further in a later book, *The Criminal Nature of the Jews,* published in 1944.[61] "The Jew does not become a criminal because he is a merchant," wrote Leers, "but rather the criminal Jew embraces the mercantile profession because he is predisposed to the crimes that are possible in this realm."[62] Leers once more took a primarily anecdotal approach to his subject, occasionally using and abusing statistics to buttress his arguments. To substantiate the accusation that Jews had dominated the prostitution trade before the war, Leers quoted figures from an antisemitic Polish publication of 1927. According to these figures, Polish authorities had prosecuted 988 Jews, but only seven Christians, on prostitution charges. The Polish publication estimated that one hundred thousand Polish Jews made their livings through the "exploitation of immorality." Leers did not explain how and from what sources such a figure was derived, yet he reproduced it as authoritative.[63]

Notwithstanding the mendacity of Leers, it was indeed a fact that Jews were heavily involved in the management of prostitution in several countries in Europe in the late nineteenth and early twentieth centuries. Jewish commentators and reformers had bemoaned this problem and urged that it be combated.[64] Leers and other antisemites were not the slightest bit reluctant to cite such internal Jewish critiques when it was convenient. Thus, to support his argument about Jewish domination of prostitution, he invoked the authority of the notable Jewish feminist Berta Pappenheim, who had been involved in a campaign against prostitution before World War I.[65] Like other Nazi scholars who tried to focus attention on Jewish involvement in prostitution, Leers considered the activity exclusively in terms of its criminal nature. He never addressed the multiple sociological factors, such as poverty, mass migration, and urban overcrowding, that a full and fair understanding of the problem would entail, as this might have suggested that something other than the essential criminal nature of the Jews was at work.

The racism that characterized Leers's work was present, although less pronounced and more qualified, in other criminological work on Jews published in the Nazi period. Two of the most prominent criminologists in Germany, Edmund Mezger and Franz Exner, both taught at the University of Munich, and both addressed in print the basis of Jewish criminal behavior, although neither scholar conducted original research on that question. Edmund Mezger occupied a chair in criminal law at Munich during the entirety of the Nazi regime. He published two editions of a survey text on criminology, which argued that race played a role in determining the criminal behavior of Jews, but he cautioned that race was "interwoven with social factors in an inextricable fashion." Social factors, he conceded, might themselves be, at least in part, the products of race. Thus, while Jewish criminality was partially the result of the social environment, the Jewish social environment itself was partially the consequence of Jewish racial characteristics. The cautious tone and circuitous reasoning ought not obscure the significant racialism inherent in Mezger's text.[66]

Mezger's colleague in Munich, Franz Exner, has been called "the most important figure in German criminology in the 1930s."[67] Exner edited a major criminological monograph series, coedited a major journal, and published his major text, *Criminal Biology*, in 1939.[68] In his book, Exner devoted a five-page section to criminal behavior among Jews. He reproduced statistics from the Reich crime survey published in 1901, but, unlike Johann von Leers, provided figures for all categories of crime, not just those in which Jews were overrepresented. This seemed more aboveboard on Exner's part, as it would now be possible for a reader to see that Jews were four times less likely than non-Jews to commit a murder or an act of vandalism, three times less likely to engage in theft, and two and a half times less likely to inflict premeditated bodily harm.[69] Moreover, Exner pointed out, the overall crime rate among non-Jews was about 17 percent higher than among Jews.[70]

All of this evidence, Exner emphasized, had to be weighed against the disproportionately high rates among Jews for crimes of a financial nature. The unavoidable central question was the extent to which Jewish crime rates could be attributed to race or to environment, and Exner left no doubt as to where he thought causation could be found. Jewish criminality, he argued, was rooted in the Jewish drive for material self-enrichment, itself a racially determined characteristic. "The picture of Jewish criminality," Exner wrote, "coincides with the basic features of Jewish nature. Just as Jews are in their social behavior more active with their heads than with their hands, so it is in their antisocial behavior. In social as in antisocial matters, [the Jew] is dominated by the strongest acquisitive drive and ruthlessly pursues his material interests."[71] Exner maintained that this "acquisitive drive" was what lay behind Jewish involvement in pornography, prostitution, and similar crimes against morality. Jews were not any less moral than others, he explained, it was merely that they found these activities to be profitable.[72]

Exner concluded his section on Jewish criminality with an argument that reflected his own highly developed capacity for either self-delusion or disingenuousness. He noted that statistical and anecdotal evidence made clear that patterns of Jewish criminality had changed over the centuries. Before emancipation, Jews had been frequently found among marauding criminal bands formed from vagrants and other "transient scum." But this kind of activity disappeared as the result of emancipation, and Jewish criminality took on new and different forms. This historical transformation would seem to be as strong an argument in favor of an environmental explanation for patterns of criminality as one could possibly imagine. Exner argued otherwise, however. Emancipation, he wrote, had enabled the Jews to "develop their delinquency in a direction more consistent with their essential nature than the marauding criminality of days gone by."[73] In the final analysis, then, there was little fundamental disagreement between Exner's scholarly position and the propagandistic rhetoric of J. Keller and Hanns Andersen—the Jews were an inherently criminal race.

The Jew as Economic Parasite: Peter-Heinz Seraphim

Most of the antisemitic social science produced in the Third Reich centered on the Jews of Germany. It was at home that the "Jewish question" was seen as being most urgent, and it was about Germany that German scholars possessed both the greatest expertise as well as the easiest access to research materials. But there was also a hunger for statistical information about Jews the world over.[74] The largest Jewish communities in Europe lay in the east, and a thorough profile of modern Jewry could not be achieved without detailed studies of the Jewish communities of Poland, the Soviet Union, Hungary, and Rumania. Basic, reliable census data would be indispensable. One of the most prolific producers of such data was the Dahlem Publication Office, an institute associated with the Prussian State Archive that focused on ethnic, cultural, and demographic issues in eastern Europe.[75] From the mid-1930s into the war years, it issued a series of statistical compilations based on published Soviet and Polish census data. These volumes provided information on the ethnic composition of hundreds of cities, towns, and villages in the east. The volume on White Russia, for example, specified how many White Russians, Jews, Russians, Poles, Ukrainians, Latvians, Germans, Lithuanians, and Tartars could be found in each community.[76] The compilations of the Publications Office were designed as reference works, and contained little in the way of interpretation or commentary. A more overtly ideological statistical survey of the Jewish population of the Soviet Union was published during the war by the Ministry for the Occupied Eastern Territories.[77] Compiled by Johannes Pohl, this pamphlet supplemented Soviet census data with information drawn from Yiddish-language studies published by Jews in the Soviet Union in the 1920s. In this case, the statistical tables were interspersed with a commentary intended to persuade the reader that the Jews of the Soviet Union were economic parasites just as they were elsewhere in Europe.

Neither the reference works put out by the Publications Office nor the essentially propagandistic tracts produced by Pohl can be regarded as serious scholarship. In contrast, the work of Peter-Heinz Seraphim on the Jews of eastern Europe constituted perhaps the most impressive fusion of Nazi antisemitism and social scientific aspiration. A political economist by training, Seraphim was arguably the most professionally and intellectually accomplished "Jew expert" in Nazi Germany.[78] His work and career exemplified several important characteristics of Nazi Jewish studies. These included the quest for scientific legitimacy; the pretense of intellectual objectivity; the self-distancing from cruder forms of Nazi anti-Jewish propaganda; the desire to make the knowledge produced by scholarship usable by the makers of policy; and, perhaps most salient, the eagerness to exploit Jewish self-knowledge.

Peter-Heinz Seraphim was born in Riga in 1902, the scion of a Baltic German family that had produced several distinguished scholars. The father, Ernst Seraphim, was a prominent historian and journalist who published several books about Baltic German history and served as chief editor of three German-language newspapers in Riga. After World War I, Ernst moved his family to Königsberg, where he published several anticommunist tomes in addition to works of Baltic German nostalgia. Some of his post-1933 publications were distinctly antisemitic.[79] Peter-Heinz's older brother by three years, Hans-Jürgen Seraphim, developed into an accomplished economic theorist whose academic appointments during the Nazi era included a term as director of the Osteuropa Institut at the University of Breslau. Specializing in agricultural economics, the elder Seraphim produced several publications during the Weimar Republic, addressing the conditions of German farmers on the eastern frontier. Soon after the advent of Nazi rule he published articles about the prospects for a regeneration of the German peasantry, and later in the 1930s he turned his attention to the study of ethnic German peasants in eastern Europe, specifically in the Baltic and in Vohlhynia.[80] Peter-Heinz's younger brother by one year, Hans-Günther, emerged after World War II as a historian and legal scholar affiliated with the University of Göttingen. He became an expert in the documentation of the Nuremberg trials, publishing detailed indexes to the materials generated by the trials of the diplomat Ernst von Weizsäcker, the industrialist Friedrich Flick, numerous executives of the I. G. Farben company, and the *Einsatzgruppen* commander Otto Ohlendorf. Hans-Günther also edited and published the political diary of the Nazi leader (and Baltic German) Alfred Rosenberg.[81]

Like many of the Nazi policy-makers and functionaries who were concerned with solving the "Jewish question," Peter-Heinz Seraphim was born too late for military service in World War I, but he did join a Free Corps paramilitary unit in the immediate postwar years. In the 1920s he was trained as a political economist. His fields of expertise were "the politics of transportation" and "east European economics," both of which were central to his first major publication, a study of the Russian railroad system that appeared in 1925, when Seraphim was still in his early twenties. Subsequent publications included monographs and articles on such topics as Polish commerce and merchant shipping in the Baltic region.[82] He published nothing on the "Jewish question" before 1937.[83] In the following year, however, he published his massive book on eastern European Jewry,[84] a work of such scope and depth that it must have been in preparation for some time. This tome marked a watershed in Seraphim's academic career. He had produced a highly impressive "scientific" study of the world's largest concentration of Jews. Moreover, the publication of his book was timely, coming as it did only a year before the Nazi regime began to extended its control over millions of eastern European Jews.

Whether Seraphim's professional retooling as a Jewry expert reflected sincere ideological commitment or mere careerist opportunism is difficult to determine. The question of personal motive notwithstanding, it should be pointed out that in the ideological and cultural context of Nazi Germany, moving from the study of eastern Europe to the study of Jews was not all that radical a shift. Already in the Weimar Republic, German academic specialists on eastern Europe had contributed through their publications and teaching to the legitimization of German territorial revanchism and cultural imperialism.[85] These scholars operated primarily in the disciplines of history, economics, geography, and literature. The climate for their work improved considerably after 1933 as a consequence of the Nazi regime's approach to academic appointments and research support. Positions and institutes dedicated to the study of eastern Europe proliferated.[86] By fashioning himself a specialist on eastern European Jewry, Seraphim positioned himself strategically at the intersection of "eastern research" (*Ostforschung*) and antisemitic Jewish studies, fields that seemed to hold out great promise for young German scholars.

Seraphim's most significant contribution to Nazi Jewish Studies appeared in 1938 in the form of a seven hundred-plus-page tome, *The Jews of Eastern Europe* (*Das Judentum im osteuropäischen Raum*). The numerous articles and brochure-sized monographs he produced thereafter tended to be think pieces, recycled sections from the original thick volume,[87] or works of anti-Jewish propaganda targeted at a middlebrow readership.[88] Several characteristics set Seraphim's book apart from most other products of Jewish research in the Nazi era. Most conspicuous were its dimensions: 732 pages, 197 statistical graphs and charts, a bibliography with 563 entries, over a thousand footnotes. Quite apart from issues of factual veracity, methodological sophistication, and ideological predetermination of conclusions, the book's size and physical impressiveness undoubtedly created an aura of unusual erudition and rigor. One contemporary review declared the book "indispensable," one without which "modern Jewish research would be unthinkable."[89] When recommending Seraphim for a professorship in 1940, the dean of the law and political science faculty at the University of Greifswald described the book as a "rigorously precise work of scholarship made possible by knowledge of the Russian and Polish languages."[90]

Seraphim was a relentless pursuer of statistical data on eastern Europe in general, and on the Jews of that region in particular.[91] He familiarized himself with statistical sources available through Jewish organizations and institutions, most notably YIVO, which was then based in Vilna.[92] Indeed, one of the hallmarks of Seraphim's large book on the Jews of eastern Europe was its extensive exploitation of Jewish scholarship. Many of its sentences opened with the phrase "nach jüdischen Angaben" ("according to Jewish sources"). Seraphim's bibliography conveniently labeled with a J works authored by Jews. Of the 563 items in the bibliography, 346, or 61 percent, were marked with the J.

To gain a more in-depth understanding of Seraphim's approach to Jewish sources, we can look at a specific example. Seraphim made extensive use of several works by Arthur Ruppin, particularly *The Jews of the Present Day (Die Juden der Gegenwart)*[93] and the two-volume *Sociology of the Jews (Soziologie der Juden)*.[94] Ruppin was cited throughout the volume, and in Seraphim's long chapter "The Jews in the Economic Life of the Peoples of Eastern Europe," Ruppin was the most frequently cited source. Seraphim treated the Jewish Ruppin respectfully, as a capable scholar who had made an important contribution to the empirical understanding of Jewish society. He accepted the reliability of Ruppin's statistics. In fact, Ruppin's documentation of Jewish participation in commerce and industry was sufficiently persuasive in its own right, and required no embellishment to be brought into accord with Seraphim's own ideological predilections. Seraphim used Ruppin's work to substantiate his argument for Jewish dominance of capitalism across eastern Europe, in every country, in almost every city, and in many branches of commerce and industry. Numerous specific examples and statistical tables, many of which were drawn directly from Ruppin, conferred an aura of quantitative rigor. When Seraphim questioned specific figures provided by Ruppin, he did so in a way that enhanced the impression of his own fairness.[95]

However, while Seraphim relied on Ruppin's statistics, he distanced himself from Ruppin's explanatory framework. In his introduction, Seraphim addressed the epistemological implications of his dependence on Jewish sources. "It cannot be doubted," he stated, "that a Jewish analyst of Jewish themes sees, indeed must see, questions, relationships, and contexts differently from a non-Jew." After a period in which the study of Jews had been dominated by Jews, he argued, non-Jewish scholars now had to aggressively seize the initiative and produce a "different, new, and more correct" portrait of Jewry.[96] In Seraphim's view, Ruppin was a prisoner of his own Jewish perspective, so Seraphim would hardly expect him to derive the "correct," that is, most damning, conclusions. Thus Seraphim invoked Ruppin's authority, and then placed his own antisemitic spin on Ruppin's data.

In his chapter "The Urbanization of Eastern European Jews," Seraphim cited Ruppin's data extensively, but challenged his conclusions about the modernizing and assimilatory consequences of Jewish urbanization. Ruppin, who wrote from a Zionist perspective, lamented assimilation, which he claimed was advancing rapidly, and which he saw as a leading cause of Jewish social and cultural degeneration in the Diaspora. Seraphim wanted to turn Ruppin's conclusion on its head. He conceded that some degree of assimilation had taken place, but he used Ruppin's own statistics to prove that most eastern European Jews had remained unassimilated. Seraphim claimed that an inbred fear of assimilation had led to a widespread voluntary self-concentration of Jews into ethnic ghettos in major cities. Moreover, Seraphim maintained, the ghetto served as the "basis of Jewish expansion," by which he meant not simply biological proliferation but also economic and cultural aggrandizement. Whereas urbanization exerted a detrimental effect on most peoples, according to Seraphim, tearing apart the fabric of tradition and culture, in the case of the Jews, the process produced the opposite effect. The Jews were by their essence an urban folk, not rooted in the soil, so urbanization actually strengthened them. In short, while Ruppin the Zionist argued that assimilation was bad for the Jews, Seraphim the antisemite argued that inassimilable Jews were bad for the people around them.[97]

Seraphim disagreed with Ruppin's basic contention that the Jewish aptitude for capitalism was a product of Jewish historical experience, and argued instead that it had a racial basis.[98] In this connection, he addressed himself to the intellectual legacy of Werner Sombart, especially Sombart's influential book of 1911, *The Jews and Modern Capitalism*.[99] Seraphim regarded himself as Sombart's intellectual heir, employing Sombart's so-called statistical and genetic methodology while enjoying access to statistical data that Sombart had not had at his disposal—that is to say, data that had been generated in the intervening years in part by

Ruppin and other Jews.[100] But Seraphim was not uncritical of Sombart. In a lengthy obituary he wrote for the recently deceased Sombart in 1941, Seraphim praised him for posing the central question about the economic nature of the Jews, but criticized his reluctance to fully accept a racial argument for Jewish economic behavior. Seraphim also looked askance at Sombart's penchant for explaining Jewish capitalism without necessarily condemning it. Sombart, in Seraphim's judgment, had been a "significant instigator" of research on the economic dimension of the "Jewish question" but ultimately had not been able to penetrate to the heart of the matter, which was race.[101]

In his own work, Seraphim tried to leave no doubt about the racial basis of Jewish capitalism. He devoted a chapter of *The Jews of Eastern Europe* to this question, which typified his method for exploiting Jewish sources.[102] In a bibliographical footnote, Seraphim summarized the theories of Elias Auerbach, Ignaz Zollschan, Samuel Weissenberg, and other Jewish scholars who had debated whether the Jews constituted a single race or could be more accurately described as a mixture of races.[103] Seraphim endorsed the position advanced by Sigmund Feist, also a Jew, in Feist's 1925 book *Jewish Ancestral Origins (Stammeskunde der Juden)*.[104] Seraphim quoted Feist at length: "The Ashkenazic Jews present a mixture of various human types, which have been combined by a common culture and similar living conditions into a single type that shows a certain external uniformity, the fundamental diversity of its individual components being obscured to the superficial observer."[105] This view, Seraphim noted, was essentially similar to that of Hans F. K. Günther, the Nazi regime's most prominent race theoretician.[106] Yet Seraphim invoked the Jewish sources much more frequently than he did Günther, perhaps because he considered them more reliable, but more likely because of his eagerness to prove a point that Nazi propaganda had repeatedly emphasized through the 1930s, namely, that the Jews themselves had long expressed a strong sense of racial consciousness.

Seraphim's seeming "inside" knowledge of Jewry undoubtedly contributed to his emergence as one of Germany's key "Jew experts" after the publication of his big book. He was in demand as a consultant to policy-makers, as a contributor to journals, and as a speaker at conferences. In 1940, while serving as an economic advisor attached to the Armaments Inspectorate of the Wehrmacht in Poland, he established a connection to the Institute for German Work in the East, which Governor General Hans Frank had established in Cracow. Under the auspices of this institute, Seraphim published articles and a booklet about economic conditions in German-occupied Poland, in which he emphasized the urgency of eliminating the vestiges of Jewish commercial activity.[107]

Seraphim developed his thinking about a long-term solution to the Jewish presence in eastern Europe in a paper delivered in late March 1941 at a conference convened by Alfred Rosenberg's Institute for Research on the Jewish Question in Frankfurt. Seraphim had accepted the editorship of this institute's new journal, *Weltkampf*, and would very soon assume a full professorship at Greifswald. Seraphim's paper was entitled "Demographic and Economic Problems for a European Comprehensive Solution of the Jewish Question."[108] During the previous year the German government had contemplated territorial solutions to the "Jewish question" in Madagascar and in the Lublin region. Whereas Seraphim's paper explicitly discussed the Lublin plan, it did not mention Madagascar specifically, although the "emigration of the Jews from Europe" as part of a global "colonial reconfiguration" did figure prominently in his analysis. Seraphim's main argument favored a massive deportation of Europe's Jews to an as-yet-undetermined overseas destination. Much of his paper was devoted to demonstrating the impracticality of the alternative—a permanent Jewish reservation on the European continent. Seraphim here reiterated the point of his earlier work on the Jewish "ghetto," arguing that such a huge agglomeration of Jews could not be economically self-sufficient, hence could not be effectively quarantined from the non-Jewish population.

Whether Seraphim's arguments had any influence, even indirectly, over the evolution of policy must remain a matter of conjecture. By the time Seraphim delivered his paper in Frankfurt in late March 1941, the failure to knock Britain out of the war had led German officials to cease serious consideration of the Madagascar plan.[109] That Seraphim was advocating the shipping of several million Jews out of Europe precisely as the government was dispensing with this idea certainly suggests a very limited impact on policy. On the other hand, Seraphim's arguments against the creation of a Jewish reservation around Lublin did coincide with the persistent rejection of such a scheme by Governor General Hans Frank, who since early 1940 had complained bitterly to Berlin over the dumping of Jews from the Reich into the General Government. The ultimate rejection of a Jewish reservation in the General Government was a major step toward the decision to commit mass murder.

In late 1941, Seraphim directly addressed the implications of that mass murder. Once again attached to the Wehrmacht as an economic advisor, Seraphim prepared a memorandum concerning potential negative consequences arising from the mass executions of Jews then taking place in Ukraine, where Seraphim was stationed. Through an intermediary, the memorandum was delivered to General Georg Thomas, head of the Wehrmacht's Economic-Armament Office.[110] Seraphim complained that 150,000 to 200,000 Jews had been executed without consideration of economic consequences. The executed Jews, who presented no real threat to German forces, had constituted a productive skilled labor force. With the Jews being killed off, Soviet prisoners of war dying in large numbers, and the non-Jewish civilian population facing the threat of starvation, Seraphim wondered "who in all the world is then supposed to produce something valuable here?" But Seraphim's complaint was not limited to economic considerations.[111] "The method of these actions, which encompassed men, the aged, women, and children of all ages," Seraphim wrote, "was horrible."[112] Seraphim also expressed distress that the killings, although carried out mainly by German Order Police and Ukrainian militiamen, often attracted "the voluntary participation of members of the Wehrmacht."

If Seraphim's revulsion toward the murder of the Jews was genuine—even if only initially—then his case underscores the need for a nuanced understanding of the motives of Nazi scholars (and other Germans) who had promoted Jewish persecution and deportation. Seraphim had marshaled his considerable intellectual abilities to advocate, publicly and in print, the physical removal of millions of Jews from Europe, but the ultimate reality of the "Final Solution" shocked him. This illustrates the point that support for anti-Jewish measures in Germany and German-occupied Europe prior to the advent of the "Final Solution" should not automatically be regarded as endorsement of mass murder. Schemes like the Madagascar plan might have been delusory, but Seraphim and others took them seriously at the time. Only in retrospect did it become clear that Seraphim's scholarship, by emphasizing the urgency of removing the Jews from Europe, had helped pave the way for genocide.

Seraphim's standing as one of the Third Reich's leading academic experts on the Jewish question did not constitute much of a hindrance to his post-1945 career. After the war, Seraphim made himself useful to American occupation officials by disclosing information about German wartime research about the Soviet Union and eastern Europe. He identified published studies and unpublished research reports that the Americans might find helpful in their developing confrontation with the Soviet Union.[113] Although he was not able to secure another university professorship, Seraphim did land an enviable job as academic director of the Administrative and Economics Academy of the Ruhr region, where he oversaw the training of West German civil servants.[114] He was also able to maintain his status as a prolific publisher of books and articles. His postwar books included studies of communist collectivization in eastern Europe, the economy of eastern Germany, the industrial region of Upper Silesia, and the challenge of integrating German expellees from Poland and Czechoslovakia.[115]

Seraphim's Nazi-era books and articles about Jews magically disappeared from his postwar list of publications.[116] He also avoided mentioning Jews in his writings. One exception was his survey of *German Economic and Social History from Ancient Times to the Outbreak of the Second World War,* published in 1962. In his treatment of Nazi economic policy, Seraphim referred briefly to the Aryanization of Jewish property, the process through which Jews were pressured to sell off their assets at sharply deflated prices. To Seraphim, these measures had several negative consequences, all economic in nature. He alluded only tangentially to the "personal defamation" of the Jews.[117] A young German economics student reading Seraphim's text would have had no way of knowing that the author had devoted a substantial portion of his scholarly career to demonstrating that the Jews were dangerous economic parasites who had to be removed.

Epilogue

In 1956, the New York–based Yiddish-language newspaper *Forverts* (*Forward*) published two articles by one "P. Berman" attacking the career and work of a West German scholar of Yiddish linguistics, Franz Josef Beranek.[1] The conflict between Berman and Beranek embodied in microcosm a particularly bitter legacy of Nazi Jewish studies. "P. Berman" was the frequently used pseudonym of Max Weinreich, the guiding light of YIVO, the Jewish Scientific Institute, first in Vilna and then in New York. Although first and foremost a scholar of Yiddish linguistics, Weinreich was also an expert on the question of scholarly antisemitism in the Third Reich, which he had documented in his book *Hitler's Professors* in 1946. After World War II, he steadfastly refused to have dealings with any German scholar whom he suspected of having cooperated with the Nazi regime. When approached by German scholars, Weinreich insisted that they submit to him in writing detailed descriptions of their activities before 1945.[2] Beranek, one of the leading experts on Yiddish linguistics in postwar Germany, was one of the German scholars whom Weinreich rebuffed.

Who was Franz Joseph Beranek, and why did Max Weinreich refuse to help him establish the study of Yiddish linguistics in postwar Germany? The official version of Beranek's biography was summarized in an obituary published in a German scholarly journal in 1967.[3] An ethnic German from southern Moravia, Beranek was born in 1902 as an Austrian citizen, became a Czechoslovak citizen in 1919, and then a Reich German in 1939. He studied Germanic and Slavic linguistics at the Universities of Vienna and Prague, receiving his doctorate from the latter institution in 1930 with a dissertation on vowels in south Moravian German. In the 1930s he became interested in Yiddish linguistics, and he developed an association with YIVO in Vilna and published in its journal. The institute was interested in Beranek's ongoing research on Yiddish in the Czechoslovak region of Carpatho-Russia,[4] a study he published in 1941.[5] For his *Habilitation* at the University of Prague, which he completed in 1943, Beranek shifted his attention to German dialects in Bohemia and Moravia. He taught at Prague in 1944 and 1945, moving to Germany at the end of the war. While working in the school system in the state of Hesse, he resumed his research on German and Yiddish dialectology. Beranek was among the very small number of scholars in postwar Germany who wanted to integrate Yiddish into the university curriculum and research agenda. He edited the newsletter of the "Working Group for Yiddish Studies," twenty issues of which were published between 1955 and 1964. In 1958 he published a book on the Pinsk dialect of Yiddish.[6] He contributed to the study of Yiddish place names, which was considered important to the understanding of bi- and multilingualism as a cultural phenomenon. In recognition of these contributions, Beranek received a research stipend from the University of Giessen, where he was later allowed to transfer his *Habilitation* and thus join the teaching faculty. Starting in 1960 he lectured at Giessen on "German Philology with Special Emphasis on the Yiddish Language." Although his position was not that of a regular, full professor, he was accorded the honor of delivering an inaugural lecture, a gesture reflective of his prominence in his field. In 1965, two years before his death, he published his most important work, a dialectological atlas of western Yiddish.[7]

The sympathetic biography related in Beranek's obituary omitted a few important details. It neglected to mention that, during his student days in Vienna, Beranek had been associated with a right-wing, nationalistic student group, that he joined the Nazi party just weeks after his region of Czechoslovakia was annexed by Germany in 1938, and that he served as an officer and a press representative in a Storm Trooper (SA) unit. The obituary also did not mention the numerous articles celebrating Germanic culture that Beranek published during the Nazi occupation of the Czech lands between 1939 and 1944, part of which time he spent as director of a German ethnographic research institution in Slovakia.[8] A further detail not included in the obituary was the sponsorship of Beranek's research by the Reich Institute's Research Department for the Jewish Question. Subventions from that organization supported both the research and the printing of Beranek's 1941 book on the Yiddish dialect of Carpatho-Russia.[9] The book was mainly a technical work of dialectology, and the main body of its text showed no evidence of antisemitism. The problem lay in the preface, where Beranek explained how his study fit into the larger picture of scholarship about Jews. "The Jewish question," he noted, "stands incontrovertibly in the first rank of the problems that the new Germany must solve." It was the duty of scholarship to investigate the "racial and unique cultural foundations of Jewry," one of which was the Yiddish language. The study of Yiddish had been hitherto dominated by eastern European Jews, whose provincial perspective had caused them to concentrate on modern East Yiddish while giving less attention to the historic roots of the language in West Yiddish, which had been much more Germanic. At its base, Beranek noted, Yiddish was a "German dialect." Linguistic research into Yiddish would therefore be valuable for understanding not only the Jews but also the historical development of the German language. Beranek believed that one of the central goals of research in the field ought to be the creation of a dialectological atlas for all Yiddish dialects, covering the entire contemporary and historical region in which Yiddish had and continued to be spoken, "from Amsterdam to Rostow, from Reval to Venice."[10]

After the war, Beranek was the first German scholar to call for the integration of Yiddish into German linguistics. He lamented that Yiddish had been treated as a "stepchild" of the German language and ridiculed as a *Mischsprache*. Germans, he wrote, bore a special moral responsibility to study Yiddish because of the role they had played in its decline. The study of Yiddish would provide German scholars with an opportunity to repudiate the ideological tendencies of the past decades; it would be "evidence of good will." Moreover, Beranek, who had been associated with YIVO in the 1930s, now wanted to establish a new bridge between German linguistics and the Yiddish studies establishment at YIVO in New York. Finally, Beranek hoped that work on Yiddish could be started in Germany immediately in order that dialectological research could be conducted among Yiddish-speaking displaced persons living in Germany.[11]

In 1955 Beranek attempted to join the New York–based College Yiddish Association. The Association's chairman, Sol Liptzin of City College of New York, responded to Beranek with the following inquiry: "To what extent did you assist in the extermination of the millions of speakers of Yiddish by placing your expert knowledge of Yiddish at the service of the Nazis?"[12] Beranek responded with a copy of his denazification certificate, which had classified him as "exonerated" (*entlastet*). He maintained that his Nazi-era work on Yiddish had been in the "service of scholarship," denying that he had ever acted politically.[13] Beranek did not believe that he had any reason to regret his actions or publications of the Nazi era. He expressed this sentiment to his German colleagues, along with his deep personal disappointment over the rejection from the Yiddish studies establishment in New York.[14] Beranek attributed the rejection to an "understandable universal resentment by Jewry toward all Germans," as well as to the "complete ignorance of circumstances in Hitlerite Germany" that prevailed in the United States.[15]

It is true that the body of Beranek's 1941 book on the Yiddish of Carpatho-Russia was politically neutral. And Beranek had hardly been among the prominent Nazi antisemitic scholars, which is why Weinreich had not mentioned him in *Hitler's Professors*. But the antisemitic content of the preface and the acknowledgment to the Reich Institute were hard to overlook. Moreover, in all of his correspondence with Weinreich and other Yiddishists, Beranek was less than candid about his past, never acknowledging, for example, his membership in the Nazi party and the SA. Beranek probably did not realize the extent to which some of the embarrassing details about his biography were known to Max Weinreich. After the war, the YIVO Institute in New York had come into possession of a massive collection of the files of the Nazi party's Science Office (Amt Wissenschaft), which had kept track of personal and political details of the lives of thousands of German scholars. A document from this collection alerted Weinreich to the fact that Beranek's wife, Dr. Hertha Wolf-Beranek, had been employed as an ethnologist by the Ahnenerbe, the scientific research branch of the SS.[16] Ultimately, Weinreich went public with his dossier on Beranek, denouncing his Nazi background in the Yiddish newspaper *Forverts*.

For a person with Beranek's biography, his hope to establish cordial ties with YIVO so soon after the end of the Third Reich can only be seen as delusional. Only a few years earlier, YIVO in Vilna had been ransacked and plundered by Nazi scholars, and many of its scholars had been murdered. Somehow Beranek convinced himself that assistance might be forthcoming from this institution and its director, the author of *Hitler's Professors*. While Beranek could and did recognize that the Nazi regime had brought about the near extinction of Yiddish as a living language, he could not acknowledge that his personal activities in the field of Jewish studies had borne any connection to that catastrophe.

Post–World War II Jewish scholars of Yiddish did not take kindly to Beranek's desire to subordinate the study of Yiddish linguistics to that of German. In his scholarly work on Yiddish dialects, Beranek distinguished sharply between East Yiddish and West Yiddish. Beranek's main interest was on West Yiddish, which he referred to as *Judendeutsch*, claiming that the widely spoken East Yiddish of modern times was merely a later, Slavicized derivative of the original Germanic dialect. This view implied a denial of the existence of what Yiddishist scholars refer to as "Old Yiddish," an original Yiddish ur-language that was believed to have antedated West Yiddish. One specialist on the history of Yiddish linguistics has called Beranek's position a "remarkably patronizing Germanistic stance."[17] Max Weinreich was a leading exponent of the view that Yiddish ought not be classified primarily as a Germanic language. Weinreich held that Yiddish had originated as a synthesis of Semitic and Latin elements, created by Jews who arrived in Europe with the Roman army as traders. Yiddish, in this view, was already established as a language unto itself before it began to absorb Germanic elements in the Middle Ages.[18] Beranek's insistence on treating Yiddish as a German dialect may well have made him all the more disagreeable from Weinreich's perspective.

Even if Beranek's Nazi-era actions and writings had shown less evidence of ideological bias than those of other Nazi scholars, it is easy to understand Weinreich's distrust of a German scholar who had belonged to the Nazi party, served in the SA, and published under the aegis of a Nazi antisemitic research institute. To Weinreich, the intellectual seriousness of scholars like Beranek was not the issue; the issue was their honesty and moral integrity. With some exceptions, the scholars who participated in Nazi Jewish studies were not intellectual frauds or Nazi party hacks. They were dishonest scholars, but scholars nonetheless. Their careers and their work violated the presumption that the scholar has a responsibility to use knowledge honestly and for positive ends. In the final analysis, the great failing of the Nazi antisemitic scholars was more ethical than intellectual.

Ethical failings, not intellectual; altho didn't consider both sides of argument, started predisposed to own thesis

The antisemitic works examined here did, in many cases, possess some of the characteristics of genuine scholarship—empirical research, inductive logic, documentation of sources, and citations to previously published work. Despite their hateful purpose and tone, they contained information that sometimes proved useful even to Jewish scholars after 1945.[19] These characteristics distinguished them from out-and-out propaganda. But by advancing conclusions that were predetermined by ideological conviction, political conformism, or professional opportunism, they also violated what many regard as basic tenets of scholarship: the responsibility of acknowledging conflicting evidence, the assiduous avoidance of making up one's mind in advance, and the striving toward ideological neutrality, unattainable as this final goal might actually be. If we were to accept this admittedly "modern" definition of scholarship, it would exclude almost everything produced under the aegis of Nazi Jewish studies. In this case, Nazi Jewish studies might best be understood as having occupied a grey zone between scholarship and propaganda, a zone into which one might also place much of the academic production of the Soviet bloc, and perhaps even court and church histories of earlier centuries. If, on the other hand, we were to accept a less positivistic definition of scholarship, according to which an illusory aspiration to neutrality should be rejected in favor of open partisan and ideological engagement, then much of Nazi Jewish studies might actually qualify.

However one might wish to classify it, Nazi Jewish studies most definitely fulfilled a partisan ideological function. The antisemitic scholars did not agree with each other on many points, but they were generally in consensus when it came to the substance and direction of Nazi anti-Jewish policy. In less than a decade, policy had proceeded through several overlapping phases, beginning with the definition of the Jews as a race, proceeding to the disfranchisement and economic expropriation of the Jews, and culminating in their physical removal from German living space. Antisemitic scholarship was there to help lend intellectual respectability to every step of this process. Scholars promoted the definition of the Jews as a biological race that was different from, and inimical to, Germans and other Europeans. They underlined the physiological and behavioral differences between Jews and their "host" peoples, insisted on the existence of an instinctive mutual repulsion among members of different races, and emphasized the degenerative consequences of racial mixing. Building on an old tradition, they demonized the Jewish religion, representing it as an innate manifestation of the Jewish racial character. They described the emancipation of the Jews, and the process of assimilation that followed it, as a fateful error committed by liberal Christians. They chronicled how the Jews, freed from their medieval disabilities, could rise without restraint, expanding their already considerable economic power, exploiting it in turn to achieve a destructive political and cultural influence. Relying on the persuasive power of statistics, they quantified the pathological nature of modern Jewish society. And although they did not explicitly advocate mass murder, scholars underscored the futility of any solution to the Jewish question that did not lead to the physical removal of the Jews from Europe.

After the collapse of the Third Reich it was uncertain whether German scholarship could ever recover from the damage done to it in the Nazi years.[20] History has proven that it could, but the recovery did take some time. In the area of Jewish studies, the recovery benefited from its postwar abandonment by those who had dominated it in the Nazi years. Walter Frank killed himself in 1945, despondent over the collapse of the Third Reich and the death of his beloved Führer.[21] Gerhard Kittel, having been removed from his chair in Tübingen, died in 1948, before receiving any chance at rehabilitation. Eugen Fischer's academic career had already ended during the Third Reich. Wilhelm Grau and Johannes Pohl quietly pursued nonacademic careers. Some of the more talented of the Nazi Jewish experts were able to carry on academic careers after the war, but turned their attentions to other subjects. Otmar von Verschuer avoided questions of Jewish heredity in his work on genetics, Karl Georg Kuhn wrote about the significance of the Dead Sea Scrolls for Christians rather than about the significance of the Talmud for Jews, and Peter-Heinz Seraphim shifted his attention away from eastern European Jews and toward other issues connected with that region. The postwar successes of these scholars (among others) were symptomatic of a widespread, systemic failure to hold Nazi intellectuals accountable for their role in the Third Reich, but at least they had stopped publishing antisemitic books and articles.

There were a couple of notable exceptions to this pattern. In 1944 the young historian Heinrich Schnee had published a short but egregiously antisemitic article in Alfred Rosenberg's *Weltkampf*.[22] It discussed court Jews who had been ancestors of Heinrich Heine, the nineteenth-century German Jewish literary figure and political radical, and came out of a larger project on court Jews that Schnee had in preparation during World

War II. Between 1953 and 1967, Schnee published the complete work, a six-volume study of court finances that historians of German Jewry still regard as "indispensable," even though the first volume resonated with language reminiscent of the Nazi period.[23] Although Schnee never received a professorship in postwar Germany, he did enjoy a secure position as a secondary school (*Gymnasium*) teacher.[24]

The other exceptional case was that of Hermann Kellenbenz. After having trained under Karl Alexander von Müller at the University of Munich, Kellenbenz received a research fellowship in 1939 from the Reich Institute for a study of "Finance Jewry in Hamburg." It was not until 1958 that the book appeared, with the title *Sephardim on the Lower Elbe: Their Economic and Political Significance from the End of the Sixteenth to the Beginning of the Eighteenth Century.*[25] The book was antisemitic in neither content nor tone. It was the only work on Jews published by Kellenbenz, one of West Germany's leading economic historians, who held professorships at the Universities of Cologne and Erlangen-Nuremberg.[26]

Aside from the exceptional cases of Schnee and Kellenbenz, there was little continuity between Nazi Jewish studies and Jewish studies in postwar Germany. The systematic academic study of Jews all but disappeared, with the exception of the field known as *Judaistik,* which focused mainly on the study of Jewish religious texts, often for the purpose of elucidating early Christianity. There was no official taboo on Jewish studies in the early phase of postwar German history, but its disappearance seemed to be for the best for all concerned. Non-Jewish Germans who possessed expertise in the field were tainted by their pre-1945 records, and there was little interest in bringing Jewish refugees back to Germany for this purpose. The Jewish German community that had provided the underpinning for Jewish scholarship, had, in any event, been decimated. Moreover, in the Jewish world, priority was given to building up centers of Jewish scholarship in Israel and in the United States.

Jewish studies slowly began to reappear in West Germany in the 1960s and 1970s, when professorships were established in (West) Berlin, Frankfurt, and Cologne. The position in Cologne was connected to the *Germania Judaica,* a library devoted to German Jewish history that took its name and inspiration from an earlier project that had been initiated in 1903 by the Society for the Promotion of the Science of Jewry. A significant step toward the renewal of the field in postwar Germany was founding of the Academy for Jewish Studies in Heidelberg in 1979.

Jewish studies underwent dramatic growth in Germany in the 1990s. The decade saw the creation of important new professorships and institutes in Duisburg, Potsdam, Leipzig, Munich, and Düsseldorf. Departing from the narrow approach of *Judaistik*, these programs have embraced an interdisciplinary approach to research and teaching. There were several reasons for this renaissance. The embrace of Jewish studies embodied a powerful positive symbolism for German politicians and intellectuals. In the wake of German unification, the renewal of Jewish studies represented the fulfillment of what was seen as a special German responsibility. At the same time, it represented a normalization of German academic life, inasmuch as Germany had been an important center for Jewish studies before 1933. A hallmark of the newly emergent Jewish studies in Germany has been the close relationship between academic programs and the expanding German Jewish community, whose growth has been fueled by Jewish immigration from the former Soviet Union. Conscious of the destructive use to which knowledge about Jews and Judaism was put in an earlier era, the scholars in charge of these programs are committed to a Jewish studies that is both academically rigorous as well as empathetic to a Jewish point of view.[27]

One of the more important centers for Jewish studies in contemporary Germany is the University of Munich, where a chair for Jewish History and Culture is fully integrated into the very history department where Karl Alexander von Müller taught, and where Walter Frank, Wilhelm Grau, and other antisemitic scholars received their academic training. The research collection of the old Research Department for the Jewish Question is now integrated into the university's historical library, and is available for use by faculty, students, and visiting scholars.

Columbia University, 1998); "Schützenhilfe nationalsozialistischer Juden-politik: Die 'Judenforschung' des 'Reichsinstituts für Geschichte des neuen Deutschland' 1935–1945," in Fritz Bauer Institute, ed., *"Beseitigung des jüdischen Einflusses. . . ." Antisemitische Forschung, Eliten und Karrieren im Nationalsozialismus* (Frankfurt: Campus, 1999), pp. 17–42; "Anti-Jewish Research and the Institut zur Erforschung der Judenfrage in Frankfurt am Main between 1933 and 1945," in Jeffry M. Diefendorf, ed., *Lessons and Legacies.* Vol. 6: *New Currents in Holocaust Research* (Evanston, Ill.: Northwestern University Press, 2004), pp. 155–89.

11. Maria Kühn-Ludewig, *Johannes Pohl (1904–1960). Judaist und Bibliothekar im Dienste Rosenbergs: Eine biographische Dokumentation* (Hannover: Laurentius, 2000).

12. Dirk Rupnow, "'Arisierung jüdischer Geschichte: Zur nationalsozialistischen 'Judenforschung,'" *Leipziger Beiträge zur jüdischen Geschichte und Kultur* 2 (2004): 349–367; "Judenforschung im Dritten Reich: Wissenschaft zwischen Ideologie, Propaganda und Politik," in Matthias Middell and Ulrike Sommer, eds., *Historische West- und Ostforschung in Zentraleuropa zwischen dem ersten und dem zweiten Weltkrieg: Verflechtung und Vergleich* (Leipzig: Akademische Verlagsanstalt, 2004), pp. 107–132.

13. Weinreich, *Hitler's Professors,* p. 7.

14. Key on this issue is David Bankier, *The Germans and the Final Solution: Public Opinion under Nazism* (Oxford: Oxford University Press, 1992), and David Bankier, ed., *Probing the Depths of German Antisemitism: German Society and the Persecution of the Jews, 1933–1941* (New York: Berghahn, 2000).

15. For thoughtful consideration of this question see Jeffrey Herf, "The 'Jewish War': Goebbels and the Antisemitic Campaigns of the Nazi Propaganda Ministry," *Holocaust and Genocide Studies* 19 (Spring 2005): 51–80.

16. Weinreich, *Hitler's Professors,* p. 242.

1. An "Antisemitism of Reason"

1. Hitler to Gemlich, 16 September 1919, in Eberhard Jäckel, ed., *Hitler: Sämtliche Aufzeichnungen, 1905–1924* (Stuttgart: Deutsche Verlags-Anstalt, 1980), pp. 88–90. Adolf Gemlich was a veteran living in Ulm who had inquired with the Bavarian Army about an antisemitic organization in Berlin. His request was forwarded to Hitler, who for a time after the war had worked as a Bavarian Reichswehr political officer. For details on the origins of the letter see Joachim C. Fest, *Hitler: Eine Biographie* (Frankfurt: Propyläen, 1973), pp. 163–168.

2. "Warum sind wir Antisemiten?" in Jäckel, *Hitler: Sämtliche Aufzeichnungen,* pp. 184–204.

3. "Matthias von Buttenhausen," Stichworte zu einer Rede, in Jäckel, *Hitler: Sämtliche Aufzeichnungen,* p. 473.

4. George L. Mosse, *Toward the Final Solution: A History of European Racism* (New York: Howard Fertig, 1978).

5. Jacob Katz, *From Prejudice to Destruction: Anti-Semitism, 1700–1933* (Cambridge, Mass.: Harvard Univ. Press, 1980), pp. 303–306. Fritsch's work originally appeared under the title *Antisemite's Catechism.*

6. On this concept and the relevant historiography see Ian Kershaw, *The Nazi Dictatorship: Problems and Perspectives of Interpretation,* 4th ed. (London: Arnold, 2000), pp. 69–92.

7. For a useful summary of the topic informed by recent research see Michael Grüttner, "Die deutschen Universitäten unter dem Hakenkreuz," in John Connelly and Michael Grüttner, eds., *Universitäten in den Diktaturen des 20. Jahrhunderts: Zwischen Autonomie und Anpassung* (Paderborn: Schöningh, 2003), pp. 67–100. Among the important recent institutional studies are Steven P. Remy, *The Heidelberg Myth: The Nazification and Denazification of a German University* (Cambridge, Mass.: Harvard University Press, 2002); Uwe Hossfeld, Jürgen John, and Rüdiger Stutz, eds., *"Kämpferische Wissenschaft": Studien zur Universität Jena im Nationalsozialismus* (Cologne: Böhlau, 2003); and Horst Junginger, *Von der philologischen zur völkischen Religionswissenschaft: Das Fach Religionswissenschaft an der Universität Tübingen von der Mitte des 19. Jahrhunderts bis zum Ende des Dritten Reiches* (Stuttgart: Franz Steiner, 1999). Tensions between professors who sought to Nazify academic life and those who opposed this project are documented in the following works by Frank-Rutger Hausmann: *"Vom Strudel der Ereignisse verschlungen": Deutsche Romanistik im "Dritten Reich"* (Frankfurt: Klostermann, 1944); *Die Rolle der Geisteswissenschaften im Dritten Reich: 1933–1945* (Munich: Oldenbourg, 2002); and *Anglistik und Amerikanistik im "Dritten Reich"* (Frankfurt: Klostermann, 2003).

8. "Die Judenfrage an den deutschen Hochschulen," 1944, Bundesarchiv Berlin, Bestand NS 15, file 349.

9. "Bibliographie deutscher Dissertationen über die Judenfrage 1939–1942," *Weltkampf* 21, no. 2 (May–August 1944): 103–105. See also Philipp Bouhler, ed., *Nationalsozialistische Bibliographie. 4. Beiheft: Hochschulschrifttum, Verzeichnis von Dissertationen und Habilitationsschriften* (n.p., 1939).

10. The best source on organizational details about the Reich Institute is Patricia von Papen, "'Scholarly' Antisemitism" during the Third Reich: The Reichinstitut's Research on the Jewish Question" (Ph.D. diss., Columbia University, 1998). Helmut Heiber, *Walter Frank und sein Reichsinstitut für Geschichte des neuen Deutschlands* (Stuttgart: Deutsche Verlags-Anstalt,

164   *Notes to Pages 12–14*

1966), contains a wealth of information but lacks an interpretive framework and is very difficult to use.

11. Walter Frank speech delivered at the opening of the Forschungsabteilung Judenfrage, 19 November 1936, published as *Deutsche Wissenschaft und Judenfrage* (Hamburg: Hanseatische Verlagsanstalt, 1937).

12. Siegfried Lokatis, *Hanseatische Verlagsanstalt: Politisches Buchmarketing im "Dritten Reich"* (Frankfurt: Buchhändler-Vereinigung, 1992). See especially pp. 66–74 for a discussion of the press's close relationship with Frank's Institute.

13. On the origins of the Frankfurt institute see Dieter Schiefelbein, "Das Institut zur Erforsching der Judenfrage Frankfurt am Main: Antisemitismus als Karrieresprungbrett im NS-Staat," in Fritz Bauer Institute, ed., *"Beseitigung des jüdischen Einflusses . . ." Antisemitische Forschung, Eliten und Karrieren im Nationalsozialismus* (Frankfurt: Campus, 1999), pp. 43–71.

14. This was particularly true at the opening conference of the Institute of March 1941, at which the plan to remove the Jews of German-controlled Europe to Madagascar or some other location was discussed. See the published versions of the papers in *Weltkampf* 1, 2 (April–September 1941).

15. Prior to 1941, Rosenberg had published a much more popularly oriented magazine called *Der Weltkampf*. The definite article "der" was dropped from the title when the magazine was reconstituted as an allegedly scientific journal.

16. Susannah Heschel, "When Jesus was an Aryan," in Robert P. Ericksen and Susannah Heschel, eds., *Betrayal: German Churches and the Holocaust* (Minneapolis: Fortress, 1999), pp. 68–89.

17. Michael Burleigh, *Germany Turns Eastwards: A Study of Ostforschung in the Third Reich* (Cambridge: Cambridge University Press, 1988).

18. Hans-Walter Schmuhl, ed., *Rassenforschung an Kaiser-Wilhelm-Instituten vor und nach 1933* (Göttingen: Wallstein, 2003).

19. Michael H. Kater, *Das "Ahnenerbe" der SS 1935–1945: Ein Beitrag zur Kulturpolitik des Dritten Reiches*, 3rd ed. (Munich: Oldenbourg, 2001).

20. Burleigh, *Germany Turns Eastwards*, pp. 254–290; Anetta Rybicka, *Institut Niemieckiej Pracy Wschodniej: Kraków 1940–1945* (Warsaw: Wydawn. DiG, 2002).

21. Jürgen Matthäus, "'Weltanschauliche Forschung und Auswertung': Aus den Akten des Amtes 7 im Reichssicherheitshauptamt," *Jahrbuch für Antisemitismusforschung* 5 (1996): 287–330; Joachim Lerchenmueller, "Die 'SD-mässige' Bearbeitung der Geschichtswissenschaft," in Michael Wildt, ed., *Nachrichtendienst, politische Elite und Mordeinheit: Der Sicherheitsdienst des Reichsführers SS* (Hamburg: Hamburger Edition, 2003), pp. 160–189. See also the useful document collection edited by Michael Wildt, *Die Judenpolitik des SD 1935 bis 1938: Eine Dokumentation* (Munich: Oldenbourg, 1995).

22. On Nazi propaganda in general see David Welch, *The Third Reich: Politics and Propaganda* (London: Routledge, 1993) and *Propaganda and the German Cinema, 1933–1945* (Oxford: Oxford University Press, 1983). On Der Stürmer see Dennis Showalter, *Little Man What Now? Der Stürmer in the Weimar Republic* (Hamden, Conn.: Archon Books, 1982). Key works on the reception of antisemitic propaganda in German society include David Bankier, *The Germans and the Final Solution: Public Opinion under Nazism* (Oxford: Oxford University Press, 1992), and *Probing the Depths of German Antisemitism: German Society and the Persecution of the Jews, 1933–1941* (New York: Berghahn, 2000); Otto Dov Kulka, "'Public Opinion' in Nazi Germany and the 'Jewish Question,'" *Jerusalem Quarterly* 25 (Fall 1982), pp. 121–144. Especially useful is the lucid discussion in Saul Friedländer, *Nazi Germany and the Jews: The Years of Persecution, 1933–1939* (New York: HarperCollins, 1997).

23. Publications of this genre are analyzed extensively in Claudia Koonz, *The Nazi Conscience* (Cambridge, Mass.: Harvard University Press, 2003). Circulation figures, which are for 1937, are drawn from *Sperlings Zeitschriften-u. Zeitungs-Adressbuch,* 1937 edition (Leipzig: Börsenverein der deutschen Buchhändler, 1937).

24. Gregory P. Wegner, *Anti-Semitism and Schooling under the Third Reich* (New York: Routledge, 2002).

25. 1937 circulation figures from *Sperlings.*

26. "Judenforschung ohne Juden," *Illustrierter Beobachter,* 30 April 1942.

27. *Völkischer Beobachter,* 18 December 1937.

28. *Völkischer Beobachter,* 13 January 1939.

29. Heiber, *Walter Frank,* p. 629.

30. "Freie Forschung im Kampf gegen das Weltjudentum," *Völkischer Beobachter,* 27 March 1941.

31. Victor Klemperer, *Ich will Zeugnis ablegen bis zum letzten: Tagebücher 1933–1945,* 2 vols. (Berlin: Aufbau, 1995), vol. 1, p. 415.

32. This appeared after the war. Victor Klemperer, *LTI: Notizbuch eines Philologen* (Berlin: Aufbau, 1947).

33. See the following in the *Völkischer Beobachter*: "Judentum, Politik und Kultur," 6 July 1938; "Biologie und Statistik des Judentums," 7 July 1938; "Judentum und Antisemitismus," 8 July 1938.

34. Wegner, *Anti-Semitism and Schooling,* and Gilmer W. Blackburn, *Education in the Third Reich: Race and History in Nazi Textbooks* (Albany: State University of New York Press, 1985).

35. Max Weinreich, *Hitler's Professors: The Part of Scholarship in Hitler's Crimes against the Jewish People* (New York: YIVO, 1946; reprint, New Haven: Yale University Press, 1999), p. 242, implies the desirability of prosecuting the scholars.

36. Götz Aly and Susanne Heim, *Vordenker der Vernichtung: Auschwitz und die deutschen Pläne für eine neue europäische Ordnung* (Hamburg: Hoffman und Campe, 1991). Much of this recent work arises from what some younger German scholars believe is their moral responsibility to inculpate in the act of genocide their professional forebears who so far have been let off the hook.

37. John Efron, *Defenders of the Race: Jewish Doctors and Race Science in Fin-de-Siecle Europe* (New Haven: Yale University Press, 1994).

2. Racializing the Jew

1. Jirí Weil, *Mendelssohn Is on the Roof*, translated by Marie Winn (Evanston, Ill.: Northwestern University Press, 1998).
2. Michael Burleigh and Wolfgang Wippermann, *The Racial State: Germany 1933–1945* (Cambridge, Mass.: Cambridge University Press, 1991).
3. Two key works remain Paul Weindling, *Health, Race and German Politics between National Unification and Nazism, 1870–1945* (Cambridge: Cambridge University Press, 1989), and Robert Proctor, *Racial Hygiene: Medicine under the Nazis* (Cambridge. Mass.: Harvard University Press, 1988). As is common in the scholarship on Nazi race theory, these works deal with the Nazi understanding of the Jewish race only briefly, concentrating more on issues connected to eugenics.
4. Hans F. K. Günther, *Rassenkunde des jüdischen Volkes* (Munich: Lehmann, 1930).
5. There is no book-length biography of Günther. For a brief treatment of his life and career, see Elvira Weisenburger, "Der 'Rassepapst': Hans Friedrich Karl Günther, Professor für Rassenkunde," in Michael Kissener and Joachim Scholtyseck, eds., *Die Führer der Provinz: NS-Biographien aus Baden und Württemberg* (Konstanz: Universitätsverlag Konstanz, 1997), pp. 161–199. A key work on Günther's Nordic ideology is Hans-Jürgen Lutzhöft, *Der Nordische Gedanke in Deutschland 1920–1940* (Stuttgart: E. Klett, 1971).
6. On Lehmanns see Gary Stark, *Entrepreneurs of Ideology: Neoconservative Publishers in Germany, 1890–1933* (Chapel Hill: University of North Carolina Press, 1981), and Sigrid Stöckel, *Die "rechte Nation" und ihr Verleger: Politik und Popularisierung im J. F. Lehmanns Verlag, 1890–1979* (Berlin: Lehmanns, 2002).
7. On Günther's appointment in Jena, see Uwe Hossfeld, "Von der Rassenkunde, Rassenhygiene und biologischen Erbstatistik zur synthetischen Theorie der Evolution: Eine Skizze der Biowissenschaften," in Uwe Hossfeld et al., *"Kämpferische Wissenschaft": Studien zur Universität Jena im Nationalsozialismus"* (Cologne: Bohlau, 2003), pp. 519–574.

8. On the decision to write the book, see Günther, *Rassenkunde des jüdischen Volkes,* p. 7.
9. The most thorough study of this issue is Annegret Kiefer, *Das Problem einer "jüdischen Rasse," eine Diskussion zwischen Wissenschaft und Ideologie (1870–1930)* (Frankfurt: Peter Lang, 1991). Also useful is Niels C. Lösch, *Rasse als Konstrukt: Leben und Werk Eugen Fischers* (Frankfurt: Peter Lang, 1997), pp. 278–280, and John David Smith, "W. E. B. Du Bois, Felix von Luschan, and Racial Reform at the Fin de Siècle," *Amerikastudien* 47, 1 (2002): 23–38.
10. Günther, *Rassenkunde des jüdischen Volkes,* p. 7.
11. Ibid., pp. 13–14.
12. Ibid., map p. 39.
13. Ibid., p. 219, n. 2.
14. Ibid., pp. 22–26.
15. Ibid., p. 26.
16. Ibid., p. 30.
17. Ibid., pp. 31–32.
18. Ibid., p. 33.
19. Ibid., p. 36.
20. Ibid., pp. 159–171.
21. The work of Paul Schultze-Naumburg, a contemporary of Günther, has become especially notorious in this regard. See Pamela M. Potter, *Most German of the Arts: Musicology and Society from the Weimar Republic to the End of Hitler's Reich* (New Haven: Yale University Press, 1998). For Schultze-Naumburg's tribute to Günther see Paul Schultze-Naumburg, "Hans F. K. Günther zum 50. Geburtstage," *Volk und Rasse* 16, 2 (February 1941): 1–2.
22. Günther, *Rassenkunde des jüdischen Volkes,* pp. 63–68.
23. Ibid., pp. 68–71.
24. Ibid., pp. 78–79.
25. Ibid., p. 80.
26. Ibid., p. 118.
27. Ibid., photos p. 109.
28. Ibid., pp. 136–143.
29. Ibid., p. 173.
30. Ibid., pp. 174–176.
31. Ibid., p. 194.
32. Ibid., p. 178.
33. Ibid., p. 195. In this regard, Günther emphasized a disagreement with Luschan, who, according to Günther, overstated the degree to which the Jews had racially sealed themselves off after Nehemiah and Ezra.
34. Ibid., pp. 182–189.

35. Ibid., p. 191.
36. John Efron, *Defenders of the Race: Jewish Doctors and Race Science in Fin-de-Siècle Europe,* (New Haven: Yale University Press, 1994), pp. 91–122.
37. Günther, *Rassenkunde des jüdischen Volkes,* pp. 200–202.
38. Ibid., pp. 211–212.
39. Ibid., p. 208.
40. Ibid., pp. 212–213.
41. Ibid., p. 215.
42. Ibid., p. 215.
43. Ibid., pp. 216–217. Günther did not elaborate on this argument. He may have been referring to the high percentage of Rumanian Jews among the immigrants to North America, or perhaps even to the Sephardic Jews who had settled in North America before the nineteenth century, although in the latter case Günther would have had to make the very implausible argument that a good deal of mixing had taken place between the Sephardic Jewish-Americans and the eastern European immigrants.
44. Ibid., p. 217.
45. Ibid., p. 219.
46. Ibid., p. 222.
47. Ibid., pp. 219–221.
48. On Fishberg see Mitchell B. Hart, *Social Science and the Politics of Modern Jewish Identity* (Stanford: Stanford University Press, 2000), pp. 158–169.
49. Günther, *Rassenkunde des jüdischen Volkes,* pp. 225–239.
50. In fact, some scholars working in the field of Jewish studies have recently devoted a good deal of attention to precisely such behaviors among Diaspora Jews. See especially Sander L. Gilman, *Creating Beauty to Cure the Soul: Race and Psychology in the Shaping of Aesthetic Surgery* (Durham, N.C.: Duke University Press, 1998), and *Making the Body Beautiful: A Cultural History of Aesthetic Surgery* (Princeton: Princeton University Press, 1999).
51. Günther, *Rassenkunde des jüdischen Volkes,* p. 248.
52. Peter Loewenberg, *Walther Rathenau and Henry Kissinger: The Jew as Modern Statesman in Two Political Cultures* (New York: Leo Baeck Institute, 1980).
53. Günther, *Rassenkunde des jüdischen Volkes,* pp. 251, 254.
54. On flat feet as a marker of Jewish difference in antisemitic discourse see Sander L. Gilman, *The Jew's Body* (New York: Routledge, 1991), chap. 2.
55. The work of Salaman cited by Günther is *Eugenics in Race and State,* vol. 2 (1923). On Salaman see Hart, *Social Science,* pp. 185–188.
56. Günther, *Rassenkunde des jüdischen Volkes,* acknowledgment to Salaman, p. 8.
57. Ibid., p. 252.

58. Ibid., p. 253.

59. Hans Peter Althaus, *Mauscheln: Ein Wort als Waffe* (Berlin: de Gruyter, 2002).

60. On the question of anti-Jewish stereotypes in Wagner's operas, see Marc A. Weiner, *Richard Wagner and the Anti-Semitic Imagination* (Lincoln: University of Nebraska Press, 1995).

61. Günther, *Rassenkunde des jüdischen Volkes*, p. 257.

62. Ibid., pp. 264–265.

63. Ibid., p. 262.

64. Ibid., pp. 260–267.

65. Ibid., p. 324.

66. Ibid., p. 300.

67. Ibid., p. 298.

68. Ibid., p. 305.

69. Ibid., p. 305.

70. Ibid., p. 345.

71. Tom Segev, The *Seventh Million: The Israelis and the Holocaust*, translated by Haim Watzman (New York: Hill and Wang, 1993), p. 19.

72. For a useful comprehensive study of the origins and implementation of the Nuremberg laws see Cornelia Essner, *Die "Nürnberger Gesetze" oder die Verwaltung des Rassenwahns, 1933–1945* (Paderborn: Schöningh, 2002).

73. The experiences of these *Mischlinge*, long a neglected subject, are the subject of the recent massive study by Beate Meyer, *"Jüdische Mischlinge": Rassenpolitik und Verfolgungserfahrung, 1933–1945*, 2nd ed. (Hamburg: Dölling und Galitz, 2002). See also James F. Tent, *In the Shadow of the Holocaust: Nazi Persecution of Jewish-Christian Germans* (Lawrence: University Press of Kansas, 2003.)

74. About 53,000 marriages between Christians and Jews were registered in Germany between 1875 and 1932. Meyer, *"Jüdische Mischlinge,"* p. 25.

75. Wilhelm Stuckart and Hans Globke, *Kommentare zur deutschen Rassengesetzgebung* (Munich: C. H. Beck, 1936).

76. On Stuckart's role at the Wannsee conference see Essner, *"Nürnberger Gesetze,"* pp. 400–410. For a short biographical sketch see Kurt Pätzold and Erika Schwarz, *Tagesordnung: Judenmord: Die Wannsee-Konferenz am 20. Januar 1942* (Berlin: Metropol, 1992), pp. 241–245.

77. At first it seemed that nobody noticed or cared that Globke had been the coauthor of the most important legal commentary on the Nuremberg legislation. This past came back to haunt him after the East Germans published a sensationalistic exposé that was intended to embarrass the Adenauer government of West Germany. There is no full-scale study of the Globke affair. For an overview see Daniel E. Rogers, "The Chancellors

of the Federal Republic of Germany and the Political Legacy of the Holocaust," in Alan E. Steinweis and Daniel E. Rogers, eds., *The Impact of
Nazism: New Perspectives on the Third Reich and Its Legacy* (Lincoln: University of Nebraska Press, 2003), pp. 234–236. Some details are in Essner,
"Nürnberger Gesetze," pp. 113–117.

78. Stuckart and Globke, *Kommentare,* p. 12.
79. Ibid., p. 1.
80. Ibid., p. 3.
81. Ibid., p. 15.
82. Ibid., p. 14.
83. Ibid., p. 15.
84. Ibid., p. 17.
85. Ibid., p. 15.
86. Ibid., p. 15.
87. Erwin Baur, Eugen Fischer, and Fritz Lenz, *Menschliche Erblehre und
Rassenhygiene,* 4th ed., 2 vols. (Munich: Lehmanns, 1936).
88. Heiner Fangerau, *Etablierung eines rassenhygienischen Standardwerkes,
1921–1941: Der Baur-Fischer-Lenz im Spiegel der zeitgenössischen Rezen-
sionsliteratur* (Frankfurt: Peter Lang, 2001), p. 52.
89. On Fischer's early career see Bernhard Gessler, *Eugen Fischer (1874–1967):
Leben und Werk des Freiburger Anatomen, Anthropologen und Rassenhygie-
nikers bis 1927* (Frankfurt: Peter Lang, 2000).
90. Fischer, Baur, and Lenz, *Menschliche Erblehre,* pp. 148–149.
91. Lösch, *Rasse als Konstrukt,* pp. 284–286. On Gross see Essner, *"Nürnberger Gesetze",* pp. 66–69.
92. Eugen Fischer, "Rassenentstehung und älteste Rassengeschichte der He-
bräer," *Forschungen zur Judenfrage* 3 (1938): 121–136.
93. Baur, Fischer, and Lenz, *Menschliche Erblehre,* p. 747.
94. Ibid., p. 748.
95. Ibid., p. 756.
96. Ibid., p. 750.
97. Ibid., p. 748.
98. Ibid., p. 753.
99. A particularly good example of how Verschuer's postwar publications referred back to his Nazi-era research in a highly selective and self-serving
way is his *Die Frage der erblichen Disposition zum Krebs* (Wiesbaden:
Steiner, 1956).
100. Otmar von Verschuer, "Was kann der Historiker, der Genealoge und der
Statistiker zur Erforschung des biologischen Problems der Judenfrage
beitragen?" *Forschungen zur Judenfrage* 2 (1937): 216–222; "Rassenbiologie der Juden," *Forschungen zur Judenfrage* 3 (1938): 137–151.

101. Verschuer, "Was kann der Historiker," p. 219.

102. For example, in 1932, Rafael Becker had published "Die Geistes-erkrankungen bei den Juden in Polen," *Allgemeine Zeitschrift für Psychiatrie und psychisch-gerichtliche Medizin*, according to which Polish Jews suffered from such conditions with disproportionately high frequency. A 1935 summary of that work endows the data with an antisemitic flavor absent in the original. See "Zeitschriftenschau," *Archiv für Rassen- und Gesellschaftsbiologie* 29, 4 (1935): 480.

103. Verschuer, "Rassenbiologie," pp. 144–145.

104. On this question I have relied on the following works: Benno Müller-Hill, "Das Blut von Auschwitz und das Schweigen der Gelehrten," in Doris Kaufmann, ed., *Geschichte der Kaiser-Wilhelm-Gesellschaft in National-sozialismus: Bestandsaufnahme und Perspektiven der Forschung*, 2 vols. (Göttingen: Wallstein, 2000), vol. 2, pp. 189–227; Carola Sachse and Benoit Massin, *Biowissenschaftliche Forschung an Kaiser-Wilhelm-Instituten und die Verbrechen des NS-Regimes: Informationen über den gegenwärtigen Wissensstand* (Berlin: Max-Planck-Gesellschaft, 2000), pp. 23–28; Benoit Massin, "Rasse und Vererbung als Beruf. Die Hauptforschungsein-richtungen am Kaiser-Wilhelm-Institut für Anthropologie, menschliche Erblehre und Eugenik im Nationalsozialismus," in Hans-Walter Schmuhl, ed., *Rassenforschung an Kaiser-Wilhelm-Instituten vor und nach 1933* (Göttingen: Wallstein, 2003), pp. 190–245; and Achim Trunk, *Zweihundert Blutproben aus Auschwitz: Ein Forschungsvorhaben zwischen Anthropologie und Biochemie 1943–1945* (Berlin: Max-Planck-Gesellschaft, 2003).

105. Verschuer's sworn statement of 10 May 1946, cited in Sachse and Massin, *Biowissenschaftliche Forschung*, p. 23.

106. Trunk, *Blutproben*, p. 8.

107. This suggestion is implicit in Müller-Hill," "Blut von Auschwitz," p. 207. In *Blutproben*, p. 4, Trunk casts doubt on it.

108. Hans-Peter Kröner, "Das Kaiser-Wilhelm-Institut für Anthropologie, menschliche Erblehre und Eugenik und die Humangenetik in der Bundesrepublik Deutschland," in Kaufmann, ed., *Geschichte der Kaiser-Wilhelm-Gesellschaft*, 2:653–666.

109. Lösch, *Rasse als Konstrukt*, p. 287.

110. Eugen Fischer and Gerhard Kittel, "Das antike Weltjudentum," *Forschungen zur Judenfrage* 7 (1943), pp. 1–236. The Fischer/Kittel piece consti-tuted this entire issue.

111. Robert P. Ericksen, *Theologians under Hitler: Gerhard Kittel, Paul Althaus, and Emanuel Hirsch*. (New Haven: Yale University Press, 1985).

112. Fischer and Kittel, "Das antike Weltjudentum," p. 10.

113. Ibid., p. 162.

114. Lösch, *Rasse als Konstrukt,* p. 340.
115. Fischer and Kittel, "Das antike Weltjudentum," p. 163.
116. Lösch, *Rasse als Konstrukt,* pp. 333, 378.
117. Walter Dornfeldt, "Studien über Schädelform und Schädelveränderung von Berliner Ostjuden und ihren Kindern" (Ph.D. diss., University of Berlin and Kaiser-Wilhelm-Institut für Anthropologie, menschliche Erblehre und Eugenik), published in *Zeitschrift für Morphologie und Anthropologie* 39, 2 (1941): 290–373.
118. Ibid., p. 295.
119. Ibid., p. 370.
120. Alexander Paul, "Jüdisch-deutsche Blutmischung: Eine sozial-biologische Untersuchung" (Ph.D. diss., University of Berlin, 1939), published in the series *Veröffentlichungen aus dem Gebiete des Volksgesundheitsdienstes* (Berlin: Richard Schoetz, 1940). Paul also published a short précis of his dissertation, "Erbbiologische Begleiterscheinungen bei jüdisch-deutscher Blutmischung," *Volk und Rasse* 16, 1 (January 1941): 34–36.
121. Paul, "Jüdisch-deutsche Blutmischung," p. 5.
122. Gisela Lemme, review of "Jüdisch-deutsche Blutmischung" by Alexander Paul, in *Archiv für Rassen- und Gesellschaftsbiologie,* 35, 4 (1941): 334–336.
123. Fritz Zschaeck, review of "Jüdisch-deutsche Blutmischung" by Alexander Paul, in *Weltkampf* (October–December 1941): 185–186.
124. Statistics on the *Mischling* population are contained in Meyer, *"Jüdische Mischlinge,"* pp. 162–165. Paul cited the census figure correctly.
125. Paul, "Erbbiologische Begleiterscheinungen," p. 35.
126. See, for example, Ernst Rodenwalt, "Vom Seelenkonflikt des Mischlings," *Zeitschrift für Morphologie und Anthropologie* 34 (1935): 364–375.
127. Paul, "Jüdisch-deutsche Blutmischung," pp. 102–105.
128. Ibid., pp. 159–160.
129. After extended internal debate and bureaucratic maneuvering, the regime decided against this, mainly out of concern over damaging the wartime morale of the "Aryan" relatives of the *Mischlinge.* Essner, *"Nürnberger Gesetze,"* pp. 384–444.
130. A standard work on this subject is Alexander Mitscherlich and Fred Mielke, *Medizin ohne Menschlichkeit: Dokumente des Nürnberger Ärzteprozesses,* rev. ed., (Frankfurt: Fischer, 1995). The work was originally published in 1948 as a report distributed to West Germany physicians.
131. Maria Teschler-Nicola and Margit Berner, "Die anthopologische Abteilung des naturhistorischen Museums in der NS-Zeit: Berichte und Dokumentation von Forschungs- und Sammlungsaktivitäten 1938–1945," unpublished manuscript, Abteilung für archäologische Biologie und Anthropologie, Naturhistorisches Museum, Vienna.

132. Claudia Spring, "Staatenloses Subjekt, vermessenes Objekt: Anthropologische Untersuchungen an staatenlosen Juden im September 1939," *Zeitgeschichte* 30, 3 (2003): 163–170.

133. Teschler-Nicola and Burner, "Anthropologische Abteilung," pp. 4–5.

134. "Das Posener Tagebuch des Anatomen Hermann Voss," in Götz Aly et al., eds., *Biedermann und Schreibtischtäter: Materialien zur deutschen Täter-Biographie* (Berlin: Rotbuch, 1987), diary entries for 26 April, 27 April, and 19 May 1942, and biographical sketch on pp. 15–21.

135. Elfriede Fliethmann, "Vorläufiger Bericht über anthropologische Aufnahmen an Judenfamilien in Tarnow," in *Deutsche Forschung im Osten: Mitteilungen des Instituts für Ostarbeit Krakau* 2 (1942): 92–111. The case is discussed in Götz Aly and Susanne Heim, *Vordenker der Vernichtung: Auschwitz und die Pläne für eine neue europäische Ordnung* (Hamburg: Hoffmann und Campe, 1991), pp. 198–202. For a critique of the methodologies employed in the study see Gretchen E. Schafft, *From Racism to Genocide: Anthropology in the Third Reich* (Chicago: University of Illinois Press, 2004), pp. 32–34.

136. The most detailed account is in Michael Kater, *Das "Ahnenerbe,"* pp. 245–255. The investigation and prosecution of the case is examined in Irmtrud Wojak, "Das 'irrende Gewissen' der NS-Verbrecher und die deutsche Rechtsprechung: Die 'jüdische Skelettsammlung' am Anatomischen Institut der 'Reichsuniversität Strassburg'," in Fritz-Bauer-Institut, ed., *"Beseitigung des jüdischen Einflusses,"* pp. 101–130. Several key documents are printed, in some cases in condensed form, in Mitscherlich and Mielke, *Medizin,* pp. 225–235. Original documents published in microfiche, in Klaus Dörner et al., eds., *Der Nürnberger Ärzteprozess 1946/47: Wortprotokolle, Anklage- und Verteidigungsmaterial, Quellen zum Umfeld* (Munich: Saur, 1999), fiches 169, 173–174, 189.

137. "Betr.: Sicherstellung der Schädel von jüdisch-bolschewistischen Kommissaren . . . ," NO-085, in Dörner et al., *Nürnberger Ärzteprozess,* fiche 169, frames 04325–04326.

138. Universities and museums are in the process of returning bones and other relics under the provisions of the Native American Graves Protection and Repatriation Act (NAGPRA). Extensive documentation available at www.cr.nps.gov/nagpra (accessed 4 April 2005).

139. For an account of a recent attempt to identify the victims selected for murder and preservation see Hans-Joachim Lang, *Die Namen der Nummern* (Hamburg: Hoffmann und Campe, 2004).

140. Theodor Mollison, "Das Anthropologische Institut der Universität München," in the "Kleine Beiträge" section of *Zeitschrift für Rassenkunde* 9 (1939): 275–277. Mollison was Fleischhacker's mentor at Munich.

141. Wojak, "Das irrende Gewissen," p. 114.

142. Hirt to Brandt, 5 September 1944, NO-088, in Dörner et al., *Nürnberger Ärzteprozess,* fiche 169, frame 04340.

143. For details of the legal proceedings and judgments see Wojak, "Das irrende Gewissen," pp. 112–119.

3. The Blood and Sins of Their Fathers

1. Adolf Hitler, *Mein Kampf,* translated by Ralph Manheim (Boston: Hougton Mifflin, 1971), p. 65.

2. Henry Wassermann, ed., *Bibliographie des jüdischen Schriftums in Deutschland, 1933–1943* (Munich: Sauer, 1989).

3. See especially Horst Junginger, *Von der philologischen zur völkischen Religionswissenschaft: Das Fach Religionswissenschaft an der Universität Tübingen von der Mitte des 19. Jahrhunderts bis Ende des Dritten Reiches* (Stuttgart: Franz Steiner, 1999).

4. On the neopagan movement in Weimar and Nazi Germany see Richard Steigmann-Gall, *The Holy Reich: Nazi Conceptions of Christianity* (Cambridge: Cambridge University Press, 2003).

5. Ibid., pp. 257–267; also numerous references to Otto Huth in Michael H. Kater, *Das "Ahnenerbe" der SS 1935–1945: Ein Beitrag zur Kulturpolitik des Dritten Reiches,* 3rd ed. (Munich: Oldenbourg, 2001).

6. See especially J. Wilhelm Hauer, ed., *Glaube und Blut: Beiträge zum Problem Religion und Rasse* (Leipzig: Boltze, 1938); Junginger, *Von der philologischen zur völkischen Religionswissenschaft,* pp. 192–193.

7. Susannah Heschel, "The Theological Faculty at the University of Jena as 'a Stronghold of National Socialism,'" in Uwe Hossfeld et al., eds., *"Kämpferische Wissenschaft": Studien zur Universität Jena im Nationalsozialismus* (Cologne: Böhlau, 2003), pp. 452–470, and "When Jesus Was an Aryan," in Robert P. Ericksen and Susannah Heschel, eds., *Betrayal: German Churches and the Holocaust* (Minneapolis: Fortress, 1999), pp. 68–89.

8. Walter Grundmann, *Jesus der Galiläer und das Judentum* (Leipzig: Wigarnd, 1940.)

9. Heschel, "When Jesus was an Aryan."

10. Leonore Siegele-Wenschkewitz, *Neutestamentliche Wissenschaft vor der Judenfrage: Gerhard Kittels theologische Arbeit im Wandel deutscher Geschichte* (Munich: Chr. Kaiser, 1980.)

11. Robert P. Ericksen, *Theologians under Hitler: Gerhard Kittel, Paul Althaus, and Emanuel Hirsch* (New Haven: Yale University Press, 1985).

12. This phase of Kittel's career is emphasized in Henry Wassermann, *False Start: Jewish Studies at German Universities during the Weimar Republic*

(Amherst, N.Y.: Humanity, 2003), pp. 171–201. I believe that Wassermann understates the racism of Kittel's Nazi-era writings.

13. Ericksen, *Theologians under Hitler,* pp. 74–76.
14. Ibid., p. 38.
15. Gerhard Kittel, *Die Judenfrage* (Stuttgart: Kohlhammer, 1933).
16. Ibid., pp. 10–11.
17. Ibid., p. 24.
18. Ibid., p. 13.
19. Ibid., p. 14.
20. Ibid., pp. 14–18.
21. Ibid., pp. 19–37.
22. Ibid., pp. 39–40.
23. Ibid., p. 40.
24. Ibid., p. 42.
25. On the Editors Law see Josef Wulf, *Presse und Funk im Dritten Reich: Eine Dokumention* (Frankfurt: Ullstein, 1982).
26. Kittel, *Die Judenfrage,* pp. 48–51. On purge of Jewish doctors see Michael Kater, *Doctors under Hitler* (Chapel Hill: University of North Carolina Press, 1989). On the purge of Jewish lawyers see Konrad H. Jarausch, *The Unfree Professions: German Lawyers, Teachers, and Engineers, 1900–1950* (Oxford: Oxford University Press, 1990).
27. Kittel, *Die Judenfrage,* p. 60.
28. Ibid., p. 57.
29. Ibid., p. 66.
30. Ibid., p. 70.
31. Ibid., p. 72.
32. Ericksen, *Theologians under Hitler,* p. 32.
33. Doris Bergen, *Twisted Cross: The German Christian Movement in the Third Reich* (Chapel Hill: University of North Carolina Press, 1996), p. 86.
34. Gerhard Kittel, "Die Entstehung des Judentums und die Entstehung der Judenfrage," *Forschungen zur Judenfrage* 1 (1936): 43–63.
35. Ibid., p. 43.
36. Ibid., p. 63.
37. Ibid., p. 44, n. 3.
38. Kittel embraced Günther's emphasis on the racial impact of the conversion to Judaism of the Khazars in the eighth century. Ibid., p. 49, n. 4.
39. Note the positive treatment of Strack in the *Encyclopedia Judaica* (Jerusalem: Keter, 1971), vol. 15, pp. 418–419. See also Alan T. Levenson, *Between Philosemitism and Antisemitism: Defenses of Jews and Judaism in Germany, 1871–1932* (Lincoln: University of Nebraska Press, 2004).
40. Kittel, "Entstehung," pp. 44–51.

41. Ibid., pp. 51–56. Note also Kittel's citations to Strack-Billerbeck on pp. 49, 53, 54, and 58.

42. Ibid., pp. 56–59; quoted passage is on pp. 57–58.

43. Gerhard Kittel, "Das Konnubium mit den Nicht-Juden im antiken Judentum," *Forschungen zur Judenfrage* 2 (1937): 30–62. Kittel published another article in 1937 containing the same argument, but without the documentation. See Gerhard Kittel, "Das Urteil über die Rassenmischung im Judentum und in der biblischen Religion," *Die Biologie* 6, 1 (1937): 342–352.

44. Gerhard Kittel, "Die ältesten Juden-Karikaturen. Die 'Trierer Terrakotten,'" *Forschungen zur Judenfrage* 4 (1940): 254–258.

45. Eugen Fischer and Gerhard Kittel, "Das Antike Weltjudentum," *Forschungen zur Judenfrage* 7 (1943): 1–225. Fischer's contribution is discussed in Chapter 2.

46. Ibid., p. 5.

47. Gerhard Kittel, "Die Behandlung des Nichtjuden nach dem Talmud," *Archiv für Judenfragen* (1943): 7–17.

48. Ibid., p. 7.

49. Article on Sanhedrin, *Encyclopedia Judaica*, 14:839.

50. Kittel, "Behandlung," p. 11.

51. Relevant material in Bundesarchiv Berlin, Bestand R55, records of the Reichsministerium für Volksaufklärung und Propaganda, files 373 and 841.

52. Max Weinreich, *Hitler's Professors: The Part of Scholarship in Hitler's Crimes against the Jewish People* (New York: YIVO, 1946; reprint, New Haven: Yale University Press, 1999), p. 216, suggests that Kittel already had knowledge of the killings, but Ericksen, *Theologians under Hitler*, p. 67, calls this into question.

53. For an especially useful explanation of the nature of the Talmud and the potential pitfalls of misinterpretation, see *The Steinsaltz Talmud: A Reference Guide* (New York: Random House, 1996), pp. 92–93.

54. Quoted in Ericksen, *Theologians under Hitler*, p. 51.

55. The most detailed analysis of this genre is Hannelore Noack, *Unbelehrbar? Antijüdische Agitation mit entstellten Talmudzitaten* (Paderborn: University Press of Paderborn, 2004).

56. Erich Bischoff, *Das Buch vom Schulchan Aruch* (Leipzig: Hammer-Verlag, 1929).

57. Dennis Showalter, *"Little Man, What Now?" Der Stürmer in the Weimar Republic* (Hamden, Conn.: Archon, 1982); Fred Hahn, ed., *Lieber Stürmer: Leserbriefe an das NS-Kampfblatt 1924 bis 1945* (Stuttgart: Seewald, 1978). For an insightful analysis of *Stürmer* propaganda see Dirk Rupnow, "'Der Judenmord': Bausteine zur Lektüre eines Stürmer-Artikels," in *Jahrbuch*

des Nürnberger Instituts für NS-Forschung und jüdische Geschichte des 20. Jahrhunderts (2002): 38–52.

58. E.g., Johannes Pohl, "Der Talmud," *Nationalsozialistsche Monatshefte* 10 (March 1939): 226–237.

59. Walter Fasolt, *Papstherrschaft: Der Machtkampf des Priesters* (Breslau: Pötsch, 1937).

60. Gerhard Utikal, *Der jüdische Ritualmord: Eine nichtjüdische Klarstellung* (Berlin: Pötsch, 1935). The quotations are drawn from an advertisement for the book appearing at the end of Fasolt, *Papstherrschaft.*

61. The following biographical information on Kuhn is drawn from "Spruch," Staatskommissariat für die politische Säuberung Tübingen-Lustnau, Spruchkammer für den Lehrkörper der Universität Tübingen, 18 October 1948, and "Spruch," Spruchkammer 7 Stgt.-Feuerbach, 21 September 1948. University of Heidelberg Archive (UAH), PA 4717 (K. G. Kuhn). I am grateful to Professor Steven Remy for providing me access to his copy of Kuhn's Heidelberg personnel file.

62. Helmut Heiber, *Walter Frank und sein Reichsinstitut für Geschichte des neuen Deutschlands* (Stuttgart: Deutsche Verlogs-Anstalt, 1966), pp. 453–455.

63. See Horst Junginger, *Von der philologischen zur völkischen Religionswissenschaft,* app. 5, pp. 322–328, for a semester-by-semester list of courses on religion offered at Tübingen.

64. Fritz Werner, "Das Judentumsbild der Spätjudentumsforschung im Dritten Reich," *Kairos* 13 (1971): 161–194.

65. Hermann Schroer, *Blut und Geld im Judentum. Dargestellt am jüdischen Recht (Schulchan Aruch)* (Munich: Hoheneichen, 1936).

66. Ibid., p. xii.

67. Karl Georg Kuhn, review of *Blut und Geld im Judentum* by Hermann Schroer, *Historische Zeitschrift* 156 (1937): 313–316.

68. Karl Georg Kuhn, "Die Entstehung des talmudischen Denkens," *Forschungen zur Judenfrage* 1 (1936): 64–80.

69. Ibid., pp. 64–65.

70. Ibid., p. 66.

71. Ibid., pp. 66–67.

72. Ibid., pp. 67–69.

73. Ibid., p. 79.

74. Ibid., pp. 72–74.

75. Ibid., p. 78.

76. Ibid., p. 74.

77. Ibid., p. 80.

78. Karl Georg Kuhn, "Weltjudentum in der Antike," *Forschungen zur Judenfrage* 2 (1937): 9–29.

79. Ibid., p. 9.
80. Ibid., p. 13.
81. Ibid., pp. 24–25.
82. Ibid., pp. 15–18.
83. Ibid., pp. 18–23.
84. Ibid., pp. 25–27.
85. Ibid., p. 29.
86. Karl Georg Kuhn, "Ursprung und Wesen der talmudischen Einstellung zum Nichtjuden," *Forschungen zur Judenfrage* 3 (1938): 199–234.
87. Ibid., p. 203.
88. Ibid., pp. 205, 211.
89. Ibid., p. 214.
90. Ibid., pp. 214–215.
91. Ibid., pp. 210–212, 216–234.
92. Ibid., p. 229.
93. Ibid., p. 234.
94. Karl Georg Kuhn, *Die Judenfrage als weltgeschichtliches Problem* (Hamburg: Hanseatische Verlagsanstalt, 1939).
95. "Die Gedenkakrobatik des Talmuds," *Völkischer Beobachter,* 21 January 1939.
96. Kuhn, *Die Judenfrage als weltgeschichtliches Problem,* pp. 5–6.
97. Ibid., p. 8.
98. Ibid., pp. 21–26.
99. Ibid., pp. 21–22.
100. Ibid., pp. 29, 33.
101. Ibid., pp. 46–47.
102. The following account is based mainly on Philip Friedman, "The Karaites under Nazi Rule," *Roads to Extinction: Essays on the Holocaust* (New York: Jewish Publication Society of America, 1980), pp. 153–175. The article originally appeared in 1960. Friedman mentions Kuhn's memorandum in a note. See also Martin Broszat, "Behandlung der jüdischen Sekte der Karaiten (Krim) im Rahmen der nationalsozialistischen Judenverfolgung," in *Gutachten des Instituts für Zeitgeschichte* (Stuttgart: Deutsche Verlags-Anstalt, 1966), vol. 2, pp. 2–43. Nazi authorities had solicited scholarly opinions on several such groups on the margins of Jewry. See Patricia von Papen, "Schützenhilfe nationalsozialistischer Judenpolitik: Die 'Judenforschung' des 'Reichsinstituts für Geschichte des neuen Deutschlands' 1935–1945," in Fritz Bauer Institute, ed., *"Beseitigung des jüdischen Einflusses . . ." Antisemitische Forschung, Eliten und Karrieren im Nationalsozialismus* (Frankfurt, Campus, 1999), p. 32.
103. These included Philipp Friedman in Lwow and Zelig Kalmanovitch in Vilna.

104. Kuhn's memorandum could not be located. Its contents are reported in "Spruch," Staatskommissariat für die politische Säuberung Tübingen-Lustnau, Spruchkammer für den Lehrkörper der Universität Tübingen, 21 September 1948, UAH, PA 4717 (K. G. Kuhn). Kuhn's participation as a consultant for the Reich Ministry for the Occupied Eastern Territories is noted in "Vermerk," 3 June 1942, Bundesarchiv Berlin, R6 (RMfdbO)/142.

105. Junginger, *Von der philologischen zur völkischen Religionswissenschaft,* p. 328.

106. The following is based largely on the two Spruchkammer files noted above. An abbreviated account of the story appears in Steven P. Remy, *The Heidelberg Myth: The Nazification and Denazification of a German University* (Cambridge, Mass.: Harvard University Press, 2002), pp. 221–222.

107. Dekan to Nied. Kultusminister, 3 March 1949, UAH, PA 4717 (K. G. Kuhn).

108. Letter to Kultusmin. Baden-Württemberg, 1 March 1954, UAH, PA 4717 (K. G. Kuhn).

109. Karl Georg Kuhn, "Widerruf," *Evangelische Theologie* 2 (1951/52), reproduced in Rolf Seeliger, ed., *Braune Universität: Dokumentation mit Stellungnahmen* (Munich: Seeliger, 1968), p. 53.

110. Seeliger, *Braune Universität,* p. 55.

111. Gert Jeremias, Heinz-Wolfgang Kuhn, and Hartmut Stegman, eds., *Tradition und Glaube: Das frühe Christentum in seiner Umwelt* (Göttingen: Vandenhoeck und Ruprecht, 1971).

112. See e.g. *Kürschners Deutscher Gelehrten-Kalender 1970* (Berlin: de Gruyter, 1970), p. 1643.

4. Dissimilation through Scholarship

1. Claudia Koonz, *The Nazi Conscience* (Cambridge, Mass.: Harvard University Press, 2003), p. 209.

2. Christhard Hoffmann, "Wissenschaft des Judentums in der Weimarer Republik und im 'Dritten Reich,'" in Michael Brenner and Stefan Rohrbacher, eds., *Wissenschaft vom Judentum: Annäherungen nach dem Holocaust* (Göttingen: Vandenhoeck und Ruprecht, 2000), pp. 25–41. See also Henry Wassermann, ed., *Bibliographie des jüdischen schriftums in Deutschland, 1933–1943* (Munich: Sauer, 1989), pp. xi–xxvii.

3. The following information is drawn from the *Jahresberichte für deutsche Geschichte,* vols. 9–13, 1933–1937 (Leipzig: Kohler, 1936–1939).

4. Frank, *Deutsche Wissenschaft und Judenfrage* (Hamburg: Hanseatische Verlagsanstalt, 1937), p. 9.

5. Although von Müller was a key figure among academic historians in the Third Reich, we lack a full-scale, critical study of his life and career. For a brief biological sketch see Rüdiger Hohls and Konrad H. Jarausch, eds.,

Versäumte Fragen: Deutsche Historiker im Schatten des Nationalsozialismus (Stuttgart: Deutsche Verlags-Anstalt, 2000), p. 464.

6. Frank, *Deutsche Wissenschaft und Judenfrage*, pp. 24–25.

7. Ibid., p. 29.

8. Wilhelm Grau, *Die Erforschung der Judenfrage: Aufgabe und Organisation*, (Munich: Hoheneichen, 1943), pp. 14–15. The piece was originally published September 1935 in *Deutsches Volkstum*.

9. Frank, *Deutsche Wissenschaft und Judenfrage*, p. 30.

10. Helmut Heiber, *Walter Frank und sein Reichsinstitut für Geschichte des neuen Deutschlands* (Stuttgart: Deutsche Verlags-Anstalt, 1966), p. 26.

11. Ibid., pp. 938–1225.

12. Walter Frank, *Hofprediger Adolf Stoecker und die christsoziale Bewegung*, 2nd ed. (Hamburg: Hanseatische Verlagsanstalt, 1935).

13. Ibid., p. 9.

14. For example Richard S. Levy, *The Downfall of the Anti-Semitic Political Parties in Imperial Germany* (New Haven: Yale University Press, 1975), pp. 269, n. 30, and 271, n. 55; Shulamit Volkov, *The Rise of Popular Antimodernism in Germany: The Urban Master Artisans, 1873–1896* (Princeton: Princeton University Press, 1978), p. 220; Peter G. J. Pulzer, *The Rise of Political Anti-Semitism in Austria and Germany*, rev. ed. (London: Halban, 1988), p. 119, n. 2. In his annotated bibliography, p. 341, Pulzer refers to Frank's book as a "standard work" on Stoecker.

15. Frank, *Hofprediger Adolf Stoecker*, pp. 74–75.

16. Ibid., p. 75.

17. Walter Frank, *Nationalismus und Demokratie im Frankreich der dritten Republik (1871 bis 1918)* (Hamburg: Hanseatische Verlagsanstalt, 1933).

18. Walter Frank, *Händler und Soldaten: Frankreich und die Judenfrage in der "Affäre Dreyfus"* (Hamburg: Deutsche Hausbücherei, 1933).

19. For an overview of Grau's career see Patricia von Papen, "Vom engagierten Katholiken zum Rassenantisemiten: Die Karriere des Historikers 'der Judenfrage' Wilhlem Grau, 1935–1945," in Georg Denzler and Leonore Siegele-Wenschkewitz, eds., *Theologische Wissenschaft im "Dritten Reich"* (Frankfurt: Haag und Herchen, 2000), pp. 68–113.

20. Wilhelm Grau, *Antisemitismus im späten Mittelalter. Das Ende der Regensburger Judengemeinde, 1450–1519* (Munich: Duncker und Humblot, 1934).

21. On the complex question of the relationship of pre-1945 *Volksgeschichte* to postwar *Sozialgeschichte* see Willi Oberkrome, "Zur Kontinuität ethnozentrischer Geschichtswissenschaft nach 1945," *Zeitschrift für Geschichtswissenschaft* 49, 1 (2001): 50–61.

22. Raphael Straus, "Antisemitismus im Mittelalter. Ein Wort pro domo," *Zeitschrift für die Geschichte der Juden in Deutschland* 6 (1935): 17–24, and Wilhelm Grau, "Antisemitismus im Mittelalter. Ein Wort contra Rafael

Straus," *Zeitschrift für die Geschichte der Juden in Deutschland* 6 (1935): 186–198.

23. Wilhelm Grau, *Wilhelm von Humboldt und das Problem des Juden* (Hamburg: Hanseatische Verlagsanstalt, 1935).

24. Ibid., pp. 9–10.

25. Ibid., p. 9.

26. Ibid., pp. 13–14.

27. Ibid., p. 17.

28. Ibid., pp. 41–55.

29. Papen, "Vom engagierten Katholiken zum Rassenantisemiten," pp. 111–113.

30. Wilhelm Grau, *Die geschichtlichen Lösungsversuche der Judenfrage* (Munich: Heneichen, 1943). The pamphlet appeared in the series "Kleine Weltkampfbücherei," the stated intention of which was to elucidate "open questions about the ideological and historical problem of the Jewish question and its solution."

31. Klaus Schickert, *Die Judenfrage in Ungarn: Jüdische Assimilation und antisemitische Bewegung im 19. und 20. Jahrhundert* (Essen: Essener Verlagsanstalt, 1937).

32. Ibid., note inside of front cover.

33. Ibid., p. 7.

34. Ibid., pp. 12–13.

35. Ibid., pp. 30–31.

36. Ibid., p. 88.

37. Ibid., p. 102.

38. Ibid., p. 106.

39. Klaus Schickert, *Die Judenfrage in Ungarn: Jüdische Assimilation und antisemitische Bewegung im 19. und 20. Jahrhundert*, 2nd ed., (Essen: Essener Verlagsanstalt, 1943).

40. Ibid., p. 296.

41. This was related to a falling out between Frank and Grau. See Papen, "Vom engagierten Katholiken zum Rassenantisemiten," pp. 90–102.

42. Ursula Wiggershaus-Müller, *Nationalsozialismus und Geschichtswissenschaft: Die Geschichte der Historischen Zeitschrift und des Historischen Jahrbuchs 1933–1945*, 2nd ed. (Hambug: Kovac, 2000), pp. 128–133.

43. Wilhelm Grau, "Geschichte der Judenfrage," *Historische Zeitschrift* 153 (1936): 336–349.

44. Ibid., p. 336.

45. Abraham Heller, *Die Lage der Juden in Russland von der Märzrevolution 1917 bis zur Gegenwart*, Schriften der Gesellschaft zur Förderung der Wissenschaft des Judentums 39 (Breslau: Marcus, 1935).

46. Grau, "Geschichte der Judenfrage," p. 337.

47. Ibid., p. 337.

48. Ibid., p. 339.
49. Ibid., p. 342.
50. Ismar Elbogen, *Geschichte der Juden in Deutschland* (Berlin: Lichtenstein, 1935).
51. Grau, "Geschichte der Judenfrage," 343.
52. *Germania Judaica: Von der ältesten Zeit bis 1238* (Breslau: Marcus, 1934).
53. *Kürschners Deutscher Gelehrten-Kalender 1940* (Berlin: de Gruyter, 1940), p. 1558.
54. *Historische Zeitschrift* 154 (1936): 104–107.
55. *Historische Zeitschrift* 154 (1936): 572–590.
56. Biographical information on Euler in Heiber, *Walter Frank*, p. 446.
57. Wilfried Euler, "Das Eindringen jüdischen Blutes in die englische Oberschicht," *Forschungen zur Judenfrage* 6 (1941): 104–252.
58. Ibid., p. 250.
59. See, for example, the acknowledgments of Euler in Dolores L. Augustine, *Patricians and Parvenus: Wealth and High Society in Wilhelmine Germany* (Oxford: Berg, 1994), p. xii, and Werner E. Mosse, *The German-Jewish Economic Elite, 1820–1935: A Socio-Cultural Profile* (Oxford: Clarendon, 1989), p. vii.
60. Papen, "Vom engagierten Katholiken zum Rassenantisemiten," p. 111. Euler's Institut zur Erforschung historischer Führungsschichten in Bensheim is known today as the Friedrich-Wilhelm-Euler-Gesellschaft für personengeschichtliche Forschung.
61. For biographical details on Craemer, who died in 1941, see Heiber, *Walter Frank*, pp. 459–460. On his connection with the much more well-known Rothfels students Theodor Schieder and Werner Conze, see Ingo Haar, "Die Genesis der Endlösung aus dem Geiste der Wissenschaften: Volksgeschichte und Bevölkerungspolitik im Nationalsozialismus," *Zeitschrift für Geschichtswissenschaft* 49, 1 (2001): 13–31, p. 21.
62. Rudolf Craemer, "Benjamin Disraeli," *Forschungen zur Judenfrage* 5 (1941): 22–147. On Disraeli see Todd M. Endelman and Tony Kushner, eds., *Disraeli's Jewishness* (London: Vallentine Mitchell, 2002).
63. *Historische Zeitschrift* 157 (1938): 546–557.
64. Ibid., pp. 547–548.
65. Johannes Heckel, "Der Einbruch des jüdischen Geistes in das deutsche Staats- und Kirchenrecht durch Friedrich Julius Stahl," *Historische Zeitschrift* 155 (1937): 506–541. Heckel had published an earlier version in *Forschungen zur Judenfrage* 1 (1937): 110–136.
66. Heckel was coeditor of the "Kirchenrechtliche Abhandlungen," a leading publication in his field. *Kürschners Deutscher Gelehrten-Kalender 1940*, p. 502.
67. Heckel, "Einbruch," p. 516.

68. Ibid., pp. 533–535. For a thorough discussion of antisemitic legal thinking in the Third Reich see Raphael Gross, *Carl Schmitt und die Juden* (Frankfurt: Suhrkamp, 2005).

69. Josef Müller, "Die Entwicklung des Rassenantisemitismus in den letzten Jahrzehnten des 19. Jahrhunderts. Dargestellt hauptsächlich auf der Grundlage der 'Antisemitischen Correspondenz' " (Ph.D. diss., University of Marburg, 1939).

70. Irmgard Müller, "Saphir in München: Eine Untersuchung über das Eindringen und den Einfluss jüdischer Journalisten in dem Münchener Pressewesen 1825–1835" (Ph.D. diss., University of Munich, 1939).

71. Margarete Dierks, "Die preussischen Altkonservativen und die Judenfrage, 1810–1847" (Ph.D. diss., University of Rostock, 1938) (Rostock: Hinstorff, 1939).

72. Hans Pieper, "Die Judenschaft in Münster (Westfalen) im Ablauf des 19. Jahrhunderts (unter besonderer Berücksichtigung freimaurerischer Einflüsse" (Ph.D. diss., University of Münster, 1938).

73. Eckhard Günther, "Das Judentum in Mainfranken" (Ph.D. diss., University of Würzburg, 1942).

74. Hans Schuster, "Die Judenfrage in Rumänien" (Ph.D. diss., University of Leipzig, 1939).

75. Waltraute Sixta, "Josef Unger als Sprechminister, 1871 bis 1879" (Ph.D. diss., University of Vienna, 1941).

76. Frank, *Deutsche Wissenschaft und Judenfrage*, p. 10.

77. On Sommerfeldt's role in the *Institut für deutsche Ostarbeit*, see Michael Burleigh, *Germany Turns Eastwards: A Study of Ostforschung in the Third Reich*, (Cambridge: Cambridge University Press, 1988), pp. 272–274.

78. Josef Sommerfeldt, ed., *Hie Bürger, Hie Jude: Eine Krakauer Kampfschrift aus dem Jahr 1618* (Cracow: Burgverlag, 1941).

79. Ibid., p. 86.

80. Ibid., p. 87.

81. Ibid., p. 87.

82. Josef Sommerfeldt, "Die Judenfrage als Verwaltungsproblem in Südpreussen" (Ph.D. diss., University of Berlin, 1942).

83. Ibid., p. 196.

84. Ibid., pp. 198–199.

85. Volkmar Eichstädt, *Bibliographie zur Geschichte der Judenfrage*, vol. 1, *1750–1848* (Hamburg: Hanseatische Verlagsanstalt, 1938).

86. Volkmar Eichstädt, "Die Judenfrage in deutschland," in Albert Brackmann and Fritz Hartung, eds., *Jahresberichte für deutsche Geschichte: 1936* (Leipzig: Koehler, 1937), pp. 338–343, and *1937* (Leipzig: Koehler, 1939), pp. 361–366.

87. Eichstädt, "Die Judenfrage in Deutschland," p. 343.

88. Eichstädt, *Bibliographie zur Geschichte der Judenfrage*, reprint ed. (Westmead, England: Gregg International, 1969).

89. Volkmar Eichstädt, "Das Schriftum zur Judenfrage in den deutschen Bibliotheken," *Forschungen zur Judenfrage* 6 (1941): 253–264.

90. Ibid., pp. 253–255.

91. Ibid.

92. Ibid., p. 263.

93. The fields of library science and library history have produced a significant body of scholarly literature, mainly articles, on the Nazi plunder of Jewish libraries. The most comprehensive overview is Dov Schidorsky, "Das Schicksal jüdischer Bibliotheken im Dritten Reich," in Peter Vodosek and Manfred Komorowski, eds., *Bibliotheken während des Nationalsozialismus*, vol. 2 (Wiesbaden: Harrassowitz, 1992), pp. 189–217.

94. The basic work on Rosenberg remains Reinhard Bollmus, *Das Amt Rosenberg und seine Gegner: Zum Machtkampf im nationalsozialistischen Herrschaftssystem* (Stuttgart: Deutsche Verlags-Anstalt, 1970).

95. The following biographical sketch of Pohl is drawn from Maria Kühn-Ludewig, *Johannes Pohl (1904–1960). Judaist und Bibliothekar im Dienste Rosenbergs: Eine biographische Dokumentation* (Hannover: Laurentius, 2000).

96. This is Kühn-Ludewig's interpretation in *Johannes Pohl*.

97. Memorandum by Pohl, 12 July 1943, in *Trial of the Major War Criminals before the International Military Tribunal*, 42 vols. (Nuremberg: International Military Tribunal, 1948), vol. 25, pp. 242–46, document 171-PS.

98. Martin Granzin, "Die Kiewer 'Jüdische Sektion' (Sammlung jüdischer Akten)," *Weltkampf* (October–December 1942): 300–304.

99. David E. Fishman, *Embers Plucked from the Fire* (New York: YIVO, 1996).

100. Herman Kruk, *Togbukh fun vilner geto* (New York: YIVO, 1961). Excerpted passages translated into English have been published as Herman Kruk, "Diary of the Vilna Ghetto," *YIVO Annual of Jewish Social Science* 13 (1965): 9–78. I have relied mainly on the translations from Yiddish into German provided in Kühn-Ludewig, *Johannes Pohl*, pp. 187–196.

101. The diary has been partially published as Zelig Kalmanovitch, "A Diary of the Nazi Ghetto in Vilna," *YIVO Annual of Jewish Social Science* 8 (1953): 9–81.

102. Kruk, "Diary of the Vilna Ghetto," entries for 19 February, 3 March, 23 April 1942.

103. Ibid., 19 May 1942.

104. Johannes Pohl, "Die jiddische Presse in Südafrika," *Zentralblatt für Bibliothekswesen* 60 (1943/44): 168–170. Kühn-Ludewig, *Johannes Pohl*, p. 263, notes that Kalmanovitch produced the translation, but according to Kalmanovich, *Diary*, entry for 19 May 1942, the translator was Leo Bernstein.

105. Kalmanovitch, *Diary*, 18 June, 13 July, and 21 August 1942.

106. Ibid., 25 April 1943.

107. Kalmanovitch, *Diary*, 2 August and 13 August 1942.

108. Schidorsky, "Schicksal jüdischer Bibliotheken," p. 207.

109. Fishman, *Embers*, p. 23.

110. On the Vienna case, see Richard Hacken, "The Jewish Community Library in Vienna: From Dispersion and Destruction to Partial Restoration," *Leo Baeck Institute Yearbook* 47 (2002): 151–172, and Otto Seifert, "Bücherverwertungsstelle Wien 1, Dorotheergasse 12," *Jahrbuch des Dokumentationsarchiv des österreichischen Widerstandes* (1998): 88–94.

111. Schidorsky, "Schicksal jüdischer Bibliotheken," pp. 194–196.

112. See the important anthologies Peter Schöttler, ed., *Geschichtsschreibung als Legitimationswissenschaft, 1918–1945* (Frankfurt: Suhrkamp, 1997), and Winfried Schulze and Otto Gerhard Oexle, eds., *Deutsche Historiker im Nationalsozialismus* (Frankfurt: Fischer, 1999). Significant monographs on this subject are Ingo Haar, *Historiker im Nationalsozialismus: Deutsche Geschichtswissenschaft und der "Volkstumskampf" im Osten* (Göttingen: Vandenhoeck und Ruprecht, 2000), and Michael Fahlbusch, *Wissenschaft im Dienst der nationalsozialistischen Politik?* (Baden-Baden: Nomos, 1999). For an insightful overview of the controversy see Konrad H. Jarausch, "Unasked Questions: The Controversy about Nazi Collaboration among German Historians," in Jeffrey M. Diefendorf, ed., *Lessons and Legacies*, vol. 6: *New Currents in Holocaust Research* (Evanston, Ill.: Northwestern University Press, 2004), pp. 190–208.

113. Ingo Haar has explored the antisemitic dimension of Ostforschung in "Deutsche 'Ostforschung' und Antisemitismus," *Zeitschrift für Geschichtswissenschaft* 48, 6 (2000): 485–508, and "Genesis der Endlösung."

114. Götz Aly, "Theodor Schieder, Werner Conze oder die Vorstufe der physischen Vernichtung," in Schulze and Oexle, *Deutscher Historiker im Nationalsozialismus*, pp. 163–182, 172–174.

115. Angelika Ebbinghaus and Karl Heinz Roth, "Vorläufer des 'Generalplans Ost.' Eine Dokumentation über Theodor Schieders Polendenkschrift vom 7. Oktober 1939," *1999: Zeitschrift für Sozialgeschichte des 20. und 21. Jahrhunderts* 7, 1 (1992): 62–91; p. 71, n. 34.

5.   Pathologizing the Jew

1. Michael B. Hart *Social Science and the Politics of Modern Jewish Identity*, (Stanford: Stanford University Press, 2000).

2. Götz Aly and Karl-Heinz Roth, *Die restlose Erfassung: Volkszählen, Identifizieren, Aussondern im Nationalsozialismus*, rev. ed. (Frankfurt: Fischer Taschenbuch Verlag, 2000).

3. Statistisches Reichsamt, *Volkszählung: Die Bevölkerung des Deutschen Reichs nach den Ergebnissen der Volkszählung 1933*, vol. 5: *Die Glaubensjuden im Deutschen Reich* (Berlin: Verlag für Sozialpolitik, Wirtscahft und Statistik, 1936).

4. Aly and Roth, *Restlose Erfassung*, pp. 36–39.

5. Friedrich Burgdörfer, "Die Juden in Deutschland und in der Welt: Ein statistischer Beitrag zur biologischen, beruflichen, und sozialen Struktur des Judentums in Deutschland," *Forschungen zur Judenfrage* 3 (1938): 152–198.

6. Ibid., pp. 152–155.

7. Ibid., pp. 170–171.

8. Aly and Roth, *Restlose Erfassung*, p. 70.

9. Burgdörfer, "Die Juden in Deutschland," pp. 187–188.

10. Ibid., p. 182.

11. Werner T. Angress, "Das deutsche Militär und die Juden im ersten Weltkrieg," *Militärgeschichtliche Mitteilungen* 19 (1976): 77–146.

12. Burgdörfer, "Die Juden in Deutschland," p. 184 (his assertion), app. illus. 9 ("Frauenüberschuss"), and p. 183, table 8 (age cohorts).

13. Ibid., p. 186. Felix Teilhaber, *Der Untergang der deutschen Juden*, 2nd ed. (Berlin: Jüdischer Verlag, 1921). On Teilhaber see Hart, *Social Science*.

14. Burgdörfer, "Die Juden in Deutschland," pp. 162–167.

15. Fritz Arlt, *Volksbiologische Untersuchungen über die Juden in Leipzig* (Leipzig: Hirzel, 1938), published as 4. Beiheft zum Archiv für Bevölkerungswissenschaft und Bevölkerungspolitik, 7, vol. 7.

16. Fritz Arlt, "Das schlesische Landesamt für Rassen-, Sippen-, und Bevölkerungswesen," *Zeitschrift für Rassenkunde* 9 (1939): 284.

17. Götz Aly and Susanne Heim, *Vordenker der Vernichtung: Auschwitz und die deutschen Pläne für eine neue europäische Ordnung* (Hamburg: Hoffman und Campe, 1991). Arlt published an apologetic autobiography in response to Aly and Heim: Fritz Arlt, *Polen-Ukrainer-Juden-Politik* (Lindhorst: Taege, 1995).

18. Arlt, *Volksbiologische Untersuchungen*, p. 5.

19. Ibid., p. 5.

20. Ibid., pp. 7–8.

21. Ibid., p. 17.

22. Ibid., p. 20.

23. Ibid., p. 21.

24. A. Harrasser, review of *Volksbiologische Untersuchungen* by Fritz Arlt, *Archiv für Rassen-und Gesellschaftsbiologie* 32, 2 (1938): 183–184.

25. Arlt, *Volksbiologische Untersuchungen*, p. 24.

26. Ibid., p. 23.

27. Ibid., p. 23.

28. Ibid., p. 29.
29. Ibid., p. 32.
30. Rudolf Euler, "Zur Frage der jüdischen Durchsetzung innerhalb der ländlichen Bezirke Kurhessens," *Archiv für Rassen- und Gesellschaftsbiologie* 29, 1 (1935): 73–82.
31. Ibid., p. 76.
32. Ibid., p. 76.
33. Ibid., pp. 76–77.
34. Ibid., p. 80.
35. Ibid., p. 81.
36. Theodor Deneke, "Berufswahl und Volkscharakter der Juden," *Archiv für Rassen- und Gesellschaftsbiologie* 29, 4 (1935): 437–458.
37. Ibid., p. 451.
38. Edeltraut Bienek, "Statistik über die Todesursachen bei der jüdischen Bevölkerung von Breslau in den Jahren 1928–1937," *Archiv für Rassen- und Gesellschaftsbiologie* 34, 2 (1940): 126–154.
39. Ibid., p. 131.
40. Ibid., p. 138.
41. Ibid., pp. 152–153.
42. As was common in Nazi Germany, Bienek used an asterisk to designate Jewish-authored works appearing in her bibliography. While Auerbach and Fishberg are marked as Jews, Bienek neglected to include the asterisk for Weissenberg.
43. Bienek, "Statistik," p. 153.
44. Ibid., pp. 142–143.
45. Ibid., p. 153.
46. Daluege quoted on p. 53 of Robert G. Waite, "'Judentum und Kriminalität': Rassistische Deutungen in kriminologischen Publikationen 1933–1945," in Manfred Weissbecker and Reinhard Kühnl, eds., *Rassismus, Faschismus, Antifaschismus: Forschungen und Betrachtungen gewidmet Kurt Pätzold zum 70. Geburtstag* (Cologne: PapyRossa, 2000), pp. 46–62. Paradoxically, a book published the following year by Daluege, *Nationalsozialistischer Kampf gegen das Verbrechertum* (Munich: Eher, 1936), does not address Jewish criminality in any systematic way, although it does specify the Jewish background of some of the criminals discussed.
47. Collection of Institut zur Erforschung der Judenfrage, YIVO Institute archives, New York, Folder 54. The contents of the files suggest that much of the information was derived from articles in *Der Stürmer*, the vicious antisemitic newspaper published by Julius Streicher.
48. Richard F. Wetzell, *Inventing the Criminal: A History of German Criminology, 1880–1945* (Chapel Hill: University of North Carolina Press, 2000);

and "Kriminalbiologische Forschung an der deutschen Forschungsanstalt für Psychiatrie in der Weimarer Republik und im Nationalsozialismus," in Hans-Walter Schmuhl, ed., *Rassenforschung an Kaiser-Wilhelm-Instituten vor und nach 1933* (Göttingen: Wallstein, 2003), pp. 68–98.

49. Wetzell, *Inventing the Criminal*. Among the many works on Lombroso is the useful recent Mary Gibson, *Born to Crime: Cesare Lombroso and the Origins of Biological Criminology* (Westport, Conn.: Praeger, 2002).

50. Max Mikorey, "Das Judentum in der Kriminalpsychologie," in *Das Judentum in der Rechtswissenschaft*, vol. 3, *Judentum und Verbrechen* (Berlin: Deutscher Rechts-Verlag, 1936). For a more detailed assessment see Wetzell, *Inventing the Criminal*, pp. 188–190.

51. Rolf Seeliger, *Braune Universität: Deutsche Hochschullehrer gestern und heute* (Munich: Seeliger, 1964), 1964, pp. 46–47.

52. J. Keller and Hanns Andersen, *Der Jude als Verbrecher* (Berlin: Nibelungen, 1942).

53. Keller had written articles on the "Jewish question" for the Nazi newspaper *Völkischer Beobachter*, the SS publication *Das Schwarze Korps*, and Joseph Goebbels's newspaper *Angriff*. He died slightly before *The Jew as Criminal* appeared. See the "Nachruf in Keller and Anderson, *Der Jude*," pp. 211–212.

54. Keller and Anderson, *Der Jude*, p. 9.

55. On von Leers see the following three articles in Uwe Hossfeld, Jürgen John, and Rüdiger Stutz, eds., *"Kämpferische Wissenschaft": Studien zur Universität Jena im Nationalsozialismus* (Cologne: Böhlau, 2003): Herbert Gottwald, "Die Jenaer Geschichtswissenschaft in der Zeit des Nationalsozialismus," pp. 913–942; Willy Schilling, "NS-Dozentenschaft und Nationalsozialistischer Deutscher Dozentenbund an der Universität Jena," pp. 180–201, especially pp. 192–197; and Annett Hamann, "'Männer der Kämpfenden Wissenschaft': Die 1945 geschlossenen NS-Institute der Universität Jena," pp. 202–234, especially pp. 210–213.

56. The conference is described in Horst Göppinger, *Juristen jüdischer Abstammung im "Dritten Reich,"* 2nd ed. (Munich: Beck, 1990), 153–163. Biographical information on von Leers on p. 155.

57. Johann von Leers, "Die Kriminalität des Judentums," in *Das Judentum in der Rechtswissenschaft*, vol. 3, *Judentum und Verbrechen*, pp. 5–60.

58. Ibid., pp. 53–54.

59. Figures contained in *Reichskriminalstatistik 1901*.

60. See, for example, Rudolf Wasserman, *Beruf, Konfession und Verbrechen: Eine Studie über die Kriminalität der Juden in Vergangenheit und Gegenwart* (Munich: Reinhardt, 1907).

61. Johann von Leers, *Die Verbrechernatur der Juden* (Berlin: Hochmuth, 1944).

62. Ibid., p. 4.

63. Ibid., pp. 108–109.

64. See, for example, (Rabbi) L. Rosenack, *Zur Bekämpfung des Mädchenhandels* (Frankfurt: n.p., 1903). Keller and Andersen quote Rosenack in *Der Jude*, p. 130, as follows: "it is disheartening that a good number of the prostitution ringleaders [Mädchenhändler] are Jews."

65. Berta Pappenheim, "Das Interesse der Juden am V. Internationalen Kongress zur Bekämpfung des Mädchenhandels," *Ost und West*, August 1913, cited by Leers in *Verbrechernatur*, p. 109.

66. Edmund Mezger, *Kriminalpolitik auf kriminologischer Grundlage*, 2nd ed. (Stuttgart: Enke, 1942), pp. 146–147. My reading of Mezger follows the discussion in Wetzell, *Inventing the Criminal*, pp. 211–212, although I think that Wetzell might understate the racialism of Mezger's argument.

67. Wetzell, *Inventing the Criminal*, p. 214.

68. Franz Exner, *Kriminalbiologie in ihren Grundzügen* (Hamburg: Hanseatische Verlagsanstalt, 1939).

69. Ibid., p. 68, see figures.

70. Ibid., p. 67.

71. Ibid., pp. 69–70; translation taken from Wetzell, *Inventing the Criminal*, pp. 218–219.

72. Exner, *Kriminalbiologie*, p. 69.

73. Ibid., p. 71.

74. For an early example of a statistical summary of world Jewry see S. Wellisch, "Die Zahl der Menschen jüdischer Abstammung," *Zeitschrift für Rassenkunde* 2 (1935): 198–203.

75. Michael Burleigh, *Germany Turns Eastwards: A Study of Ostforschung in the Third Reich* (Cambridge: Cambridge University Press, 1988).

76. *Bevölkerungsstatistik Weißrutheniens* (Berlin: Selbstverlag der Publikationsstelle, 1942).

77. Johannes Pohl, *Juden in der Sowjetunion zu Beginn der Herrschaft Stalins* (Tilsit: Holzner, 1942).

78. Only a small number of major works of scholarship on the Holocaust have recognized Seraphim's importance. Notable among them are Saul Friedländer, *Nazi Germany and the Jews: The Years of Persecution, 1933–1939* (New York: HarperCollins, 1997), p. 187, and Aly and Heim, *Vordenker der Vernichtung*.

79. Biographical details in Gerhard Lüdtke, ed., *Kürschners Deutscher Literatur-Kalender auf das Jahr 1930* (Berlin: de Gruyter, 1930), pp. 1169–1170. For an example of Ernst Seraphim's antisemitism in the Nazi era see his "Zar Nikolaus II. und Graf Witte: Eine historisch-psychologische Studie," *Historische Zeitschrift* 161 (1940): 277–308, especially the positive evaluation of the tsar's antisemitism on p. 285.

80. *Kürschners Deutscher Gelehrten-Kalender 1940/41* (Berlin: de Gruyter, 1941), p. 773.

81. *Kürschners Deutscher Gelehrten-Kalender 1976* (Berlin: de Gruyter, 1976).

82. Biographical information drawn from Personalakte 433, Peter Heinz Seraphim, University Archive, University of Greifswald Archive; *Kürschners Deutscher Gelehrten-Kalender 1940/41*, 774; further details in Aly and Heim, *Vordenker der Vernichtung*, pp. 96–97, and Max Weinreich, *Hitler's Professors: The Part of Scholarship in Hitler's Crimes against the Jewish People* (New York: YIVO, 1946; reprint, New Haven: Yale University Press, 1999), p. 77.

83. In October 1937 Seraphim delivered a lecture on the Jews of eastern Europe at a small conference of German scholars who specialized in eastern Europe. The lecture possessed something of the quality of a premiere for Seraphim's work of the subject. See "Das Judentum im osteuropäischen Raum," in Peter-Heinz Seraphim, ed., *Einige Hauptprobleme deutscher Ostwissenschaft* (Königsberg: Osttreffen Deutscher Dozenten, 1937), pp. 52–62. See also his article "Das ostjüdische Ghetto," *Jomsburg* 1 (1937): 439–465.

84. *Das Judentum im osteuropäischen Raum* (Essen: Essener Verlagsanstalt, 1938).

85. David T. Murphy, *The Heroic Earth: Geopolitical Thought in Weimar Germany, 1918–1933* (Kent, Ohio: Kent State University Press, 1997).

86. Burleigh, *Germany Turns Eastwards*. A very large scholarly literature about Ostforschung in the Nazi era has emerged in the past several years. A useful bibliography and methodological assessment can be found in Rudolf Jaworski and Hans-Christian Petersen, "Biographische Aspekte der 'Ostforschung': Überlegungen zu Forschungsstand und Methodik," *Bios* 15, 1 (2002): 47–62.

87. "Der Antisemitismus in Osteuropa," *Osteuropa* 14 (1938/39): 332–346; "Die Judenfrage als Bevölkerungsproblem in Osteuropa," *Archiv für Bevölkerungswissenschaft und Bevölkerungspolitik* 9 (1939): 167–180.

88. *Das Judentum: Seine Rolle und Bedeutung in Vergangenheit und Gegenwart* (Munich: Deutscher Volksverlag, 1942); "Die Judeneinwanderung nach den USA aus den Judengebieten Osteuropas," *Weltkampf,* 1942, pp. 40–45.

89. Reinhard Maurach, review of *Das Judentum im osteuropäischen Raum* by Peter-Heinz Seraphim, *Weltkampf* 18 1, 2 (April–September 1941): 118.

90. Dekan to Reichsminister für Wissenschaft, Erziehung und Volksbildung, 10 December 1940, Personalakte 433, Peter-Heinz Seraphim, University of Greifswald Archive.

91. See, for example, his critical survey of statistical data in "Von Wesen und Wert der Statistik in Osteuropa," *Deutsches Archiv für Landes- und Volksforschung* 379 (1939): 194–207.

92. Seraphim, *Judentum im osteuropäischen Raum,* p. 678, indicates that he did actually use materials acquired from YIVO.

93. Ruppin, Arthur, *Die Juden der Gegenwart: Eine sozialwissenschaftliche Studie* (Cologne: Jüdischer Verlag, 1911).

94. Ruppin, Arthur, *Soziologie der Juden,* 2 vols. (Berlin: Jüdischer Verlag, 1930/31).

95. See, for example, p. 416, n. 170, in which Seraphim questions Ruppin's statistics on Jewish divorce rates.

96. Seraphim, *Judentum im osteuropäischen Raum,* 9.

97. Ibid., pp. 354–355.

98. Ibid., p. 629.

99. For an insightful examination of Sombart's theories and the responses they elicited from Jewish and Gentile critics, see Derek J. Penslar, *Shylock's Children: Economics and Jewish Identity in Modern Europe* (Berkeley: University of California Press, 2001), pp. 163–173.

100. Seraphim, *Judentum im osteuropäischen Raum,* p. 13.

101. Peter-Heinz Seraphim, "Zum Tode Werner Sombarts (19.5.1941)," *Weltkampf* , Vol. 18, no. 3/4 (October–December 1941), pp. 177–178.

102. Seraphim, *Judentum im osteuropäischen Raum,* chapter 5: "Die Ostjuden als rassische Gruppe," pp. 405–412.

103. Ibid., p. 405, n. 155. On the work of these writers see John Efron, *Defenders of the Race: Jewish Doctors and Race. Science in Fin-de-Siècle Europe* (New Haven: Yale University Press, 1994).

104. Sigmund Feist, *Stammeskunde der Juden: Die jüdischen Stämme der Erde in alter und neuer Zeit* (Leipzig: Hinrich, 1925).

105. Seraphim, *Judentum im osteuropäischen Raum,* pp. 405–06.

106. Ibid., pp. 405, n. 155, 406.

107. Peter-Heinz Seraphim, *Die Wirtschaftsstruktur des Generalgouvernements* (Cracow: Institut für deutsche Ostarbeit, 1941), pp. 85–89.

108. "Bevölkerungs- und wirtschaftliche Probleme einer europäischen Gesamtlösung der Judenfrage," *Weltkampf* 1, 2 (April–September 1941): 43–51.

109. Christopher Browning, *The Final Solution and the German Foreign Office* (New York: Holmes and Meier, 1978), pp. 35–43.

110. Rue in Ukraine, Inspecteur, to General Thomas, 3 December 1941, with attached undated memorandum by Seraphim, in *Trial of the Major War Criminals before the International Military Tribunal,* 42 vols. (Nuremberg: *International Military Tribunal,* 1948), document 3257-PS, vol. 32, pp. 71–75.

111. Raul Hilberg has cited this document at some length. Seraphim's single-minded attention to the economic ramifications of policy provides compelling evidence for Hilberg's central argument about the persistence of the Germans' bureaucratic impulse. But Hilberg omits the passage in which Seraphim expresses his moral concerns. Raul Hilberg, *The Destruc-*

tion of the European Jews, 3 vols. (New York: Holmes and Meier, 1985), vol. 1, p. 276.

112. "Die Art der Durchführung der Aktionen, die sich auf Männer und Greise, Frauen und Kinder jeden Alters erstreckte, war grauenhaft. Die Aktion ist in der Maßenhaftigkeit der Hinrichtungen so gigantisch wie bisher keine in der Sowjetunion vorgenommene gleichartige Massnahme."

113. Memorandum, "In Deutschland vorliegendes Material über wirtschaftliche Fragen der UdSSR (Aufgezeichnet nach dem Gedächtnis von Prof. Dr. P. H. Seraphim)," n. d., probably 1945 or 1946, Institut für Zeitgeschichte, Munich, ED 368/1.

114. Details of Seraphim's post-1945 career up to 1956 are summarized in Ilse Girard, "Prof. P. H. Seraphim: 'Wissenschaftlicher' Wegbereiter faschistischer Ideologie unter Hitler und unter Adenauer," *Dokumentation der Zeit* 126 (September 1956): 355–374. Notwithstanding the ideological spin and political motives of this East Germany publication, the account of Seraphim's career is generally accurate. See also the denunciation of Seraphim in Seeliger, *Braune Universität*, pp. 66–68.

115. Peter-Heinz Seraphim, *Das Genossenschaftswesen in Osteuropa* (Neuwied: Raiffeisen, 1951); *Die Wirtschaft Ostdeutschlands vor und nach dem 2. Weltkrieg* (Stuttgart: Brentano, 1952); *Ostdeutschland und das heutige Polen* (Braunschweig: Westermann, 1953); *Industriekombinat Oberschlesien: Das Ruhrgebiet d. Ostens. Das großoberschlesische Industriegebiet unter sowjet. Führung* (Cologne: Müller, 1953); *Die Heimatvertriebenen in der Sowjetzone Deutschlands* (Bonn: Bundesministerium für gesamtdeutsche Fragen, 1955).

116. *Kürschners Deutscher Gelehrten-Kalender 1954* (Berlin: de Gruyter, 1954), p. 2224.

117. Peter-Heinz Seraphim, *Deutsche Wirtschafts- und Sozialgeschichte: Von der Frühzeit.bis zum Ausbruch des zweiten Weltkrieges* (Wiesbaden: Gabler, 1962), p. 228.

Epilogue

1. P. Berman [Max Weinreich], "The Excuses of the German Yiddish Researcher Beranek," *Forverts,* 30 March 1956, and "Who Are the Germans Who Research the Jewish Language?" *Forverts,* 10 June 1956.

2. Dina Abramowicz, conversation with author, 1995.

3. Hans Peter Althaus, "Franz Josef Beranek (1902–1967)," *Onoma* 12 (1966/67): 2–3.

4. This detail from "Session of the Board of Directors of YIVO," 8–9 October 1938, YIVO Institute for Jewish Research Archive, RG 1.1, folder 15. I am grateful to Cecile Kuznitz for making me aware of this document.

5. Franz J. Beranek, *Die jiddische Mundart Nordostungarns* (Brno: Rohrer, 1941). By the time the book appeared, the region had become part of Hungary.

6. Franz J. Beranek, *Das Pinsker Jiddisch und seine Stellung im gesamtjiddischen Sprachraum* (Berlin: de Gruyter, 1958).

7. *Westjiddischer Sprachatlas* (Marburg: Elwert, 1965).

8. "Wissenschaftl.-charakterliche-politische-Beurteilung des NSD.-Dozentenbundes," for Beranek, 15 October 1942, National Archives of the United States microfilm publication T-81, Records of the National Socialist German Labor Party, roll 51, frames 54342–54343.

9. Beranek, *Jiddische Mundart Nordostungarns,* p. 8.

10. Ibid., pp. 5–7, 11.

11. Beranek, "Die Erforschung der Jiddischen Sprache," *Zeitschrift für deutsche Philologie* 701(1947/48): 163–174.

12. Liptzin to Beranek, 7 April 1955, Max Weinreich Collection, YIVO Archive, RG 584, folder 690.

13. Beranek to Liptzin, 11 May 1955, and accompanying "Spruch" from Spruchkammer Büdingen 2, 9 December 1946, Max Weinreich Collection, YIVO Archive, RG 584, folder 690.

14. Hans Peter Althaus, letter to author, 16 March 1997.

15. Beranek to Florence Guggenheim, 20 April 1955, Max Weinreich Collection, YIVO Archive, RG 584, folder 690.

16. Beranek to Auslandsamt der Dozentenschaft der deutschen Universitäten und Hochschulen, 3 March 1942, Max Weinreich Collection, YIVO Archive, RG 584, folder 690.

17. Jerold C. Frakes, *The Politics of Interpretation: Alterity and Ideology in Old Yiddish Studies* (Albany: State University of New York Press, 1989), p. 115.

18. Frakes, *Politics of Interpretation;* Marian Aptroot, "Yiddish Studies in Germany Today," in Gennady Estraikh and Mikhail Krutikov, eds., *Yiddish in the Contemporary World* (Oxford: Legenda, 1999). Another useful summary of the debate: "Scholars Debate Roots of Yiddish, Migration of Jews," *New York Times,* 29 October 1996.

19. See the discussion of Bruno Blau in Mitchell B. Hart, *Social Science and the Politics of Modern Jewish Identity* (Stanford: Stanford University Press, 2000), pp. 230–231. In 1995 I was informed by Dina Abramowicz that Peter-Heinz Seraphim's book on eastern European Jewry, which contained extensive statistical information, had sometimes been consulted as a reference work at YIVO in New York.

20. Max Weinreich, *Hitler's Professors: The Part of Scholarship in Hitler's Crimes against the Jewish People* (New York: YIVO, 1946; reprint, New Haven: Yale University Press, 1999), p. 241.

21. Helmut Heiber, *Walter Frank und sein Reichsinstitut für Geschichte des neuen Deutschlands* (Stuttgart: Deutsche Verlags-Anstalt, 1966), p. 1211.
22. Heinrich Schnee, "Heinrich Heine's Ahnen als Hofjuden deutscher Kirchenhöfe," *Weltkampf* 2, (1944): 91–94.
23. Heinrich Schnee, *Die Hoffinanz und der moderne Staat. Geschichte und Systeme der Hoffaktoren an deutschen Fürstenhöfen im Zeitalter des Absolutismus,* 6 vols. (Berlin: Duncker und Humblot, 1953–1967). The reference to the indispensability of the work is from Stefan Rohrbacher, "Jüdische Geschichte," in Michael Brenner and Stefan Rohrbacher, *Wissenschaft vom Judentum: Annäherungen nach dem Holocaust* (Göttingen: Vandenhoeck und Rupprecht, 2000), p. 167.
24. *Kürschner's Deutscher Gelehrten-Kalender 1966* (Berlin: de Gruyter, 1966), vol. 2, p. 2194.
25. Hermann Kellenbenz, *Sephardim an der unteren Elbe. Ihre wirtschaftliche und politische Bedeutung vom Ende des 16. bis zum Beginn des 18. Jahrhunderts* (Wiesbaden: Steiner, 1958).
26. On Kellenbenz's relationship to the Reich Institute see Heiber, *Walter Frank,* pp. 456–457. For the judgment on the fairness of his 1958 book see Rohrbacher, "Jüdische Geschichte," p. 167. On his postwar accomplishments see *Kürschner's Deutscher Gelehrten-Kalender 1976* (Berlin: de Gruyter, 1976), p. 1522.
27. Brenner and Rohrbacher, *Wissenschaft vom Judentum.*

Acknowledgments

Perhaps the most gratifying part of completing a book is the opportunity to thank institutions, friends, and colleagues whose assistance helped make it possible. This project was suggested to me by the late Sybil Milton, and one of my deepest hopes is that the end result honors her memory. The thematic breadth of the study compelled me to turn for advice to many colleagues in both the German and Jewish history fields. I received useful suggestions from Richard S. Levy, who read the manuscript in its entirety, bringing to bear his unparalleled command of the modern history of antisemitism. Two outside readers commissioned by Harvard University Press recommended revisions that improved the book significantly. Joyce Seltzer, my editor at Harvard University Press, compelled me to think more about the broader implications of my research. Patricia von Papen-Bodek selflessly shared her vast knowledge of Nazi Jewish studies. Susannah Heschel commented on various aspects of my work on countless occasions, and her own research on Nazi theologians has provided a model of impeccable scholarship. I would also like to thank the following people for questions, insights, and information: Hans Peter Althaus, Marion Aptroot, Doris Bergen, Michael Berkowitz, Richard Breitman, Michael Brenner, Christopher Browning, Steve Burnett, Nina Caputo, John Efron, Bob Ericksen, Norbert Frei, Henry Friedlander, Philipp Gassert, Martin Geyer, Geoffrey Giles, Mitch Hart, Peter Hayes, Ulrich Herbert, Jeffrey Herf, Hans Günter Hockerts, Konrad Jarausch, Detlef Junker, Claudia Koonz, Cecile Kuznitz, Christiane Kuller, Jodi Magness, Jürgen Matthäus, Anson Rabinbach, David Rechter, Steve Remy, Dirk Rupnow, Hans-Dieter Schmid, Ron Smelser, Frank Stern, Claus Stolberg, Winfried Süss, Gregory Wegner, and Gerhard Weinberg.

I benefited enormously from the research collections and staff expertise at the YIVO Institute for Jewish Research in New York. Zachary Baker granted me unfettered access to Max Weinreich's own collection of Nazi writings on Jews, and the late Dina Abramowicz helped guide me through it. I wrote a large portion of this book in the reading room of the Institute for Contemporary History (Institut für Zeitgeschichte) in Munich, where the librarians always proved hospitable. I am also grateful to the interlibrary loan specialists at the Love Library of the University of Nebraska–Lincoln, who efficiently tracked down many esoteric items.

Financial support from the German Academic Exchange Service and the Fulbright program enabled me to have valuable research time in Germany. A fellowship from the Skirball Foundation underwrote a semester at the Oxford Center for Hebrew and Jewish Studies, where I had time to read and reflect. The Simon Dubnow Institute at the University of Leipzig covered the costs of my participation in an important conference on Nazi Jewish studies in January 2004, where I had the opportunity to discuss my work with knowledgeable German colleagues. At the University of Nebraska-Lincoln, the Department of History, the Harris Center for Judaic Studies, and the College of Arts and Sciences provided travel support and allowed me to spend time in Germany, Britain, and New York.

My greatest debt is to my wife and colleague Susanna Schrafstetter. Had some of her intelligence and discipline not rubbed off on me, this book would probably never have been completed.

Index

Made in the USA
San Bernardino, CA
05 October 2013